A NEW PARADIGM IN THINKING, UNDERSTANDING, AND TREATMENT.

The Magic of
Cholesterol
Numbers

[*A step away from the cholesterol-lowering drugs*]

"What's the big deal about cholesterol,
and why does everyone want to lower it?"

SERGEY A. DZUGAN, MD, PhD
KONSTANTINE S. DZUGAN

The Magic of Cholesterol Numbers

ISBN: 978-0-615-50744-6

Printed in the United States of America

This book is dedicated to my family: my wife Yelena and three sons Sergey, Alexander, and Konstantine.

Foreword

Robert Wiley, M.D.
Ophthalmologist, Anti-Aging Physician

Asya Mikulinsky, M.D.
Anesthesiologist, Anti-Aging Physician

Jose Roberto Araujo Lima, M.D.
Doctor of Nutrologia

Robert Wiley, M.D.
Ophthalmologist, Anti-Aging Physician

"Talent hits a target no one else can hit; Genius hits a target no one else can see."

Arthur Schopenhauer quotes (German Philosopher, 1788-1860)

Disruptive:

"Dad, you might want to attend a two day, physician seminar taught by Dr. Sergey Dzugan, December 3 & 4, 2010." And so it began – my retirement was about to end. My son, William Wiley, M.D., had purchased my ophthalmology practice seven years earlier. But it took me only one day (December 3, 2010) to realize that Dr. Dzugan was a brilliant scientist with disruptive ideas. Ideas that I wanted to know more about.

I am attracted to innovative, out-of-the-box thinking. I was one of the first surgeons in the United States to be involved with many new and disruptive technologies: microscopic outpatient cataract surgery, combined cataract and glaucoma surgery, no-stitch cataract surgery, and RK refractive and LASIK eye surgery. Dr. Dzugan's ideas are every bit as revolutionary as LASIK eye surgery was twenty years ago. Dr. Dzugan has the potential to have a major impact on the practice of every practicing physician.

In 1985, Drs. Michael Brown and Joseph Goldstein won the Nobel Prize for their discovery of the underlying mechanisms of cholesterol metabolism (see 1). These discoveries led to the development of the HMG-CoA reductase inhibitors, better known as statin drugs. Some of the more common statin drugs are: Lipitor (atorvastatin,), Crestor (rosuvastatin), Vytorin (contains a statin - ezetimibe/simvastatin), Zocor (simvastatin), and Livalo (*pitavastatin*).

It is hard to over emphasize the impact that this class of drugs has had over the past quarter century. In terms of both public awareness and revenue generated for the pharmaceutical companies, statins are big business. Indeed, as Dr. Sekar Kathiresan, Director of Preventive Cardiology at Massachusetts General Hospital said, "Statins have had the largest impact of any medicine ever developed, short of penicillin." (see 2 – personal communication confirming this quote with permission to use).

However, as Mark Twain once said, "It ain't what you don't know that gets you into trouble. It's what you know for sure that just ain't so."

It is accepted as conventional wisdom that "a lower cholesterol number is always better" and "drugs are the best way to lower cholesterol." This book will challenge these "Truths". The concepts presented in this book are disruptive to the current cholesterol paradigm.

For the past few months my physiology has benefited from Dr. Dzugan's theory - my cholesterol is now nicely managed by improved managed physiology, no longer by statins. I am grateful to Dr. Dzugan for showing me a whole new way to look at Medicine, and for inviting me to see firsthand the benefits of physiology based medicine.

If a reliable method of cholesterol management, based on pharmacology, is worthy of Nobel recognition, then certainly a method of cholesterol management based on sound physiology management, with the added benefit that a balanced system is a healthier system, is also worthy of Nobel recognition. Many physicians feel the Dzugan approach to cholesterol, and his approach to basic human physiology, is a game changer.

If your goal is to understand complex, organic chemistry interactions, Dr. Dzugan's approach and clear explanations will help demonstrate the practical applications of biochemistry, thus making these complex interactions easier to understand. Over 40 years ago, I majored in Chemistry at the University of Michigan. Even though I had additional biochemistry courses at the University of Virginia Medical School, statements like this, taken from page 19 of this book, are very difficult to comprehend: *"Chylomicrons consist of about 85-88% triglycerides, 3% cholesteryl esters and 1% cholesterol, 8% phospholipids, and 1-2% proteins."* But much of the "magic" in The Magic of Cholesterol Numbers is Dr. Dzugan's ability to make very difficult concepts understandable (something that is also accomplished in his other books).

Following the quote above, Dr. Dzugan helps us better understand what a chylomicron is, with a well-illustrated diagram and these words:
"These are also the biggest [lipoprotein] at 1000 nm (nanometers, or one billionth of a meter), which of course isn't very big at all. The primary purpose of chylomicrons is to transport the triglycerides and cholesterol taken in from food that is absorbed in the intestines. They are also the least dense of the transport particles."

Even if you are a physician, as you read this book, you will find yourself frequently saying: "I didn't know that" ... but, of course, that is why you want to read this book.

An example is found on page 58: *Patients with the lowest cholesterol levels [less than 165 mg/dL (4.27 mmol/l)] had more than six times the risk of committing suicide compared to the highest levels [greater than 223 mg/dL (5.77 mmol/l)].* [30]

Or, page 63, another surprising fact:

Individuals with total cholesterol levels below 160 mg/dL had the highest rate of death from CHD [coronary heart disease], while those with levels above 240 mg/dL had the lowest risk of death from CHD.

Dr. Dzugan is a scientist first! He is a scientist with a good sense of humor. Every few pages you will be rewarded with a little chuckle: (ref. page 47 of this book)

Regarding the scientific method: *At no point in this procedure does it say that further testing to reach a conclusive hypothesis can be replaced by a survey based on opinion that can be employed for the application of action in regards to the hypothesis. To find the truth, you can't be a voter. You need to be an observer, investigator, and analyst. … yet here we are, voting on cholesterol.*

Or, from page 119

Potential improvements in Parkinson's are certainly nice, but what about something with a bit more force? Evidence suggests that progesterone may be a factor in the clinical treatment of traumatic (is there any other kind?) brain injury with its wealth of neuroprotective functions.

Dr. Dzugan presents a timely, cautionary message that we do not have the facts correct when we think we know Cholesterol. Are we correct in labeling HDL and LDL, "good cholesterol" and "bad cholesterol"?

In fact, maybe "up is down" and "down is up":

As reported in many journals and media venues in May, 2011, a drug trial conducted by the National Institutes of Health (NIH) studying the effects of Abbott's Niaspan (a high-dose, extended release form of niacin), which raises HDL, in combination with a statin on patients with heart and vascular diseases was ended 18 months earlier than planned after data showed the combination did not reduce the risk of cardiovascular events. A data-safety monitoring board overseeing the study concluded that "high dose, extended-release niacin offered no benefits beyond statin therapy alone in reducing cardiovascular-related complications in this trial."

The board also said there was a "small and unexplained increase in ischemic stroke rates" in the Niaspan group, which contributed to the decision to stop the trial early.

Some might say that Dr. Dzugan's approach to medicine is "alternative medicine," but his approach is better described as "back to basics," and back to health care, as opposed to the disease care model so prevalent today.

Dr. Dzugan's hormonal balancing technology is DISRUPTIVE! Most physicians and those uneducated in physiology based medicine will initially resist it.

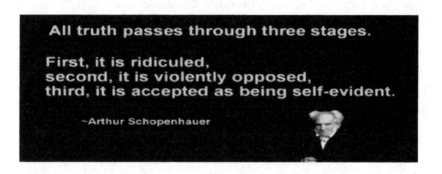

All truth passes through three stages.

First, it is ridiculed,
second, it is violently opposed,
third, it is accepted as being self-evident.

~Arthur Schopenhauer

Whenever a new discovery is reported to the scientific world, they say first, "It is probably not true".

Thereafter, when the truth of the new proposition has been demonstrated beyond question, they say, "Yes, it may be true, but it is not important".

Finally, when sufficient time has elapsed to fully evidence it's importance, they say, "Yes, surely it is important, but it is no longer new".

Montaigne (1533-1592)

The statin drug companies have marketed, with innovative methods and with unprecedented financial gain, not only to physicians, but directly to the public. The public now demands to know their cholesterol number. Doctors are not immune to this public pressure, and the pharmaceutical companies know this.

It is important that patients and doctors know that there is another side to the Cholesterol Story. In The Magic of Cholesterol Numbers, Dr. Dzugan helps tell the other side of the story. What would happen if, instead of asking "what is my cholesterol number?" patients asked their doctor, "Do statin drugs help patients live longer?" or, "Is it true that patients who take statins have a higher incidence of cancer and hemorrhagic stroke?" Asking these types of questions may help to change the view that "cholesterol is bad" and "statins are good". Well educated patients and their targeted questions will help shift the paradigm about cholesterol and, one by one, doctors will learn that **optimum physiology is the key to normalized cholesterol and good health.**

Bob Wiley
Robert G. Wiley, M.D.
Executive Director, International Physiology Optimization Medical Society (iPOMS)
Toledo, Ohio

1. http://www.utsouthwestern.edu/utsw/home/about/nobel/
2. Sekar Kathiresan, MD
http://www2.massgeneral.org/cvrc/faculty_kathiresan_about.html

Asya Mikulinsky, M.D.
Anesthesiologist, Anti-Aging Physician

The importance of asking the right question cannot be overestimated. It's a foundation of every scientific hypothesis, theory, and study. The rest only follows. It requires an unbiased and clear vision, a deep understanding of the matter at hand, an ability to focus, and last but not least a lot of courage. This is exactly reflected in the value that Dr. Dzugan's work brings to the world and the medical community today.

The significant subject matter in this book that is being discussed is investigated very thoroughly, thoughtfully, and from all possible aspects. This investigation ranges from observing the nature of the issue from something as in depth as chemical structures and even analyzing how the study of cholesterol has evolved our understanding of it.

Today, every single middle aged person who has access to medical care is required to have their cholesterol level tested by conventional medicine, even if they are completely healthy. If the results are unfavorable to the accepted standard, then medical intervention is usually used, often to detrimental effects. If we as a society really care about our health, it is imperative to understand "The Magic of Cholesterol Numbers" and act accordingly to reach optimal health and not just focus on a number game. Cholesterol is used extensively by the body for optimal function and these levels are being manipulated by medications without a thorough understanding of the underlying forces at work.

Top scientists have conducted multiple investigations into the matter of cholesterol, utilizing the best in modern technology and equipment. The amount of information gained from this is enormous and leads to further studies by pharmaceutical companies and the creation of standards of medical care by medical societies based on this information. Dr. Dzugan's ability to seek answers to the right questions, his vision, courage, and hard work brings great clarity to the matter. He took the road never travelled.

The very simple question of "What are we actually treating when we address high cholesterol?" guides the analysis of his own professional experience as a heart surgeon and as a specialist in immunorestorative therapy at the Cancer Center where he engaged in this exquisite investigative work to find the answers behind cholesterol. He follows the standard of basic physiology taught in medical schools, an analysis of conclusions of recent research on the subject, and his own experience to create this fantastic book for people to use.

This incredible line of inquiry brought to life a very practical tool – the approach developed by Dr. Dzugan - as a process that uses the restoration of hormones to optimize the physiology of the body. The program created by the Dzugan methodology is designed for each person based on their specific information in the form of blood tests, their medical history, and physical examinations. It approaches the "issue" of cholesterol by taking all the pertinent facts into consideration.

The elements used in the program are the same ones that are already in the human body, creating an optimal balance and harmony for optimal health. While drugs operate on physical pathways that are foreign to the body, these substances utilized by the program use the very same physical pathways that the body already uses. There is no forceful and foreign approach in the attempt to repair the body, but instead a natural one. This foreign approach can cause side effects to the rest of the body, so that even if one issue is fixed another can arise. This concept of using the naturally pre-existing pathways to restore optimal physiologic function deserves special recognition. Dr. Dzugan's book includes medical histories and stories of numerous people who had their lives turned around after their initiation in the Dzugan program.

All of this indicates visionary work: scientific theory is confirmed by results of practical application where substantial results are gained and observed. Dr. Dzugan's technique of physiologic regulation approaches cholesterol in a logical method that keeps in mind the very important role that cholesterol plays in the body and not as a number that needs to be kept down. This brings benefits to people that suffer from very common conditions caused by physiologic breakdown associated with the simple aging process such as hypertension, diabetes, atherosclerosis, coronary artery disease, and cerebro-vascular diseases. It can also help in managing depression, fibromyalgia, migraine, chronic fatigue syndrome and many, many other conditions that are linked to a breakdown of optimal function.

The human body is very powerful and even more so when physiology is optimized with science, knowledge, experience, and attention to detail. I was fortunate enough to be present at Dr. Dzugan's presentations at medical conventions, where I began to learn about the significance of this new approach to a very common issue.

His ability to deliver the message in a vision with clarity, focus, and undeniable logic left me inspired and excited. I really hope that this book will find readers everywhere and get them excited to a completely different level, one that is aided by understanding and logic. I know that the Dzugan program gets people to a new level of functioning, satisfaction with their lives, happiness, and participation in their own lives as well as the community. The healthy body includes the happy person as he or she functions in his own community, leading to a lot of good overall.

Finally, I'd like to thank Dr. Dzugan for making a huge difference in my own life with his program for myself. I would also like to express my deepest respect, admiration and appreciation to Dr. Dzugan for this brilliant scientific work and the honor I have at being asked to write this foreword.

Jose Roberto Araujo Lima, M.D.
Doctor of Nutrologia

From the moment that we attend Schools of Medicine, we learn how to treat diseases in order to treat them to relieve suffering. We are overloaded with concepts that leave us confused until our experience has grown to a point where we can discern the severity of diseases and make sense of it fully. Today, health may be the most important of our assets. It is a priority for us to change our life style and to incorporate habits such as having good meals, trying to eliminate or reducing stress, doing exercises, and taking mineral and vitamin supplements to help us avoid the disease. With this action we can at least delay the onset and increase the chance of having better quality of life.

Prof. S. Dzugan is one of those pioneering doctors in the study of measures that can be taken to improve health, while not bothering to suffer criticism from more "orthodox" medical practitioners who refuse to admit changes in concepts in the treatment of patients. From a deep understanding of cellular function, Dr. Dzugan learned how to explain and act upon the mechanisms of immune defenses, which leads to a better understanding of things that can cause cancer, and thus, establish guards and measures that are able to act in the prevention of such a terrible disease.

In this book, cholesterol is demystified as a villain in heart disease and rises up as a courageous agent that breaks paradigms in medicine. While the pharmaceutical industry encourages the continued use of drugs to reduce cholesterol levels, Dr. Dzugan manages to show the biological importance of this substance for everyday life as well as its importance in nearly all bodily functions once it is present in all of our cells. Many studies have shown that very low cholesterol levels increase mortality from various causes, contrary to what the medical "establishment" would like to admit and that new ways of thinking about the causes of cardiovascular disease should be placed on the agenda to reach new conclusions.

This book reconfirms that we can only treat patients holistically, that is to mean seeing them as a WHOLE, and not as a collection of symptoms. The super-specialization of medical science has made methods of diagnosis and treatment more expansive but lacking in what concerns the welfare of patients. Unanimity in science is a myth.

Ameghino said: "I will change my mind as many times as necessary as I'm provided with new knowledge." Dr. Dzugan certainly faces criticism due to the concepts that he presents in this book, but science will respect him more and more once these concepts become better analyzed, and therefore accepted. Dr. Dzugan has studied, done research and surveys, and has collaborated a great deal to improve the quality of life for many patients around the world.

Table of Contents

INTRODUCTION

Picking up this book you might glance at the cover, see that essential word in the title, and skip ahead to this introduction. After all, another book on cholesterol? How tired can those get? Maybe it's some sort of guide on "eating right" or a book talking about the dangers of this evil substance. So many texts, all singing the same old song – let's lower our cholesterol! Let's push that devil into submission so that we can all be healthy!

If that actually was the book you are looking for, then we are sorry to disappoint you, because this isn't one of those. The subject of this book is indeed cholesterol, but perhaps in a different light than you might be used to seeing. Here, cholesterol is the hero, and not so much the villain. Well, not at all in fact, which we will show in due time.

Consider this a handbook of sorts into this very unique and very misunderstood agent. This isn't an epic tome full of mind numbing scientific data worthy of a medical school classroom, revised each year with very little added information that for some reason sells for the same price as the previous edition. Nor is this a heavy excursion into understanding cholesterol, filled with lots of words and unnecessary descriptions. Instead, what you will find here is a book that will try to explain exactly what cholesterol is, why it is so very important to everyone's health, and what the actual facts are behind the numbers that all those commercials tell us to get to.

You will not find a story at every turn that takes several pages to describe the workings of one simple fact. We are here to give you the facts, backed up by scientific data and studies, all wrapped up in our own observations and explanations, and sometimes a bit of raw data. We want this to be concise and to the point. We want to give you the most information possible without holding your hand the entire way, but we don't want you to fall asleep reading either. In fact, once you realize how ridiculous this barrage of bile is against cholesterol, you just might have a laugh at how ridiculous this situation is. It might get so ridiculous that you might even cry, but we aren't here to make you cry. We are here to give you the knowledge to make the right decisions, and more importantly your own decisions, about cholesterol.

We're not here to force a biased viewpoint down your throat either. We speak out of our mouths (and nowhere else) about the actual scientific evidence, the biological inner workings of the body, our own experience, and our own hypothesis about cholesterol. We will also touch briefly on our method and how it fits in with all this. Why is all of this so important? Why are so many people obsessed with cholesterol?

Coronary heart disease is still the leading cause of mortality (measure of the rate of death in a population) in developed countries.[1-3] Various studies have shown that hypercholesterolemia is a major risk factor for coronary atherosclerosis (hardening of arteries due to the buildup of fatty substances) and myocardial infarction.[4,5] Although myocardial infarction is usually simply referred to as a "heart attack," the literal meaning of this term is the death of heart muscle tissue. Physicians and their patients have attempted for years to solve this dilemma, trying to find out ways to lower their cholesterol levels, whether it is via cholesterol lowering drugs or dietary methods. In fact, numerous countries currently have strategies in place for public health that attempt to lower and control the level of cholesterol.[6]

Though success has been gained in the treatment of hypercholesterolemia, atherosclerosis is still a serious problem in the Health Care System. As such, the lowering of cholesterol is the main method to prevent cardiovascular disease. This would be an excellent contribution to public health if cholesterol lowering drugs actually targeted the cause of hypercholesterolemia. However, the key issue here is that these drugs only treat the symptoms of the disease.

Though there is plenty of debate on the benefits of such drugs, the use of these agents has risen greatly in most countries.[7,8] Perhaps the most important fact to take away from the various studies regarding these drugs is that although they are effective in primary prevention, the matter of long term tolerability is still a matter of controversy and dispute.[9,10] Tolerability, in this instance, refers to the fact that as the length of drug use is increased in an individual, the body's acceptance of these agents becomes more strained and a variety of side effects can occur. As we all surely know, side effects are no picnic as evident anytime the commercial announcer starts to speak quickly to cover all the side effects. Eventually, the boiling point is reached where the side effects eclipse the actual "problem" that the drug is trying to solve. To compound the frustration behind this matter, studies suggest that as total cholesterol is lowered in the body, the incidence of coronary heart disease is decreased, but at the same time there is not such an analog in total mortality.[11,12] In other words, the cholesterol level is decreased but the overall amount of death going on is not impacted. We would think that this is a serious problem, since no patient would want to be in the group that has the higher mortality.

Recommendations for lowering serum cholesterol are numerous, but lowered serum cholesterol is associated with poorly understood morbidity (ill health), as well as increased mortality from hemorrhagic stroke and violent deaths.[14-17] The occurrence of serious side effects associated with cholesterol lowering drugs is seen in 4-38% of patients which resulted in discontinuations and reductions of dosages.[18-20] Most patients who begin a course of lipid-lowering therapy stop it within one year, and only about a third of patients reach their treatment goals.[21] 60% of patients discontinued their medication over 12 months.[22]

Serious problems, such as diminished quality of life, severe rhabdomyolosis (destruction of skeletal muscle), kidney failure, and even death clearly demonstrate the need to find a better treatment for the elevation of total cholesterol.[23,24] This is something that we will touch upon as we briefly observe the cholesterol witch hunt. All the people hear is that cholesterol is bad, they don't so much hear that if they try to lower their cholesterol by the conventional means there is an oh so slight chance that their kidneys will fail and they will die.

With all this data presented (or not presented, as the case may be) to us as potential medical consumers, what are we to make of all this information? Clearly, hypercholesterolemia is an issue and should be taken care of, but from what perspective and how do we go about this mission without leaving a devastated body behind?

What are we treating?

We should put the tape player (or mp3 player, if you wish) on pause at this point and ask a very serious question? What actually causes high cholesterol? This is an "unknown" (although as you will see later on, we have more than a very good idea). So, if we do not know what causes elevated cholesterol, then what in the world are we treating? The answer is simple and frustratingly ineffective: the symptoms rather than the root cause. In this book, we will try to show a potential cause of high cholesterol and a method which can effectively help fight this cause, and not the symptom.

All this talk about cholesterol leaves out a very important part of the great chain of production in the human body that is responsible for our steroid hormones. Whenever cholesterol is spoken of as the big bad, steroid hormones are sitting on the sideline, forgotten. This is odd, considering that these agents, which are essential to life, are created from cholesterol. This is where our method comes into play.

We should make clear here that the primary focus of this book is not on our method, but rather on education and to shed light on the side of cholesterol that few speak about. This is information that your doctors and other people very rarely talk about. It is very nice to possess actual information so that informed decisions can be made on a personal basis. The inclusion of our method here is to reinforce our hypothesis and provide evidence outside of simple words and thoughts.

We use reinforcement of the body's own natural supply lines to correct the production of cholesterol. But we'll get to that later. The first and foremost course of action is to remove that horrible miasma lingering around cholesterol's bad reputation and to show just how important it is. We don't quite know why after medical school we forget what our physiology, or how our body works, is. We also don't understand why cholesterol is not looked upon as an essential part of our life and is instead considered as an object to be suppressed.

How did this journey begin?

As a former heart surgeon, I always look at the information surrounding atherosclerosis and coronary heart disease. After all, if I didn't keep up with such matters then I would probably be considered bad and uninterested in my own field. Numerous times as a heart surgeon I posed the question to myself as to why so many individuals who had a heart attack had normal cholesterol. Whenever a biological malfunction occurs the most logical next step is to find the scientific explanation behind this event.

When I worked with Dr. Arnold Smith at the North Central Regional Cancer Center in Greenwood, Mississippi, we used immunorestorative therapy for cancer patients. The core element of immunorestorative therapy is hormonorestorative therapy. In other words, we tried to restore the immune system in large part by restoring hormone levels. One of these experiences stuck with me and turned into a very strong idea.

A particular patient had advanced non-small cell lung cancer. He had an inoperable tumor with multiple metastases (when disease or cancer spreads to other parts of the body) in the brain, chest, and lymph nodes in the neck. He underwent radiation treatment and then we proceeded with the immunorestorative therapy. For many years, he had a cholesterol level of more than 300 mg/dL, was on statin drugs, and took a large dose of insulin due to his insulin dependent diabetes.

After his cancer treatment, he got his cholesterol level tested which revealed that his level had normalized. He jokingly mentioned to me why he had to go through the terrible ordeal of cancer just to get his cholesterol level under control. I started thinking and realized that he was not the only one whose cholesterol was normalized after treatment. Then I thought about and looked at the pathway of cholesterol metabolism and I noticed some very interesting things.

Hormone production decreases with age, and the body increases cholesterol production. What occurs during pregnancy? Cholesterol greatly increases for the elevated levels of hormones in the mother as well as for the healthy growth process of the fetus. At all times cholesterol tries to pick up where the body is lacking by increasing. After all, nobody would ever dream of recommending lowering cholesterol for a pregnant woman.

If we were to restore hormones to optimal levels, what would occur? If youthful hormone levels are restored, then logically the natural feedback mechanisms of the body would go into effect, which would mean that cells should stop the production of cholesterol because the need for this increase is not there anymore. To see what would happen, we tried out a study on a small group with the use of hormonorestorative therapy and were amazed at the results.

All the patients in the study had a normalization of cholesterol. We were shocked because these results were unexpected from the established scientific data, but were expected from this new train of thought that we had established. We immediately formulated a hypothesis linking the restoration of hormone levels with the optimization of cholesterol and sent it off to the Medical Hypothesis journal, where it was reviewed and published by Dr. David Horrobin.

This hypothesis is termed the hormonodeficit hypothesis of hypercholesterolemia. It attempts to explain increased cholesterol levels, in particular the elevated levels that are brought on with age. In short, cholesterol is a precursor of steroid hormones. As the systems in place for adequate hormone production break down, cholesterol levels are elevated in an attempt to fix it. Thus, cholesterol becomes a very important biomarker for a large variety of impaired function. We will not only be covering the true functions behind cholesterol but also how our hypothesis takes into account a vast array of measurements and blood tests based on our own clinical experience.

THE MAGIC OF CHOLESTEROL NUMBERS

CHAPTER 1

The Cholesterol Story

There is an extremely large amount of confusion surrounding the entire area of cholesterol. In fact, there is almost as much confusion as there is misguided hatred. How are we to make sense of all this?

So what is this seemingly dangerous enemy, demonized from many sides as a catalyst to the destruction of a healthy body? Is it some foreign substance that invades the body and causes morbidity? What precisely is cholesterol, the target of so many attacks and bad press? Surely with all the negativity surrounding it, cholesterol must be the bad apple of the bunch, the diseased fruit hanging on the healthy tree? Let's explore further and talk about what cholesterol is, which is so much easier said than done even on the surface identification.

Intelligence for the Cholesterol War

Cholesterol spits in the face of any convention that tries to classify what it is. Quite often it is referred to as a lipid, steroid or fat. The problem here is that it does not solidly fit into any of those categories. It is also referred to as a sterol, which is a combination of an alcohol and a steroid, but it does not behave like alcohol. The precise chemical term for the cholesterol

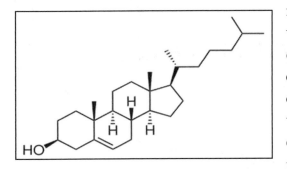

molecule thus remains without an exact definition. We could of course just call it cholesterol, but that would probably be too easy. After all, to fight the enemy, we must know the enemy.

With identification so far out of our reach, maybe it would be a good idea to determine the production sites of cholesterol, so that instead of fighting a war against an enemy of great multitude that is popping up everywhere, we can simply sabotage the means of production. So where precisely are these terrible manufactories? 25% of cholesterol is localized within the brain, with most of it present in the myelin (more on this vital structure in a bit). All cholesterol in the brain is a product of local synthesis since plasma lipoproteins are unable to cross the blood-brain barrier.[1] In essence, all cholesterol in the brain is also made in the brain due to this impediment.[2] Well, we put up a valiant defense, but the foe is in our brain. It seems that it is time to find the undertaker, because the unit controlling our bodies has been corrupted by that vile, unclassifiable agent of destruction.

Unfortunately, here we run into a slight obstacle. There is an issue with the previously mentioned blood-brain barrier. The blood-brain barrier refers to the fact that brain capillaries have endothelial cells (that line blood vessels) which are very tightly grouped, which does not allow for the passive transport of certain agents (such as bacteria and large molecules that can be dissolved in water) from the blood. This allows some agents to pass through without energy expenditures while others are kept out. Other agents can enter through via active transport. The difference between active and passive transport lies in the name, because quite simply passive transport happens without the expenditure of energy while active transport requires the use of energy for the transport of molecules. A very simple example, although certainly not the only one, of passive transport is diffusion.

Diffusion works on the principle of a concentration gradient and varying concentrations on either side of a barrier. Consider a cell membrane and varying amounts of a substance on either side of this loose barrier. Through random motion, the molecules from the higher concentration will move towards the lower concentration in an effort to create a balance, thus negating this concentration gradient. A simpler example occurs when that one co-worker who bathes in aftershave comes into the elevator. Quite soon, the powers of diffusion make the entire elevator fill with the dreadful odor, as the high concentration of molecules around his neck attempt to fill out the rest of the space. Other examples of passive transport include facilitated diffusion (usage of transport agents but still without the use of energy), filtration (variable water pressures allowing water and molecules to pass through), and osmosis (diffusion of water).

Something seems very wrong here. Is the brain somehow being tricked into creating a harmful substance? How could cholesterol even accomplish this? The infestation goes deeper. Cholesterol is actually embedded in myelin. Myelin forms a sheath around some axons (which conduct impulses to other nerve cells) and helps regenerate cut axons. As you can see in the attached illustration of a neuron, the myelin is extremely vital in the facilitation of nerve impulses throughout the nervous system. It appears that not only has cholesterol tricked the brain into producing more cholesterol, but it has also managed to sneak into a very important part of nerve function. Is it actually serving in a beneficial function here, to offset the damage it does

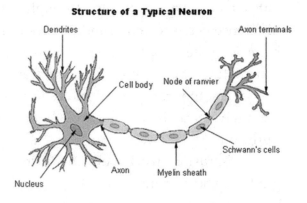

Structure of a Typical Neuron

Dendrites

Axon terminals

Cell body

Node of ranvier

Schwann's cells

Axon

Myelin sheath

Nucleus

elsewhere so that the body can keep going to create more cholesterol? Regardless, the brain is the brain, a most vital part of our body, so we certainly can't attack it as a source of cholesterol. Perhaps we can look around the body to see where else cholesterol can be countered.

The liver, then, can be next on the inquiry list. Synthesis of cholesterol and triglycerides occurs in the liver, after which cholesterol is transported all over the body, putting a bad mark in its favor. However, cholesterol is also transported back to the liver, where it can be excreted in bile. This seems contradictory. If the liver is sending these cholesterol molecules out and about to destroy our body, why is it also accepting some cholesterol back to help us out of our trouble? To muddle the water further, some of the cholesterol in the bile is not expelled out of the body but is instead reabsorbed right back into it, to be reused. What exactly is bile, other than the bile surrounding cholesterol (we apologize for that one)?

Bile is a fluid produced in the liver which aids in the digestion of lipids. A major function of bile is to help absorb all the fat that we take in via diet, because as much as we might not like fat in our bodies, our bodies certainly like and need fat to operate properly. Without this beneficial action of bile, the majority lipids would not be properly absorbed. Bile also helps in the absorption of certain vitamins (due to the fact that some dissolve in water while others are dissolved in fat). Bile acids (which are of course a part of bile) split endotoxins into harmless substances. This prevents their entry into the bloodstream. An endotoxin is a toxin which is a part of the cell wall of microorganisms. For our purpose here, such a microorganism is something such as bacteria. Bile certainly is much more important than the association with its name would seem to imply.

Here the evil plan seems clear, the liver is only getting rid of the faulty cholesterol and salvaging what is left to send out more cholesterol back in the body. But the liver also serves important functions such as detoxification of blood, metabolism of carbohydrates, and protein synthesis, as well as the aforementioned bile which has further use in the body. Well, we can't attack the liver as a source of production then either, and must find a way to battle cholesterol in some other way.

Upon further investigation it becomes apparent that cholesterol is present in all cells in the body. Is everyone a walking time bomb? Is our deadly enemy so anchored in our bodies that we are just giant walking risk factors just waiting to expire? The brain, the liver, all of our cells, we seem betrayed by our own body.

A Misguided Crusade

At this point, this train of thought starts to look a bit foolish. If we replaced key terms we could have a great science fiction novel about an alien invader destroying the human race from within. It seems funny, until enough thought is applied to the matter (then it starts to be sad). Then, we begin to realize that something is very strange in this entire matter. If cholesterol is present everywhere, why is our body, for lack of a better word, so dumb? Why is it not only allowing cholesterol to be everywhere but even producing it all over the place?

This is where a great problem lies in the popular conceptualization of cholesterol. We aren't even talking about the nature of cholesterol, which we will talk about shortly. Think back to anytime someone mentions cholesterol. You're at a party, someone drinking a glass of cheap wine makes a joke about cholesterol and everyone laughs. How does the joke go? Invariably it talks about cholesterol clogging the arteries (we're sure it was a very bad joke that wasn't well thought out) and then the heart attacks set in.

This is the first thing that comes to mind for most people when cholesterol is mentioned. Commercials with complex three dimensional diagrams of how cholesterol is blocking all the arteries, those fancy posters at the doctor's office with color coded areas where more artery blockage is happening, and people regurgitating this information to everyone they find to spread the news about how bad cholesterol is, all of these factors and more disseminate information about one thing that can happen under bad circumstances that are initiated by the breakdown of other functions within the body.

What we are trying to say is that yes, cholesterol is linked to such blockages, but this occurs in crucial times and for reasons that are never touched upon, and on top of that during times of elevated cholesterol. That is another important distinction – popular belief would have us think that as soon as cholesterol is created in any quantity, it is on the warpath to block our arteries and kill us. This whole association is one giant mess so let's clear up things one at a time. We can begin by seeing what cholesterol actually does.

The Constructor of our Bodies

It turns out that cholesterol is one of the most important molecules in the body. It is a major building block from which cell membranes are created, something that is vital to cellular production. Why are cell membranes so important? They cover our cells, for one, which some people would say is a good thing to occur. It isn't a simple cellophane wrap analog though, and can carry out quite a few more functions than some protective plastic wrap. A much better comparison is a skin layer, letting things in and out as needed for optimal function.

The important fact to take away from this is that the cell membrane is a complex structure responsible for many different aspects of everyday cellular function and much like a human would expire without skin, so would a cell. Cholesterol is also important in the routine repair of tissues because not only is it the building block of cell membranes, it is also present in the finished product, and the organelles within cells are rich in cholesterol. Furthermore, it is used to make very important substances such as steroid hormones, which regulate many vital actions throughout the body. Cholesterol is the most produced molecule in our body and to attack it is a bad idea indeed. It is produced in such large quantities because it is important for a normally functioning physiology. Physiology is simply the science of the functions of living organisms and their component parts.

Before going further, a distinction needs to be made about steroid hormones. When a person hears steroids, automatically the mind goes to bodybuilders who say they only drink protein while having uncontrollable anger, impaired kidney function, and stunted skeletal growth. Another example could be steroids given in a hospital for certain dangerous issues that require a rather hardy anabolic boost to the system, or ones given for the suppression of inflammation or for allergic reactions. At all times, the popular perception of steroids is bad, which is unfortunate.

The steroids one is liable to always hear about are the synthetic steroids which physiologically speaking, have absolutely no place in the human body. These are manmade productions designed to mimic, but never replicate the natural steroids that are present in the human body. This is why when the word "steroid" is heard, all the bad connotations with these synthetic creations are by default piled on top of the word, regardless of context or origin. The steroid hormones in the body are created by the body itself, being a natural part of normal function.

There is also the issue of synthetic steroid such as prednisone. Doctors use prednisone for a variety of functions including allergies, infections, and autoimmune diseases, to name some. There are certainly indications for the application of such an agent for such issues, but we must understand that there are serious side effects that are associated with their long term use.

The issues with synthetic steroids have given a bad name to all steroids, natural or otherwise. The steroid hormones in the body are simply steroids that carry the function of hormones, and are not analogous to synthetics. We make this distinction very clear because we will be covering steroid hormones in great detail later on. What exactly are hormones?

The Regulators and Controllers

Hormones escape an all-inclusive classification due to the large amount of functions that they are responsible for. To use a broad definition, hormones are the most powerful molecules in the regulation of an optimal physiology (the functions of living systems). They are vital parts of our neuro-endocrine-immune system.

This name is simply a reference to three major systems. The nervous system is the collection of all the neurons in the body, responsible for transmitting impulses and signals throughout the body. There are various subdivisions of the nervous system, such as the central nervous system which includes the brain and spinal cord. Other divisions include the peripheral nervous system, which itself includes important elements such as the sympathetic and parasympathetic systems.

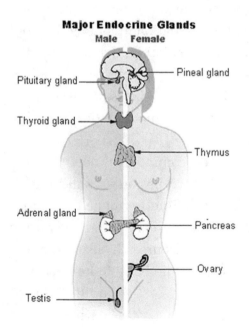

Major Endocrine Glands
Male   Female

Pituitary gland —

Pineal gland

Thyroid gland —

Thymus

Adrenal gland —

Pancreas

Ovary

Testis —

The endocrine system has perhaps a more direct application in its relationship to hormones, simply because it is directly responsible for actually creating a large variety of hormones. In broad terms the endocrine system can be thought of as a series of glands responsible for this hormonal genesis. The most common types of these glands are thyroid, pituitary, pineal, and adrenal glands, as well as the important ovaries, testes, and pancreas. The illustration shown here is simply a rough overview of the major endocrine glands and their locations, with the differences due to gender.

The thyroid gland, known much more commonly as the thyroid, is the largest gland and has important functions such as maintaining energy use throughout the body and controlling the effectiveness of other hormones by regulating how much the body reacts to them. The thyroid creates the appropriately named thyroid hormones by utilizing iodine taken in via food. A look at department store shelves in the salt section will show the label "iodized salt," and the thyroid is the reason for this. Iodine deficiency was a widespread issue (and still is in some parts of the world) that caused significant problems such as goiters (enlargement of the thyroid gland) and congenital hypothyroidism. Congenital hypothyroidism, referred to in the past as cretinism, can occur due to iodine deficiency from diet in the mother which if untreated can lead to delayed or halted physical development and mental retardation in infants. Thyroid hormones are also important in regulating metabolism, the chemical reactions that maintain living organisms. A big role for a big gland, it seems. However, in this case size is not necessarily in charge of importance. The thyroid is actually under control of the pea sized pituitary gland.

The pituitary gland, much less commonly known as the hypophysis, is a small gland with very important functions. It directly tells the thyroid how much thyroid hormone to produce by creating a hormone of its own. The pituitary gland is certainly not just in charge of the thyroid, of course. It also produces hormones that are essential in keeping the body in homeostasis. Homeostasis is simply the description of the equilibrium, or balance, that exists in an organism. Homeostasis is maintained by various feedback mechanisms, both positive and negative. Very simple (but not remotely simple in application) examples of homeostasis include the regulation of human body temperature or the acidity or alkalinity (pH) of human blood.

The adrenal glands are responsible for the production of corticosteroids, important steroid hormones which are created in the adrenal cortex from cholesterol (much more on this later). The adrenal cortex itself is a part of the adrenal gland. We will go into more detail regarding corticosteroids (in particular the more recognizable one, cortisol) at a later point. These steroid hormones are in charge of various tasks ranging from stress response to immune system function.

Ovaries and testes are probably much more recognizable because they are also the more noticeable (in the case of testes, anyway). Ovaries are responsible for the production of estrogens and progesterone. We will be going into much more detail about these further down the line, but for now we can simply say that they are important in determining female secondary sex characteristics (although this hardly scratches the surface of their many functions). Testes play a very important role in testosterone production in males. Testosterone is the all important "male" hormone and is also responsible for many functions, secondary sex characteristics being one of them. It goes without saying that both ovaries and testes are vitally important in human reproduction.

The pancreas is a very important gland that is important for both hormones and digestion. Digestive enzymes from the pancreas travel to the small intestine and help with the breakdown of agents such as carbohydrates, lipids, and proteins. It also secretes hormones such as insulin and glucagon. Insulin is responsible for lowering blood glucose, while glucagon is responsible for increasing blood glucose. It is easy to see why a properly functioning pancreas is important, lest individuals start to faint or get a bad round of diabetes.

Just because some of these hormones have localized production does not mean that they are meant for localized consumption. Hormones travel throughout the blood to all cells in the body. In cells, hormones control cell proliferation, differentiation (the process by which a cell becomes a more specialized cell), protein synthesis, metabolic rate, and more. Seeing as how we are made up of cells, hormones seem like good agents to have in our bodies. Optimal levels of hormones as well as optimal hormonal effects are essential for health and quality of life.

While areas such as the various endocrine glands can be thought of as factories of a sort, they are not magic factories. Just like in the outside world, these factories need raw materials and power to undergo a lengthy and complex assembly line process for the creation of steroid hormones. These steroid hormones are created from cholesterol, which itself is made up of many other building blocks that undergo their own complex creation procedures.

The creation of cholesterol can be extremely simplified as thus: a molecule of cholesterol is primarily synthesized (produced) from Acetyl CoA through the 3-hydroxy-3-methylglutaryl CoA (HMG-CoA) reductase pathway. HMG-CoA is acted upon by the enzyme HMG-CoA reductase to eventually create the final product of cholesterol. This highly simplified explanation (pictured below) with terms that are probably completely foreign will be explained in much greater detail at a later point. We aren't getting you ready for the exam, so rest assured that we won't explore every little and minute detail of this process. It would be unfortunate if we enlightened you about cholesterol only to have you die of boredom.

Cholesterol Biosynthesis
(simplified version)

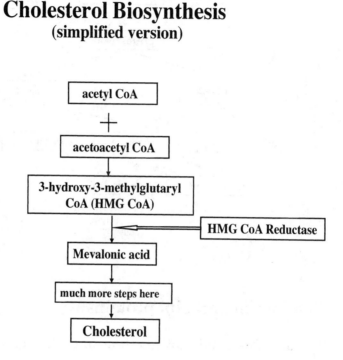

The steroid hormones originate from cholesterol in a similar fashion. Once again, this diagram is highly simplified and we will go into further detail at a later point.

Metabolism of Cholesterol
(simplified version)

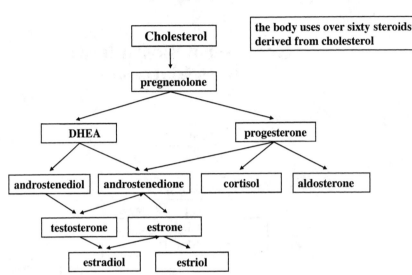

Cholesterol and Lipoproteins

We have now briefly covered how important cholesterol is to the body just by virtue of it being such a vital component in the body. So now, there must be some confusion going on. If cholesterol is obviously so important, why is it such a prime target for suppression? We put on our brainstorming hats and think back to our greatest source of information, the television commercials. Aren't they always going on about good and bad cholesterol? Problem solved!

Well, if for this time "solved" means "horribly complicated", then yes indeed it is solved. With such clear cut names like "good" and "bad" cholesterol we can single out the villainous cholesterol and leave the good one alone. So how can we target this delinquent cholesterol, this unproductive member of our body society? Surely this is the cholesterol that loiters in our blood streams, leading to blockage. Once again, we run into a problem of classification. But this is a different kind of problem than the one where we don't truly know what to classify cholesterol as. The problem here is giving the flat out wrong name to something that doesn't deserve it. The two actors of the play here, good and bad cholesterol, are wrongfully labeled due to the somewhat critical fact that neither of them is actually cholesterol. Good cholesterol is actually high density lipoprotein (HDL) and bad cholesterol is low density lipoprotein (LDL). You might recall that cholesterol has no exact terminology and it is neither a lipid nor a protein, which is what these two fine specimens are. Why are these lipoproteins called cholesterol when they're not, and why did they earn the Wild West monikers of good and bad?

The primary job of HDL and LDL is to act as carriers for lipids and cholesterol. This is the association that they have with cholesterol, as transports. So why are they called cholesterol? Well, we're at a loss here. They transport cholesterol? Yes, this makes about as much sense as having a cloth sack to carry apples, and then calling that cloth sack apples. To make matters worse when we're going to the cider distillery our cloth sack is inexplicably called bad apples and when we are bringing our leftover apples home it is called good apples when the apples in the sack are the same both ways. If you're thinking how in the world this makes sense - it doesn't.

HDL and LDL are not the only lipoproteins in town. Lipoproteins in general are made up of phospholipids, proteins, cholesteryl ester, cholesterol (which stays intact), and triglycerides. Triglycerides and cholesterol cannot be dissolved in blood, which necessitates this transport action. They need to be wrapped up and delivered to where they need to go so that they don't simply float about the blood streams. In other words, lipoproteins are the transport for insoluble cholesterol and triglycerides.

In the war against cholesterol, its cousin triglyceride is often mentioned as an accessory to whatever destructive deeds cholesterol is up to. The most common association that triglycerides have is simply with "fat," though this does not quite give justice to this molecule. In terms of energy storage, triglycerides carry more energy than even carbohydrates, which are often given all the credit as far as empowering the metabolism with power. As we will note shortly, triglycerides are an important part of the chain of lipid transports, and when their job is done they can be reabsorbed for storage or utilized for energy. Unfortunately, whenever something in the body has both a good and bad function, it seems that the public perception is much more likely to focus on the negative and neglect the positives. After all, we can't very well market drugs to target the good parts of something. How well would a cholesterol lowering drug sell if the notification on the bottle said that it interfered with the beneficial aspects of cholesterol?

Lipoproteins come in various sizes and are classified by function and composition. This handy diagram shows the players of the game, much like an illustration of the solar system (albeit one made of fats and proteins).

Lipoproteins are classified according to their density

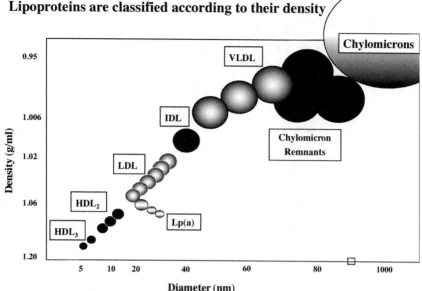

- Chylomicrons, which are also the biggest of the lot, transport fats and cholesterol from the intestines to the liver. The liver reconstructs these component parts and sends them into the bloodstream. Chylomicrons transport triglycerides from the intestines to the liver, skeletal muscle, and to adipose tissue (quite simply body fat). The liver then reconstructs component parts into very low-density lipoproteins and sends them into the bloodstream. Chylomicrons consist of about 85-88% triglycerides, 3% cholesteryl esters and 1% cholesterol, 8% phospholipids, and 1-2% proteins. These are also the biggest at 1000 nm (nanometers, or one billionth of a meter), which of course isn't very big at all. The primary purpose of chylomicrons is to transport the triglycerides and cholesterol taken in from food that is absorbed in the intestines. They are also the least dense of the transport particles.

- Very low-density lipoproteins (VLDL) are produced from the liver from the aforementioned component parts. VLDL carries newly synthesized TRG from the liver to adipose tissue. VLDL becomes an intermediate density lipoprotein particle after it has lost its triglyceride content. They consist of 50-55% triglycerides, 12-15% cholesteryl esters, 8-10% cholesterol, 18-20% phospholipids, and 5-12% protein. A key difference between chylomicrons and VLDL is that chylomicrons transport products taken in via food while VLDL transports products that are created inside the body. Size wise, VLDL is smaller than chylomicrons.

- Intermediate density lipoproteins (IDL) are short lived and consist of about 32-35% cholesteryl esters, 8% cholesterol, 24-30% triglycerides, 25-27% phospholipids, and 10-12% protein. IDL are taken back into the liver for reprocessing into component parts or lose even more triglyceride content to become LDL. It is important to note here that intermediate does not refer to a stage but rather to the density, which is between VLDL and LDL. The size of IDL is smaller than VLDL.

- LDL is the primary plasma carrier of cholesterol for delivery from the liver to all tissues. Cholesterol is further absorbed by cells around the body. LDL consists of 37-48% cholesteryl esters, 8-10% cholesterol, 10-15% triglycerides, 20-28% phospholipids, and 20-22% protein. LDL transports both cholesterol taken in via dietary means and cholesterol produced within the body. LDL is also the primary transporter of cholesterol, and accounts for more than half of lipids circulating within the blood. LDL is responsible for bringing the cholesterol to production sites where it is needed. LDL particles are involved in the formation of plaques on the walls of the arteries. Going down the list, LDL is, as expected, smaller than IDL.

- HDL molecules are made in the intestines and the liver. They help remove cholesterol from artery walls. HDL acts as a cholesterol sponge, scavenging cholesterol not utilized by cells and bringing it back to the liver. Excess cholesterol is reabsorbed by the liver and reused or excreted into bile. HDL consists of 15-30% cholesteryl esters, 2-10% cholesterol, 3-15% triglycerides, 24-46% phospholipids, and 55% protein. HDL is also the most dense in this list.[3] Without much surprise, HDL is the smallest on the list.

It must be noted here that the list above is listed in descending order of size, and that the percentages are more guidelines rather than fact. For example, an LDL molecule could well be carrying a much smaller amount of cholesterol than listed above, and the same can be said for any of the transports. They are not simply always roaring to go at full capacity, but instead allocated as needed by the body. There are no adjectives in the world of lipoproteins. The cloth sack is either good apples or bad apples, but never almost full good apples or nearly empty bad apples.

We can explain what is going on in our body in regards to LDL and HDL with a simple example. On the one side, we have the factories that are producing cholesterol. On the other side, we have the plants that produce the steroid hormones. Low levels of steroid hormones require cholesterol to create more steroid hormones. How do we deliver cholesterol from one side to the other? We of course need transports. These are LDL. When we have an excess of cholesterol near the plants that produce the hormones, we need extra transportation for the cholesterol returning to the liver. What is the name of these carriers? HDL. These transports have no conception of good and bad, they are only trying to do their job.

Measuring Cholesterol

This gallery of movers and shakers is quite a diverse group, but one question remains. With all these elements, what is total cholesterol? How is it measured? It is simple, really.

LDL + HDL + (Triglycerides/5) = Total Cholesterol

That is total cholesterol. This is that deadly number that needs to be brought down as the reassuring man in the commercial says. A question, a very just one at that, might arise at this point. Just what exactly are triglycerides doing up there? Is this another case of misplaced nomenclature as with good and bad cholesterol? Do triglycerides fall under an alternate name as some kind of "intermediate" cholesterol? Unfortunately such an alternate classification does not exist, because triglycerides are triglycerides. The division of triglycerides by 5 is the way in which VLDL is estimated. So, in essence the formula is this:

LDL + HDL + VLDL = Total Cholesterol

We make this distinction because VLDL is not always tested,

even though to get the total cholesterol value the triglyceride level is always divided by 5 (which is the VLDL estimation). Next time you look at a blood test, you can rest assured that with some simple math you can figure out what exactly is going on.

There is another matter which must be considered here. Taking a look back at the equation shows LDL, HDL, Triglycerides (VLDL) on one side, which when added together create the sum of total cholesterol, while keeping in mind that on the left side of the equation nowhere is the word "cholesterol" mentioned.

Consider the following example. An apple overseer at a regional trucking transport company is trying to keep track of all the apples that are transported via trucks. In the field, there are 76 trucks hauling apples to a warehouse, 52 trucks hauling apples away from the warehouse, and 150 trucks just driving around empty because they are serving as placeholders for 30 trucks hauling apples that aren't directly taken into account (we had a hard time with this one as well). None of these trucks that is carrying apples is full. However, when the apple overseer gets the report of apple numbers, he will see that he has 158 trucks full of apples rolling around.

This doesn't look too well for the trucking company's upcoming fiscal year. Why did we bring up this example? Unfortunately, it can be transported right from the hypothetical trucking firm to the very real local blood testing laboratory. The issue here is that LDL consists approximately 50% of cholesterol and cholesteryl esters while HDL consists approximately 30% of cholesterol and cholesteryl esters, yet in the equation they are added as having equal values associated with their cholesterol content. One would think that if we are trying to find out the value of "total cholesterol" we might make some further divisions, but such is not the case.

If HDL is the "good cholesterol," then why is its part in the equation simply as an addition to the "bad cholesterol?" Of course, we also can't forget that the LDL and HDL molecules being counted are not going to be all at full capacity, so even the arbitrary 50% and 30% cholesterol values are insignificant.

But we are in the clear now, right? We have at least the process by which we can get the information, and even if VLDL is a bit of a pain we aren't too bad off in the other parts of the equation. That would be excellent and simple, but it isn't. LDL is a calculated number as well. Another simple equation comes into play here. Get ready for this one.

Total Cholesterol – (Triglycerides/5 + HDL) = LDL

The powers of mathematics prevail again. If this was algebra class, then this is simply a modification of our original formula except in this case we are solving for variable LDL.

This equation is called the Friedewald Equation. There are some conditions that interfere with this test. If the triglyceride level is higher than 400 mg/dl then LDL cannot be accurately measured in this manner, the reason for this being that concentrations of triglycerides of more than 400 mg/dl make the laboratory sample too thick. If chylomicrons are present in the sample, then they can interfere with accurate readings as well.

Even when the equation is used under optimal conditions, the amount of LDL can be underestimated or overestimated. This occurs because the other tests are measured in an imprecise manner as well, so that by default the imprecision that is present in those tests are transferred onto the LDL value because said values are used to obtain this number.

We must make clear that this isn't some kind of grand conspiracy to spread around false cholesterol numbers (one would hope anyway). The problem with direct LDL measurement is that it is both costly and somewhat advanced. As a result, a lot of testing laboratories are not equipped to handle this more advanced procedure. In essence, this equation is used to save money and time, as well as lack of appropriate equipment. This would be much more reassuring if the cholesterol lowering industry wasn't so keen on numbers, ready at any moment to dispense advice on drug use.

At all times, whether we are figuring the VLDL by division of triglycerides or even the value of total cholesterol, we find out the estimations of current transports which are carrying variable levels of cholesterol. However, such is the testing procedure, just something worth mentioning to keep in mind when considering all the absolute numbers recommended from all sides.

The Wrong Approach?

So now it seems that cholesterol is not so bad at all, all questions regarding the way it is measured aside. In fact, it is apparent that cholesterol is vital to life and a normally functioning body. Why then, is the anti-cholesterol crusade still in full swing? There is the matter of hypercholesterolemia (high cholesterol). Cholesterol can build up in the arteries and cause severe arterial damage. That is how the often repeated story goes. However, this version of the story is quite lacking. The usual suspect, cholesterol, is of course always mentioned. But what this story always seems to neglect to mention is the fact that this is in no way a one man job. Cholesterol is certainly not the only element at play here.

In fact, the damage done to cholesterol in this instance is

quite bad due to the association. Whenever that helpful diagram of the ever increasingly clogged artery is shown on the commercial, the narrator is speaking about atherosclerotic plaque. The commercial is for cholesterol lowering drugs, so cholesterol is the primary target and is mentioned hand in hand with the name of atherosclerotic plaque. This exposure to cholesterol and the concept of atherosclerosis is either reinforced ad nauseum or is the first true exposure an individual will have to the concepts of cholesterol (other than off hand remarks here and there that cholesterol = bad, or perhaps on the package of breakfast cereal that lowers cholesterol).

Such exposure leads to an association via reinforcement by repetition. The concept of atherosclerosis brings about the image of arteries clogged with cholesterol, looking like a fat mess that needs to be cleared up or cut open. The problem here is that atherosclerosis, by definition, simply refers to the hardening of arteries. It does not mean by default that elevated cholesterol is completely bent on clogging our arteries. What of this plaque then?

The largest composition of atherosclerotic plaque actually consists of macrophages. Macrophages are rather "large" white blood cells, which are large because of their function. The Greek basis of this word literally means large and eat, and true to their name macrophages float around and eat things. What sort of things? The first that comes to mind are pathogens, the invaders of our bodies such as bacteria. Macrophages can quite simply swallow these whole and digest them. In this instance "swallowing" is more like opening up a part of the cell and engulfing the offender. However, they are not solely responsible for taking out the invaders.

Pathogens aren't the only thing on the menu for macrophages. They have the task of removing dead and damaged tissue within the body as needed. This job might seem like a lesser effort because of the way such a difference in tasks would be seen. The valiant job of fighting back invaders in the body is quite a bit more glamorous than working as a sanitation engineer taking out the garbage. Engulfing and eliminating pathogens is a much more noticeable effort and is thus the much better known action of macrophages, as learned in high school biology.

Macrophages are also fully integrated with the immune system (being a part of the immune system certainly qualifies it for this distinction). When macrophages absorb pathogens, they release the antigens (a molecule, usually present on pathogens that triggers the creation of antibodies) present in the pathogen to white blood cells. Antibodies are created from this chain of events which adhere to the antigens on other pathogens, which in turn makes their absorption easier for macrophages. The macrophages utilize substances present on pathogens themselves as a weapon against them, with the help of other agents of the immune system.

What would happen if macrophages did not help eliminate this dead tissue from the body? If the trash got left out on the curb in the real world then it would be a major eye sore, some bad smell, and attraction of all sorts of unwanted organisms, large and small. Within the body, this example would be much worse. Necrosis, or premature cell death, is a very dangerous condition because when cells undergo apoptosis, or natural cell death, they send out signals so that macrophages can take care of the matter. Cells that die via necrosis do not release such signals. Thus, necrosis is bad due to increasing amounts of dead cells. If macrophages did not take care of cells that went through apoptosis naturally, a similar and very dangerous buildup of dead tissue would ensue.

A macrophage is not always called simply a macrophage. In fact it is called this last in the general scheme of things. Since macrophages are so numerous and present in so many areas, they are named after their location and function. The majority of macrophages are thus located in such specific areas, with a lower total amount circulating randomly about the blood. These specialized macrophages include but are not limited to alveolar macrophages, histiocytes, Kupffer cells, and microglia.

Alveolar macrophages, also called dust cells, are located in the lungs, in particular in the alveoli. The alveoli are small, grape like clusters that are hollow inside and line the lungs. They are responsible for the actual gas exchange that occurs when breaths are taken. Carbon dioxide is brought to the surface of these structures and oxygen is taken inside. This oxygen and carbon dioxide transport is accomplished by the circulating blood. Alveolar macrophages, true to their other name, are responsible for capturing the dust that enters the lungs during respiration, as well as all the airborne pathogens that enter in this fashion. Due to extreme amount of contact with the outside environment, these macrophages have quite a hectic job.

Histiocytes are macrophages that are found in connective tissue. Connective tissue is one of the major types of tissues, with the four tissue types being connective, muscle, nervous, and epithelial (skin). Connective tissue has a variety of tasks and functions depending on its location. It holds organs in place and even connects epithelial tissue to other tissues. Highly specialized connective tissue includes adipose tissue (which holds fat), cartilage, bone, and even blood. Why is blood considered a type of "tissue?"

This has to do with one of the core tenets of connective tissue in that it is usually surrounded by an extracellular matrix. An extracellular matrix is simply nonliving matter among the living parts of the body. The function of this matrix is to provide support and other important tasks as needed. How does blood fit into this as a connective tissue? The cells and various agents that are in blood are suspended in the plasma, which is mostly composed of water and is thus not a living part of the body (though it is vital for life).

Kupffer cells suffer from having a non-scientific name among the macrophages, joining the ranks of such parts of the body as the Golgi Apparatus (an organelle). Being first to discover something gives a certain priority in naming schemes, and these fine individuals wasted no time in calling these finds after themselves. The case with Kupffer cells is amusing because while he was the first to discover them, he did not correctly identify their origin.

The domain of Kupffer cells is in the liver. As usual, the job is to pick up debris and microbes. Kupffer cells are particularly effective in blocking certain microbes due to their location. Occasionally, bacteria from the small intestine can make their way through tears in the intestinal lining. This covers both the "good" bacteria and potentially invading "bad" bacteria. The good bacteria are part of the human digestive system and assist the body in various tasks but they are confined to the digestive system for a reason. If they make their way to other parts of the body they can be dangerous.

If the rest of the macrophages in this list are part of the regular armed forces (and sanitation department, for that matter), then the microglia can be considered the elite special forces due to their location and the speed at which they must accomplish their tasks. The domain of the microglia is the brain and spinal cord. To say that these parts of the body are extremely important is quite an understatement. While the systems in the body are happy to go about their tasks and work to the best of their abilities, they need instructions from the brain to do so. The vast network of neurons that is responsible for the relay of information to perform all vital functions of the body, not to mention the movements you are performing right now as you read this book without even thinking about it, is a very powerful yet delicate system which must have constant upkeep. When neurons are damaged microglia promptly take care of them, along with any other debris or foreign matter, and do their job of keeping the system healthy. Damaged neurons are certainly not something that is desirable to have intact within a system which is in control of life itself.

Microglia are not simply the garbage collectors, they are also the repairmen of the brain. Through various actions they help facilitate the regeneration of those damaged neurons that are simply in need of repair and not removal. This repair even includes the re-routing of the impulse pathways. The anti-pathogen capability of microglia is very advanced due the nature of their environment. The blood-brain barrier does a very good job of keeping a majority of all invaders out, but Mongols do penetrate the Great Wall. When such invaders come into the brain, the microglia must react immediately and attempt to neutralize the threat to protect the sensitive neural tissue.

At this point, it is readily apparent that macrophages are extremely vital to the regular function of the body, and not just as repairmen and defenders. They can even combine to form "giant cells" which are referred to as granulomas in an attempt to stop pathogenic invasion in the body (a brute force approach to just block the invasion with a mass). So why did we just spend all that time describing in brief (truly in brief, because to fully describe all the actions of macrophages within the body would take a good deal more effort) what macrophages do?

The point is that nothing in the body can be taken at face value. If we were to observe macrophages only in the instance where they are the major component of atherosclerotic plaque, then we would certainly want to eliminate such a seemingly dangerous item. But, for lack of a better or proper term, that would be pretty stupid.

If we turn back the clock some 2000 years a large part of the populace believes that the sun revolves around the earth. Now we know that the earth revolves around the sun, that the sun revolves around our galaxy, and that our galaxy is part of an incredibly complex and not fully understood universe. With the evidence presented to us, the latter is the one which must be accepted as the proper interpretation. It is not logical to focus on an observation in one specific instance in order to define the function of something.

On the one hand, the macrophage can be seen as a specific agent participating in atherosclerotic plaque, while on the other hand as part of the bigger picture the macrophage is also an essential element of the body. Nobody would ever dream of a macrophage lowering drug, because that would be an act of sabotage against the body.

As we go further in depth into the nature of cholesterol it will become apparent that it suffers from such a hypothetical scenario. Unfortunately, the case is far from hypothetical and cholesterol is in exactly such a situation. To add insult to cholesterol's injury, there is another aspect of atherosclerotic plaque that is not only exempt from blame but even enjoys great acclaim.

Who is this mystery contender? Calcium! How does calcium fit in with atherosclerotic plaque? Once the buildup becomes advanced enough, calcification occurs over time which makes the outer edges harder and stiffer. But yet, calcium supplementation in large quantities is suggested on a massive scale to older individuals, with larger doses recommended for older women to pop them down like candy. Why is it that instead of additional calcium they are recommended calcium reduction therapy to help reduce the hardening of atherosclerotic plaque? After all, when calcium hardens the buildup in arteries, it becomes much more difficult to disperse the blockage.

Thus, we tread as we ever do into dangerous waters. These waters are infested not with kraken or Vikings, but with a terrible inconsistency. This is the inconsistency that stems from something being associated with something else as opposed to something being an actual direct cause of something else. Let's look at some examples.

After a long night out on the town, some mishaps happen. A few doctor visits later, it appears that HIV has been contracted. Over time, if no action is taken with something such as antiretroviral drugs, HIV will cause AIDS. As such, HIV causes AIDS. This is a simple example (which is of course never simple when one looks at the calculated precision with which HIV destroys the immune system) of an agent having direct causation to something else.

Next up is something like heavy metal poisoning. Heavy metals are important to the body in small quantities or as trace elements (an element that is needed only in the most minute of quantities for proper function). This is why all inclusive breakfast cereals show a seemingly hefty dose of iron on the side panel. While the thought of iron in our bodies might seem like a strange idea, belonging more so in a factory than a living organism, it is actually a very important element.

One important function of iron is its part in carrying oxygen in hemoglobin throughout the body. Hemoglobin is a protein in red blood cells which transports the oxygen throughout the body. In fact, hemoglobin is classified as a "metalloprotein," which shows clearly that metals are vital to the body since they have a dedicated protein type to describe such interactions. Iron isn't limited to humans either, and is present in all living organisms.

However, an iron overdose can occur. This is not a very practically occurring event, since obtaining an iron overdose through diet is more or less impossible. A much more likely scenario is an iron overdose due to over-ingestion of iron supplement capsules. The body is very well adapted to handling extra amounts of iron, but past a certain point too much circulating iron will overwhelm such precautions. In such an event, the excess iron can cause organ damage. This is an example of an agent that is normally beneficial and vital, but if it is present in too many quantities will directly cause harm to the system.

Next up we have atherosclerosis. Let's speak in broad terms for now and say that elevated cholesterol is associated with this condition. However, so are macrophages and calcium. That's the problem. We cannot pick out enemies to target within our body due to association. If we did that, then we would quickly find ourselves trying to exterminate a large part of the body because of the vast amount of associations present in our body between malaise and vital components.

These examples are very important to list because they provide a good cross examination of the attacks on cholesterol. By examining other examples of appropriate scenarios and those where attack through association makes no sense, we can get a better grasp on what is going on in the public perception of cholesterol. As we move forward we will be going much deeper into cholesterol and associated systems to see if the cholesterol war has any merits (spoiler alert - it really doesn't). As a first step, we can glance through the history of cholesterol research and discovery to see the origins of the science behind it all before proceeding further into the effects associated with variable levels of cholesterol and the end products of cholesterol metabolism.

CHAPTER 2

The Atherosclerosis – Cholesterol Axis

In this instance, by axis we of course mean the structure around which these concepts revolve, not the term that brings to mind Third Reich associations from the second World War. Before going into a brief history we'd like to stress that this is not so much a history as it is a cursory glance at how the studies of cholesterol originated, changed, established trends, and evolved over time. A written out comprehensive analysis of all cholesterol studies would well require a separate book in itself. Which is just as well, as going through the quicksand of technical language and questionable statistical analysis is not by definition having a good time.

The 1850s is the time when the ball slowly started rolling, the snowball picking up mass and speed from the top of the mountain to eventually take of all our attention. It was in this time period that Rudolph Virchow, a German doctor, developed the lipid hypothesis which suggested that blood lipid accumulation in arterial walls was the cause of atherosclerosis.[1] In 1858 Virchow showed that cholesterol did not quite start the process, but rather that it was the end product of degeneration. Damage to tissue was the first and most obvious sign observed. After the damage occurred, an accumulation of fat appeared. Then, as the scar tissue was formed, a high amount of cholesterol appeared. This is somewhat important to keep in mind, because it shows a good understanding of the basic actions of cholesterol as an agent associated with repair. For those keeping track, this happened in the Victorian Era, when Africa was still considered "The Dark Continent". For the rest of the 1800s the cholesterol front was quiet.

The early to mid-1900s can be best described as very dire times to be a rabbit due to their priority selection for laboratory testing. The pioneers of atherosclerosis research went about testing their hypothesis by feeding cholesterol to rabbits to see the results in relation to plaque buildup. There is, of course, a slight problem with this. Rabbits are herbivores, or organisms that eat plants, and as such do not consume animal cholesterol in their natural diet. Their bodies simply cannot utilize it. The results were appropriately unpleasant: anything from completely yellowed eyes to loss of fur occurred, as well as atherosclerosis in rabbits fed immense quantities of cholesterol.

While animal testing is no doubt a great asset to research in many fields, it would be somewhat ideal if there was at least a better correlation with the test subjects. We're sure no humans want to go on a scientific trial to consume lots of fats and oils to wind up expired on a dissection table for the name of science, which is why we use animals. But to use animals that do not consume meat and giving them something that they would not take in is a recipe for a bad day for rabbits and a bad day for accurate scientific research. One study from 1926, while searching for a correlation of protein and atherosclerosis, not just cholesterol, found fault with contemporary and earlier studies not because of the use of cholesterol on a herbivorous animal, but rather on the dosing and methods.[2] For some reason, the concept that herbivorous animal use in these testing scenarios was not optimal for more accurate results was not scrutinized.

The reason we spent so much time on the type of animal issue is simply because the initial stages of research in any field are crucial in establishing future research and the assumptions that are present in this field. As research progresses the methodology and experimentation improves, but the initial assumptions linger in the background. This sounds like a flawed concept on an initial analysis. When Io, one of the moons of Jupiter, was first discovered, it was thought to be a dead moon much like our own. It was not until the late last century when our space probes flew by that we found out it was an active and volcanic world. New direct scientific evidence showed us that we were wrong. The problem is rabbits are not thought of as dead moons to be discovered by our probes as active and volcanic worlds. If we feed them cholesterol today they will react just as they did some 80 odd years ago.

The Turning Point of Research

In 1950, John Gofman hypothesized that blood cholesterol was the main cause of coronary heart disease (CHD). A year later Duff and McMillian created the lipid hypothesis in its modern form.[3] In 1953 Ancel Keys published a paper that discussed saturated fats and cholesterol as the causes of heart disease.[4] At this point it was found that people who died of heart disease often had a high level of cholesterol in their blood. Numerous studies have found that elevated cholesterol levels are associated with an increased risk of atherosclerosis. However, the key word here is associated. Let's say that a bridge is in danger of future collapse, which prompts workers to improve and reinforce the bridge with new masonry. However, the bridge collapses regardless. Is the newly introduced masonry the cause of the collapse, or is it whatever problem the new masonry attempted to rectify?

In the years that followed, studies regarding cholesterol rose up left and right. One of the more important studies, though not directly related to cholesterol but to cardiovascular health in general, is the Framingham Heart Study. It is a large scale and long term study from which some information regarding CHD was hoped to be found. However, some of the results obtained were not necessarily the results that were to be expected. For example, a few decades after the Framingham study began results showed that individuals with low cholesterol had a greater morbidity from other causes of death, negating any reduced incidences of lowered coronary heart disease.[5] The prevalence of studies regarding cholesterol has significantly increased into present day, which is why attempting to list all the data here would be foolish.

With such a large body of work dedicated to the investigation of cholesterol, a large amount of time would have to be put into actually analyzing all this data. To the lay person, this is certainly a challenging or even almost impossible objective. At this statement, lay people all over might furrow their brow and deem this as an attack at their intelligence. It is anything but. A layperson to a certain field is simply an individual who has not invested a good amount of time in learning to understand all the intricate and delicate ins and outs of the discipline. There is another and very important block that bars the layperson from this information. This block exists in the form of an admittance barrier that is up to anyone who is not affiliated in some way with the source of information.

For example, take PubMed. This is a search engine of sorts to a large variety of health and medical articles and studies, with literally millions of references included. Great, you might think, give me a weekend and I can brush up on the information and be just as well versed as any of these experts. If such was the case we would have a lot more of this information floating around.

As it is, searching the database without some sort of medical login credentials will usually at most point to an abstract of an article or at worst just the name of the article and nothing more. To see the information you would need a free transcript to be available (which is quite rare) or be a member of whatever publishing body hosts the study. Even with medical login credentials this information is often barred in the form of a membership with the affiliated entity.

In other words, the cost of entry to an "outsider" of this field will usually be too prohibitive to warrant pursuing the matter further. What does this mean? Quite simply the general population simply has to accept what information is being given to them without easily being able to peruse the matter on their own. Since the quest for information is full of so many pitfalls, a quicker method of information gathering can be established by observing trends.

Temporary Trends of Constant Cholesterol

One thing associated with cholesterol we can look at first is the "cholesterol diet." First, it should be noted that the human liver synthesizes roughly 3000 mg of new cholesterol in any 24 hour period. A majority of people can handle an intake of cholesterol within the range that people normally consume (300 mg – 400 mg) without significantly altering their blood cholesterol level. People usually get 10%-30% of cholesterol through their diet. However, in most people, less than 5% of the cholesterol in the bloodstream gets there through diet.[6]

Such numbers can hardly be encouraging if an individual wishes to lose cholesterol by altering his or her diet. This is a wasted effort because the body is always looking out for itself. If an individual decreases the consumption of cholesterol through food, the actual effect on plasma cholesterol levels is minute because when this restriction occurs the body increases its own production of cholesterol to make up for this lost source.[7]

While we might be out to control our bodies, we fail to realize that there are many safeguards to put a wrench in the plans that we think are best. Consider that a person trying to lose weight by not eating for long periods of time is committing sabotage because the body notes the lack of food and goes into emergency mode so that when more food is taken in, it is more readily turned into fat to try and create a surplus.

Cholesterol lowered by diet also caused lowered levels of estradiol, testosterone, and DHEA (steroid hormones which we will cover in due time).[8] The Framingham Heart Study that we mentioned earlier tried to establish if high cholesterol levels were in fact caused by diets. To measure this, they chose 912 men and women and compared the cholesterol intake via diet to the blood cholesterol levels. There was no link in these two factors. They also measured the amount of saturated fat consumption and the total amount of calories taken in which showed that there was no link here either. The actual phrasing that the researchers used was that there appeared to be no relation between diet and the development of coronary heart disease in this particular study group.[9] What is important to remember is that this particular study was performed in 1970, and that many cholesterol "diets" came later.

Unfortunately, this study was never published. Why not?

Why not indeed.

It would appear that something that has as loose a definition as a "low cholesterol diet" can be a trend but not necessarily be based on hard scientific data. Solid and standardized numbers are often the signifiers of solid scientific research, so surely the recommended levels of cholesterol are verifiers of this notion. Prior to 1980, hypercholesterolemia was defined as any value above the 95th percentile for the population. These figures ranged from 210 mg/dL in persons younger than 20 to more than 280 mg/dL in persons older than 60.

In 1970 the normal range for cholesterol was 150-280 mg/dL.[10] In 1990, the "desirable" blood cholesterol value became anything below 200 mg/dL. In 1995, the normal range of cholesterol became 150-250 mg/dL.[11] In 1996, the recommended interval became what was before the "desirable" interval of below 200 mg/dL. In 2002 the focus came into LDL (our old friend bad cholesterol), and any value less than 100 was optimal, as well as increased focus on high triglyceride values (higher than 200 mg/dL).[12] Currently, the normal laboratory range for triglycerides is less than 150 mg/dL. In 2004, the recommended LDL level became less than 70 mg/dL for individuals with known atherosclerosis.

Before we proceed we should speak a bit on these "optimal ranges" and "high ranges." The normal range is defined as exactly what it sounds like, the range that the majority of individuals possess for a certain level. This is usually defined as 95% of the population where all is good and well. How does this factor in with cholesterol values?

As many as 5% of the population in Western countries have total cholesterol higher than 300 mg/dL, which according to the definition of normal ranges should be the real hypercholesterolemia (this figure is roughly 20% lower among Asians). But according to the recommendations from the medical community, this value is 200 mg/dL or below. There is also the issue of 120 million people with a cholesterol value greater than 200 mg/dL, as well as 60 million with cholesterol greater than 240 mg/dL, living in the United States.[13] How is it possible that so many people are not "normal"? Why the stark difference between the expected normal value and the actually suggested normal value?

The Lipid Hypothesis - Scientific Consensus

With such seemingly determined and constant changes, there must certainly be a strict scientific method behind these recommendations. One would hope, and one would assume, that we live in a land where new scientific data is accepted only after rigorous testing which determines a unified scientific consensus based on overwhelming evidence by rigorous testing. Unfortunately, the selection of these values is something decided on by a vote. This brings to mind presidential elections, except instead of one party winning, we all lose a little bit.

But a scientific consensus can be considered a good vote, can it not? After all, when a large group of scientists gathers and determines that there is a consensus they must know what is going on. Interpretation of data allowed the "lipid hypothesis" to be created by the end of the previous century. A survey was taken in 1978 that found out that a majority of researchers and practitioners were in favor of the lipid hypothesis.

In that survey, 211 top researchers in the associated field were asked if there was a connection between cholesterol levels and the development of coronary heart disease, and whether or not the available knowledge surrounding diet and heart disease was enough to recommend a change in diet for a society that allows such a change. 90% of these researchers answered in the affirmative. With such a general question, the answer can be very direct while actually not revealing concrete information.

What is science? Seems like a question with a rather obvious answer so ingrained into our understanding that if someone were to ask us, we would actually have a bit of hesitation in explaining it. Science comes from the Latin word *scientia*, which simply means knowledge. Science is knowledge gained about the physical world through the powers of observation and experimentation.

Let's consider an example that is all around us. If you let go of this book, it will drop to the floor (unless of course you are an astronaut orbiting the earth, if so we wish to thank you on your choice of reading material). This is the work of gravity. How do we know about gravity? Observation and experimentation. Numerous studies and applications of physical laws by many scientists have shaped our modern view of gravity. A group of elite scientists did not gather around a portrait of Sir Isaac Newton and have a show of hands on what was to be the accepted policy regarding gravity. Even with all of our seemingly advanced understanding of gravitational interactions, we still don't know what actually causes gravity. This sounds somewhat familiar.

The way that science works is tied into the scientific method, unsurprisingly enough. The scientific method can be thought of as overall guidelines for establishing scientific research. While it is not a set of steps written in stone to be followed by the letter with every single bit of research, it does provide an overall idea of how to go about doing this research for accepted scientific explanation.

There are four broader categories that describe the scientific method, which for the sake of simplicity can be further broken down into eight steps. The latter eight steps is probably the more familiar concept, being imprinted in the minds of elementary school children everywhere. It must be noted that when scientific research is about to commence, scientists don't have a list of the steps and go down this list in order to see what to do next. It's just that as far as good scientific research is concerned, these steps show the logical progression for optimal results.

The four broad categories themselves are not the steps, but rather the methods used in formulating scientific hypotheses. Observation, which includes both physical observation and actual data collection, gathers information not only for the creation of the experiment and hypothesis but also from the experimentation process. The hypotheses category describes the explanations formed to find meaning in the subject. Predictions are formed based on the expected outcomes and experimentation. Experimentation refers to the tests performed to try and explain all the other categories.

The eight steps that bring about the science fair flashbacks are more cut and dry. The first step is the formation of the question. The second step is observation, seeing the factors in question and collecting information about them. The next step is formation of the hypothesis, or an educated guess trying to explain what is going on. Experimentation comes next, and attempts to test the hypothesis and to gather data about the outcome. This data is then analyzed, after which the results can be interpreted for reinforcement of the hypothesis. The last steps include publication of findings and further testing. The further testing is of particular importance because it also includes tests performed by others based on the published findings to either reinforce or discredit the new hypothesis.

It's clearly evident that a lot of work goes into science. There are many steps all with the goal of trying to prove the accuracy of observations and statements made. The complex chain is rounded up by rigorous testing from numerous parties for reinforcement. At no point in this procedure does it say that further testing to reach a conclusive hypothesis can be replaced by a survey based on opinion that can be employed for the application of action in regards to the hypothesis. To find the truth, you can't be a voter. You need to be an observer, investigator, and analyst.

Democracy is great, because we can use subjective selection to determine what we think is the best choice. Logic would dictate that a subjective selection process of an objective notion is somewhat of a paradoxical concept, yet here we are, voting on cholesterol. The pain of Pluto being recently demoted from the status of planet to dwarf planet by a show of hands is brought to mind, but Pluto's definition as a planetary body has no impact on the health of millions of people.

The word medicine comes from the Latin *ars medicina*, which translates to the art of healing. Unfortunately, in the modern world medicine got a nasty habit of being somewhat the art of business. Even as we have great advances in improving healthcare, medicine is hindered by being a science with a heavy involvement of statistics and doesn't exactly have a 100% relation to the art of healing anymore.

Have we gone off the deep end at this point? Will we say that government is bad next? Of course not, because that would be foolish and make no sense. Nobody is denying that we continue to make great strides in medicine that help many.

Medicine is in no way inherently bad, it is by all means inherently good. However, the marriage of medicine and business is not a very good union.

Let's consider the example of the fluctuating cholesterol levels as they are considered optimal. By definition, the people who can be labeled as having hypercholesterolemia according to the concept of the normal range is appropriately low, or else it wouldn't be called the normal range. The entire point of a normal range is to describe the majority, or the "normal" part of the population, while taking into account the fringe members who do not fall under this label. So, let's say that hypercholesterolemia is 300 mg/dL and above, per the normal range definition. Now, let's move this number down by a significant 100 mg/dL.

What happens? First and foremost, we just corrupted the concept of normal range, so we can't call it that anymore. We can call it the "recommended range." The second event that occurs is greatly increased potential for monetary gain. Suddenly, with an extra buffer of 100 mg/dL, a significantly larger percentage of the population is "qualified" for cholesterol lowering drugs.

This is all beginning to sound vaguely like a conspiracy theory reserved for fringe lunatics and paranoids. There's no need to take out the tinfoil hats. The reason that it works in the instance of cholesterol is because it is already associated, key word being associated, with something like clogged arteries, so lowering the acceptable level would only elicit cheers from the populace. As far back as the people can remember, cholesterol has been a bit of a bad guy.

Let's mix this scenario up a bit. Consider platelets (also known as thrombocytes), which should be familiar to most people. Platelets are cell fragments circulating about in the blood that are responsible for clotting. The most popularly known function of platelets is to stop bleeding, but they also serve roles in homeostasis and even cell growth. Platelets are also carriers of serotonin, which is an extremely important neurotransmitter. Much like cholesterol, platelet levels that are too low or too high are not optimal. Levels that are too low increase the risk of excessive bleeding, while levels that are too high increase the risk of blood clots forming which can lead to events such as stroke and heart attacks.

Let's imagine for a minute that suddenly the "recommended" level of platelets drops by as significant a percentage as the recommendation for cholesterol. People would rightfully think that something is seriously wrong with that idea. Why would a sizeable portion of the normal range suddenly become not part of the recommended range? Did scientists suddenly figure out that a bunch of humans are defective and are walking stroke risks?

The reason that this sounds like a pretty bad idea is because nobody thought of platelets as inherently bad. In fact, platelets are another component of atherosclerotic plaque, just like macrophages and calcium. We tend to think of platelets as those certain life saving particles that prevent us from bleeding out. Cholesterol, on the other hand, has always been floating around as known associate to atherosclerosis. How would the cholesterol lowering drug industry do if from the beginning we were bombarded not with messages of doom and gloom about clogged arteries but instead about how cholesterol is a vital part of the body that is essential for life?

Perhaps we are making an unfair and biased comparison? Perhaps the normal range for cholesterol should be modified somewhat to account for some kind of dangerous variable that we haven't covered yet? Going forward we will consider the information behind high and low cholesterol as well as the role that cholesterol lowering drugs play in all of this. After all, perhaps the individuals voting for the stance that should be adopted towards cholesterol have some valuable information that they have considered when voicing their opinions.

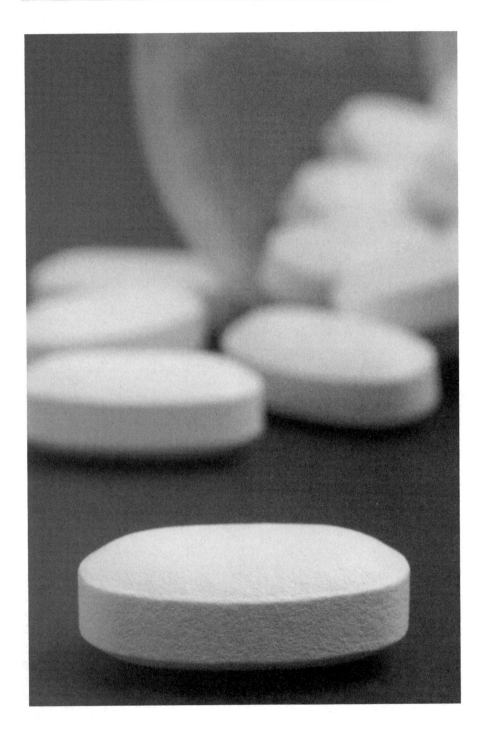

CHAPTER 3

Problems Related to High and Low Cholesterol, and Cholesterol Lowering Drugs

There are many conditions and effects associated with varying cholesterol levels, whether said levels are low or high, and whether the effects are good or bad. Since a high cholesterol level is singled out for so many issues, we would be well served to see what the effects of hypercholesterolemia are. As we mentioned previously, hypercholesterolemia is associated with atherosclerosis, which is perhaps the aspect of high cholesterol most targeted when discussions for the lowering of cholesterol are brought to the table.

That isn't to say that high cholesterol and atherosclerosis are the only links. One important thing to keep in mind while going through this section is to remember to keep cholesterol in mind as a builder and not as a scourge of the human body. We will go into great detail about this in the next section.

We can also go into greater detail about what actual medical literature (the facts) says about cholesterol as opposed to what is regularly heard from advertisements on the television and doctors. To prevent redundancy, whenever we mention facts and figures with references, we are referring to studies. So that you don't read "a study shows" a hundred times or so, we are getting that out of the way now and making this distinction.

Fueling the Fires of Creation

Hypercholesterolemia is associated with increased physiologic demand, times during which the body must prepare itself or change how it is functioning for particularly taxing tasks. Total cholesterol, LDL, and triglycerides increase significantly in women during pregnancy. Total cholesterol rises by up to 59% [which is equivalent to a mean of 314 mg/dL (8.14 mmol/l)] in the third trimester.[1-6]

That's quite a large rise to a level which would not be considered the best around. But are pregnant women dropping dead from atherosclerosis left and right? Not quite. Following delivery, total cholesterol decreases significantly within 3 months and a further decrease occurs during the following 9 months.[7] The reason for this increase goes hand in hand with the nature of pregnancy and the role of cholesterol. Growing an entirely new person inside of the body is no small feat, and cholesterol is vital for this function. There is also a great increase in the amount of steroid hormones present in the female body for this vital construction effort.

But does this high cholesterol lead to healthy births? This question is rather senseless since it is obvious that the biological response of cholesterol to pregnancy is an increase. So what happens when this level is decreased? Diminished concentrations of total cholesterol and LDL fractions were observed in women with threat of miscarriage.[8] It is quite clear that increased levels of cholesterol are essential for the most optimal and safest fetal development.

Hypercholesterolemia was found in up to 53.1% of school children in various studies.[9-13] Again, we have to reason through this and wonder: are our children dropping like flies to atherosclerosis? Even with a good dose of childhood obesity floating around this is not an issue. Most kids are likely as worried about atherosclerosis as they are worried about Communism. These elevated levels are simply a result of the natural progression of human development, as shown in pregnancy situations. There is a large increase in anabolic hormones which are important in growth and physical development into adulthood. The old saying linking teenagers to hormones is actually quite appropriate because these levels become naturally and permanently larger as they progress into adulthood, and playing loud music and disobeying the establishment somehow helps them cope.

Individuals who have significant stress during their lives have an associated increase in cholesterol.[14] An important factor here is not simply the increased buffer against mental and physical stressors. Stress has the potential to make the body go into a code red of sorts, where due to the stress the body can prepare itself for an unwanted occurrence (that might never come, but that's how the body works). This can also be associated with an increase of a specific hormone which is linked to stress, which we will cover at a later point.

High cholesterol levels may result in the enhanced delivery of lipids to cells during the immune response or tissue repair and may enhance defense against endotoxins and viruses.[15] In critically ill or injured patients, cholesterol levels fell by 33% in individuals who died as opposed to a 28% increase in survivors.[16] Decreasing or fixed cholesterol levels suggest the development of infections or organ/metabolic dysfunctions.

Conversely, an increase in cholesterol suggests that organ failure is being resolved.[17] All these instances point to the actions of cholesterol as a body-wide repairman. This association is very important to keep in mind because it will shed an exceptional amount of light on the pathophysiology (the study of the body as it is affected by disease) of atherosclerosis.

Plasma cholesterol concentrations increased by 400% during starvation, while plasma triglyceride levels declined by 50%.[18] The explanation behind this one is simple. Recall our mentioning that the body produces more cholesterol if dietary cholesterol is decreased. This increased production can also potentially point to greater hormone production to reinforce the body as it loses a major part of sustaining itself. The decrease in triglycerides is practically self-explanatory. "Fat" stores the greatest amount of energy while also existing in chemical bonds that are extremely hard to break. These powerful bonds ensure that when the body looks for energy, it looks at all the other usual suspects and considers triglycerides last. In the extreme event of starvation, the other options are exhausted and the body turns on the triglycerides to obtain the energy it needs to keep on living.

When top-class athletes train for sports such as hockey and soccer, concentrations of serum cholesterol levels showed an increase.[19] This is an important example because these athletes are supposed to be the greatest specimens of physical prowess among us. Cholesterol is important in the baseline association of the body undergoing strenuous physical activity, which is certain to cause a tear here or there. The more significant association is once again tied into steroid hormone production. The imposing physiques that these athletes obtain are not made solely by lifting weights, but due to the physical response of raised steroid hormone production to this physical activity, which is responsible for the anabolic processes of muscle building and upkeep.

Pregnancies, helping fight off disease, intense athletic training, starvation buffers… the list could go on for some time. Whether life is actually being created in the case of pregnancy, disease is being fought back, or something like organ failure, which would fall under the label of "quite serious," is being resolved, increased levels of cholesterol have a funny way of being associated with the improvement of the human body.

Upkeep of Mental Function

The importance of cholesterol for physical and psychological well-being has been recognized for several decades. Upon further investigation it has quite a strong correlation with the psychological side. There is a substantial amount of evidence that cholesterol levels may be associated with variations in the mental state or personality.[20] Hypercholesterolemia has been reported in individuals with schizophrenia, obsessive-compulsive disorder, panic disorder, generalized anxiety disorders, and post-traumatic stress disorder (PTSD).[21] In addition, decreased levels of total cholesterol were observed in children with autism.[22]

Patients with manic episodes, bipolar disorder, suicidal ideation, and depression in full remission had lower cholesterol than their controls.[23,24] Low cholesterol levels have been reported in patients with major depression, dissociative disorder, antisocial personality disorder, borderline personality disorder, and criminal violence.[25,26] Men with a cholesterol level less than 175 mg/dL (4.5 mmol/l) have a four to seven fold increased risk of severe depressive symptoms compared with subjects with a cholesterol level between 232 and 270 mg/dL (6 and 7 mmol/l).[27] Studies in psychiatric patients described an association between lower cholesterol concentrations, suicidal tendency, depression, impulsivity, and aggression.[28,29] The level of total cholesterol of 160 mg/dL or less and a level of LDL at 100 mg/dL or less were observed with individuals with suicidal behavior. Patients with the lowest cholesterol levels [less than 165 mg/dL (4.27 mmol/l)] had more than six times the risk of committing suicide compared to the highest levels [greater than 223 mg/dL (5.77 mmol/l)].[30] Lowered cholesterol levels have been associated with an increase in violent deaths in cardiovascular primary prevention studies.[31]

While severe depression and mood disorders are never something to dismiss, they tend to be perceived publicly on a lower scale than illnesses and disorders which cause actual physical damage in patients. This isn't due to insensitivity to these issues but rather because of the nature of the differences. If a patient comes into the doctor's office with a bit of disfigured flesh, then this is a physical ailment which could well be a case of leprosy. This can be seen, whether it is physical or under a microscope slide for bacterial contamination, an objective identification of visible causes. On the other hand, if someone comes in complaining of a touch of the nerves or voices in the head, then this would be a subjective measurement based on the psychologist making the prognosis. This association with lowered levels of cholesterol and suicide puts more weight on these serious mental afflictions because it actually increases mortality. Not to mention the fact that death by suicide due to severe depressive symptoms or issues such as bipolar disorder is the worst possible outcome that can occur from such situations.

Deforestation of the Morning Wood

Good health, both mental and physical, for both men and women is certainly ideal, but many men will no doubt place special emphasis on something that is an important part of what many consider "being a man." Men with total cholesterol over 240 mg/dL had 1.83 times the risk of erectile dysfunction (ED) as did men with a total cholesterol lower than 180.[32] Mean plasma cholesterol levels and LDL levels in individuals suffering from erectile dysfunction were significantly higher than in control subjects.[33,34] High levels of total cholesterol are associated with poor testicular function and were found in 65% of infertile men.[35]

At this point some men might think stop the presses, but if high cholesterol leads to erectile dysfunction then bring on the lower cholesterol, consequence be damned! There are two things we will say in this case. The first is that we are trying to provide information in a way that is the absolutely least biased on our part. We have a point to prove, but we aren't set out to hold back information after earlier having spent so much emphasis on how important access to information is. There are both positive and negative associations with high cholesterol, and the most important thing to remember here is to never accept data at face value without understanding all that goes with it. In this particular case, the erectile dysfunction in men, the actual and literal problem that causes ED is not high cholesterol. How can this be, when it seems quite apparent that this is precisely the case? This will be explained in due time. For now we are focusing on strict cholesterol level associations.

Upkeep of Cardiovascular Function

The primary reason high cholesterol is under scrutiny is due to coronary heart disease. High cholesterol is associated with atherosclerosis, so lowered cholesterol should lead to less heart issues and as such decreased overall mortality. This is what that brand of logic would dictate, anyway.

Women over the age of 60 had the lowest mortality when their cholesterol level was at 270 mg/dL (7 mmol/l), versus 5.2 times worse mortality for those at cholesterol levels of 155 mg/dL (4 mmol/l). Women who had a cholesterol level of 340 mg/dL (8.8 mmol/l) had a mortality that was 1.8 worse than the ones at 270 mg/dL (7 mmol/l).[36] In this instance, the highest cholesterol level is clearly not ideal, but the overall worst is certainly the lowest level. We are always pointing out the disparity between what is considered the "ideal" level of cholesterol and that which actually appears to be so. We can't stress enough that in this case 270 is a good 70 more than what is considered to be the peak of the "optimal range." That is 35% more than the upper limit.

High total cholesterol is associated with longevity in people older than 85 years. In a 10 year follow up study of three groups of patients in this age bracket, the main cause of death was cardiovascular disease with a similar mortality in all groups. However, mortality from cancer and infection was lower among the people who had the highest total cholesterol.[37]

Major ischemic strokes are more often seen in patients with lower cholesterol levels. Higher cholesterol levels are associated with minor strokes and post-stroke mortality is inversely related to cholesterol. That is, the higher the cholesterol level in a patient, the less likely he or she will die from the stroke.[38]

Before we go into more detail about strokes, it is essential to define precisely what a stroke is. The actual definition of a stroke is a rapid loss of brain function that occurs as a result of decreased supply of blood to the brain. When most people think of stroke, they imagine a person seizing up a bit before collapsing on the ground. Even the word itself, stemming from strike, leads itself to such a definition of the event, as if a powerful blow from a hammer suddenly hit the individual in the head. While individuals suddenly seizing up and collapsing can certainly occur from stroke, the definition must be laid out to show exactly why such a response occurs. When a stroke occurs, it is not a simple event, but rather the culmination of various factors. If anything, the base definition makes stroke seem like a somewhat drawn out affair.

Strokes can be funneled into two categories: ischemic and hemorrhagic. Ischemic strokes occur when the brain suffers from a lowered blood flow, which as is clearly seen in the events of stroke is most certainly not a good thing. This is also the type of stroke that occurs much more frequently. Origins of ischemic stroke include such complications as thrombosis, an embolism, systemic hypoperfusion, and venous thrombosis. Things can get a bit complex at this point.

Plain thrombosis occurs when an area of blockage occurs and the obstruction occurs there. For example, a blood clot may form around plaque in the arteries, and from there directly cause the obstruction. In other words, this is an obstruction due to local production. An embolism is the opposite while at the same time not quite. An embolism occurs when an obstruction originating from another location travels and causes an obstruction in another location. For example, a thrombus (blood clot that causes thrombosis) can very well break off from the point of origin and go floating about as an embolus. In other words, an embolism can be caused by the steps leading towards thrombosis.

Systemic hypoperfusion refers to a decrease of blood flow to the entire body, which of course includes the brain. The most important aspect of systemic hypoperfusion is that it is not a cessation or disruption of blood flow but a decreased amount. This in turn can lead to a decreased amount of oxygen and has the potential to affect a wide area of the brain. Systemic hypoperfusion occurs from events such as shock or myocardial infarctions, which impairs blood flow throughout the body.

The last of the events leading to ischemic strokes is caused by an event that hits a little closer to the home turf of the stroke target area. Cerebral venous sinus thrombosis is as potent as its name is long. This occurs when a blood clot occurs in the sinuses which are responsible for draining the blood from the brain. To clarify, not all sinuses have this function, but the dural venous sinuses do. Understandably enough, when a clot occurs in such an area it is quite an issue. Thankfully, this type of event leading to stroke is exceedingly rare. Complications from this event can lead to another dangerous stroke.

The complications leading to ischemic stroke are taken care of, but we have not yet covered the events that can lead up to hemorrhagic stroke. These are intracranial hemorrhage and intracerebral hemorrhage. One would assume that the second classification might seem a bit superfluous, on account of the fact that if there is bleeding going on "in the cranium," then by default it would also include bleeding within the brain. However, these divisions are necessary because bleeding within the brain as opposed to right around the brain have different attributes.

The more violent event that can lead to such bleedings is also the common sense one, because if someone gets struck in the head with a hammer that cracks skull and perforates tissue, then the laws of nature dictate that hemorrhage will occur. An easy to show distinction between intracranial and intracerebral hemorrhage is the actual location of the blow and the logical follow up of such an event. For example, in the event of bleeding with the brain itself, the flow of blood is disrupted because the brain is quite literally losing blood, which not only leads to new blood trying to replenish new blood instead of performing vital function but also the accumulation of blood leading to increased pressure. In the event of an intracranial hemorrhage, the buildup of blood pressure right outside the brain not only presses in on the brain but can also disrupt the flow of blood into the brain.

Individuals with total cholesterol levels below 160 mg/dL had the highest rate of death from CHD, while those with levels above 240 mg/dL had the lowest risk of death from CHD.[39] Elevated total cholesterol levels, low HDL, and high TC/HDL ratios did not have an association with a higher rate of mortality from all causes, mortality from CHD, or hospitalization for heart attacks.[40] Patients in the lowest total cholesterol group of less than 180 mg/dL (as compared to the group between 180 to 239 mg/dL) were at a significantly higher risk of mortality due to hemorrhagic strokes, cancer, and all causes.[41]

In men, the lowest mortality was found with cholesterol levels between 180 and 239 mg/dL. Decreasing the levels below this range could result in increased risks of death from cancer or other disease.[42] An inverse association exists between total cholesterol and hemorrhagic stroke, as well as with total and cancer mortality for men.[43] In other words, the lower the cholesterol, the greater occurrence of those other events. Follow ups of mortality revealed a sizeable excess of cancer in the individuals who were in the lowest 10% of total cholesterol level.[44] There are many items that an excess of is not ideal, and cancer certainly tops that list.

Cholesterol and Total Mortality

In the case of mortality and cholesterol levels, it would appear that high cholesterol isn't as bad as it's made out to be. In fact, it seems that in certain situations it can assume the role of the hero. As far as the balance of side effects to good and bad, the ball is still in the court of a normal and standard level of cholesterol. But so far, the focus has been on high cholesterol. It would be prudent, then, to look at what must be a bounty (increased mortality aside, of course) of good effects associated with low cholesterol, as that is the current focus of the medical field. After all, with so much effort spent on attaining this goal surely the only motivation is the wellbeing of people.

While on the subject of low cholesterol, the lowest of the low should be examined. Who are these Olympian beings, certainly safe from any manner of ailment? Unfortunately, that might be a bit of a stretch. In fact, the stretch is over and the safety harness has snapped, because the mortality of hypocholesterolemic (note hypo, the opposite of hyper) patients who have cholesterol levels less than 100 mg/dL is ten times that of the average. Individuals whose cholesterol level dropped to below 45 mg/dL simply did not survive.[45] It's not that they had some side effects here and there, or were more liable to catch a spot of the cold – they simply expired.

This is certainly disheartening information. However, extremes are hardly a good thing in any occasion and in either direction, so this doesn't really say much. It appears that both low and high total cholesterol may be associated with a higher risk of premature death.[25] Another issue is that it is simply not logical to speak about the effects of low cholesterol without taking into account the association between it and mortality. If the full nature of cholesterol is to be determined, all associations need to be considered. Just as atherosclerosis can be examined as an association of high cholesterol, so too must increased mortality be observed as an association of low cholesterol.

Mean total cholesterol levels in hospitalized patients who died were significantly lower than the levels of those who survived (a difference of mean levels of 163.6 mg/dL versus 217.8 mg/dL).[45] Hospitalized adults over the age of 65 had low cholesterol as a predictor of short term mortality. The association with mortality and cholesterol levels was 5.2% for cholesterol less than 160 mg/dL, 2.2% for cholesterol levels between 160 mg/dL and 199 mg/dL, 1.6% for levels between 200 mg/dL and 239 mg/dL, and 1.7% for levels at and above 240 mg/d.[46]

In this latter example, the matter appears to be a tad frustrating. While it is apparent that the lowest cholesterol levels in this instance are hardly ideal with their statistically significant difference between mortality associations compared to the next range, the range above 239 mg/dL is still 1.7% as opposed to 1.6% of the segment before it. In other words, it is difficult to gauge a standardized correlation of gradually decreasing percentages. However, it must be noted that the two lower level ranges are nonetheless higher in mortality (even though they are in the "recommended" interval of cholesterol) than the two higher ones.

Men with levels of cholesterol lower than 180 mg/dL were observed to have several less than optimal overall health characteristics, such as a higher occurrence of current smoking, heavy drinking, and certain gastrointestinal conditions. Children with alcohol use, substance abuse, and depression with suicidal tendencies have the lowest total cholesterol values.[47] Heroin addicts have significantly lower mean values of total cholesterol than control subjects.[48-50]

Concentrations of cholesterol of less than 185 mg/dL in men in the age range of 40 to 59 years were associated with the highest mortality from all causes. In one particular study, the men were divided into three groups. In the low cholesterol group, even after individuals with conditions such as gall bladder disease were removed, the high risk of cancer and non-cardiovascular deaths remained.[51]

We have gone somewhat in depth about the overall mortality and death due to non-cardiovascular issues, but what about the deaths that are associated with actual CHD? Surprisingly (or not, if you have been following along), some studies showed that patients with low levels of cholesterol had the highest rates of death from CHD, while those with elevated total cholesterol levels (greater than 240 mg/dL) appeared to have the lowest risk of death from CHD.[52,53] That disease that is so intent on killing people in the developed world doesn't seem all that interested in associating itself with the labels placed on it. After all, isn't one of the major points of the anti-cholesterol campaign for increased heart health?

Mean levels of cholesterol in the body increase with age.

Recall also the other association with age – that steroid hormone levels decline with age, which are produced from cholesterol. This makes the link more than apparent. However, it is important to note that mean levels of cholesterol increase with age up until around the age of 70. When 70 years is reached, cholesterol levels begin to stabilize and then decline. By the time 80 years have passed, cholesterol levels are lower still and comparative to the younger age groups (without the benefit of that groups hormonal production rates).

The Cholesterol - Age Axis

Mean standard deviation of cholesterol[54]

Age	Cholesterol
20-29	188.37
30-39	204.75
40-49	221.43
50-59	232.10
60-69	236.55
70-79	227.53
80+	218.18

Longer term studies such as the Framingham Heart Study are always a good source of data because they allow us to observe the effects of cholesterol over larger periods of time, creating more specific results than short term studies. It is, of course, odd how some of that data is represented, but we digress. The Honolulu Heart Program is an ongoing study of cardiovascular disease in 8006 men that began in Hawaii in 1965. The benefits of such a study are apparent even if just taking into account the long term observations performed (observing a population for a long time is more beneficial than short term just on account of the increased data). The study being associated with cardiovascular disease of course puts cholesterol as a variable to be measured, which means that these levels could be monitored in individuals as they aged during this long term study.

This study monitored cholesterol levels as one of the variables and showed that long term periods of low cholesterol increased mortality. The researchers also noted that this correlated to the fact that patients who had lower concentrations of cholesterol earlier had greater risks of death. In other words, a younger individual who had low cholesterol will gain cholesterol with age just as others do, but since his cholesterol is lower to begin with his mortality increases in relation to someone who had the same cholesterol but was say 10 years older. Overall, this study shows that caution must be employed in regards to any attempts to lower cholesterol in the elderly, if not outright showing evidence that lowering cholesterol is the last thing anyone should try for the elderly.[55]

Falling total cholesterol levels were accompanied by increased risks of death caused by various cancers (blood, esophageal, and prostate,) non-cardiovascular non-cancer causes (in particular liver disease), and all causes. The rate of all-cause mortality was 30% higher among individuals with a decline from the middle range (180 to 239 mg/dL) to a low range (less than 180 mg/dL) of total cholesterol, as opposed to those individuals who remained in the stable middle level.[56]

Total cholesterol levels of less than 160 mg/dL are associated with higher mortality rates from cancer, liver disease, respiratory disorders, and injuries, while advanced lung cancer, lymphoma, and cervical cancer patients demonstrated significantly lower total cholesterol in comparison to healthy control groups.[57,58] Total cholesterol levels were inversely associated (cholesterol down, other factors up) with incidence of colon, stomach cancers, and other sites in men.[59,60] There is an inverse relationship between total cholesterol and LDL levels and incidence of cancer.[61,62]

Cholesterol levels less than 160 mg/dL were associated with a significantly increased risk of death from cancer of the liver and pancreas; digestive diseases, particularly hepatic cirrhosis; suicide; and alcohol dependence syndrome. Significant inverse associations were found between cholesterol levels and cancers of the lung, lymphatic and hematopoietic systems (system of stem cells that gives rise to all blood cells), and chronic obstructive pulmonary (lung) disease (COPD).[63] COPD is another term for chronic bronchitis and emphysema, with the net effect of narrowed airways in the lungs. This is all more than quite a mouthful, with one very specific theme: cancer. All across the board, it seems, low cholesterol has a nasty habit of being associated with an increased incidence of cancer.

Is Cholesterol a Guard Against Disease?

We've already shown examples that an elevated cholesterol level can appear to be a guard against illnesses, but how far does this relationship go? Decreased levels of cholesterol are associated with increased rates of pneumonia/influenza hospitalization among men and women and chronic obstructive pulmonary disease in men.[64] Sepsis with multiple organ failure is frequently associated with a substantial decrease of cholesterol levels. Decreased cholesterol levels seem to play a crucial role in the pathophysiology (changes of normal bodily function from disease) of sepsis.[65] Although sepsis might be more "commonly" known as blood poisoning, this is not accurate. Sepsis is the inflammatory response of the body with the presence of an infection. Septicemia, or the presence of harmful agents (ranging from bacteria to viruses) in the blood stream, is what can be more closely labeled as "blood poisoning." Septicemia (which is also known as bacteraemia) leads to sepsis, which shows how the all-inclusive common label got attached to sepsis as well as septicemia.

Low total cholesterol levels are a marker of increased HIV risk in men and associated with immune dysfunction in this infection.[66,67] Total cholesterol in in-hospital patients was inversely and significantly related to urinary tract, sexually transmitted, musculoskeletal, and all infections among men; and to urinary tract, all genitourinary, septicemia or bacteraemia miscellaneous viral site, and all infections among women.[68] There is a significant relationship between preoperative hypocholesterolemia and the incidence of septic complications (infections) after surgery.[69] Clearly, the association with immune function and resistance to infection goes quite a good bit.

The most important thing to get out of all of this is quite simple really. It is extremely vital to remember that technically speaking, low and high cholesterol are not bad per se. In essence, it is whatever is causing the low or high cholesterol which is the antagonist in this case. Consider a patient who has leukemia. Depending on the type, white blood cells will be higher in count or lower, but in most cases will be higher. Are high white blood cells the cause of leukemia? This type of reasoning sounds pretty absurd if a few seconds are spent thinking about it, but why is it not absurd when it is coupled with cholesterol? Cholesterol is turned into a scapegoat for very specific reasons while the rest of the staggering amount of data associated with it is swept under the rug. Who would be the most important recipients of this data, the laypeople who are constantly worried about cholesterol because they are constantly barraged by warnings, are not given the full picture by a long shot. It almost seems like a medieval enterprise, where the regular folk are left to live in fear and uncertainty.

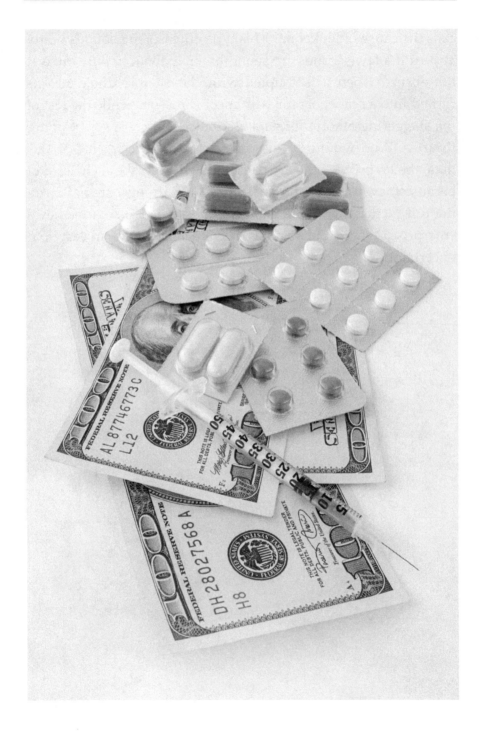

CHAPTER 4

Cholesterol Lowering Drugs

Where then, do cholesterol lowering drugs (CLD) come into the picture? After all, these drugs are the things that all the fear against cholesterol is leveraged for. Do they directly work to fix the issue which causes the rise in cholesterol? Or perhaps by lowering cholesterol they enable a mechanism to go into action to restore cholesterol to previous normal levels, which by extension fixes the issue that was associated with the abnormal level of cholesterol in the first place? Such an effect from these agents certainly would be wonderful. It would be wonderful if this is also what actually happened.

As with any agent that is said to give benefits of a certain kind, an examination of the side effects of said agent or agents needs to be made. When we see the commercials for the vast variety of drugs available, we tend to pay attention to the narrator as the voice suddenly grows quick and muted while delivering such tidbits of information as "stomach bleeding" and "permanent nerve damage." Delving into the world of CLDs, it quickly becomes apparent that there is no single CLD, but instead we find out that CLD is a blanket term for several types of agents.

The following is a list of the types of CLDs, as well as some of their variants.

Statin Drugs	
Generic Name	**Brand Name**
Atorvastatin	Lipitor
Fluvastatin	Lescol, Lescol XL
Lovastatin	Mevacor, Altoprev
Pravastatin	Pravachol
Simvastatin	Zocor
Rosuvastatin	Crestor

Statins, which are HMG CoA reductase inhibitors (we will go into further detail on this shortly), are perhaps the more famous ones, if by fame we can refer to a beastly income coupled with a large advertising budget. Statins also pack the greatest punch, as they affect the basic mechanisms of cholesterol synthesis in a major way. They actually cut off cholesterol before it can be made.

Cholesterol Absorption Inhibitors	
Generic Name	**Brand Name**
Ezetimibe	Zetia
Ezetimibe + Simvastatin	Vytorin

Selective cholesterol absorption inhibitors block the absorption of cholesterol particles into chylomicrons, which reduces the amount of cholesterol going back to the liver and has a net effect of lowering LDL. They are often combined with statin drugs for a more powerful effect.

Bile Acid Sequestrants	
Generic Name	**Brand Name**
Cholestyramine	Questran, Questran Light, Prevalite, Locholest
Colestipol	Colestid
Colesevelam	Welchol

These drugs bind themselves to bile to expel it from the body. This action forces cholesterol to be put into new bile acid production, thus lowering the overall level of cholesterol.

Fibrates	
Generic Name	**Brand Name**
Gemfibrozil	Lopid
Fenofibrate	Tricor

Fibrates work by reducing the production of VLDL in the liver, which has an overall effect of lowering triglycerides. Fibrates can also moderately increase the levels of HDL.

Niacin (nicotinic acid)	
Generic Name	**Brand Name**
Niacin	Niaspan

Niacin, although not a drug but rather an organic compound (also known as vitamin B_3 or nicotinic acid) is used as a cholesterol lowering agent. It blocks the breakdown of VLDL, which decreases the amount of LDL being created.

Statins are still the big players, and many of the non-statin drugs mentioned are used in conjunction with statin drugs as part of the cholesterol lowering process.

Side Effects from Cholesterol Lowering Drugs

Side effects, when speaking in general terms encompassing all side effects, of CLD were seen in 4-38% of patients, which resulted in their discontinuations and dose reductions.[1-5] The occurrence of adverse side effects was registered in 73.6% of users of cerivastatin and 74.9% for pravastatin.[6] Most patients who begin lipid-lowering therapy discontinue it within 1 year, and only about a third of patients reach their treatment goals.[7] 60% of patients discontinued their medications over 1 year.[8]

The most common side effects of CLD include chest pain, dizziness, weakness, fatigue, fibromyalgia, headaches, insomnia, and upper respiratory tract infections.[2,9] Statins and fibrates may cause erectile dysfunction.[10,11] This one in particular is important, and not just for the men. Earlier we noted studies where high cholesterol was present in men with erectile dysfunction. If high cholesterol was the actual cause of this issue, wouldn't it stand to reason that a lowered level of cholesterol would actually help with this instead of being a cause of it? Adverse events from CLD include poor quality of life, eczema, skin rashes, severe rhabdomyolysis (the breakdown of skeletal muscle tissue), renal failure, and death.[12-16]

Lupus-like syndrome, pleurisy, and arthralgia were also documented.[17] We felt that we should spend some time explaining these, as they may not be common terms one hears every day and shows how varied the side effects of these drugs can be. Lupus is an auto-immune disease that attacks the host body's own tissues, which isn't the best thing for an immune system to do. This can result in inflammation and tissue damage. Pleurisy is inflammation of the lining of the lungs and chest. This can cause chest pain. While arthralgia is not a household name, most are familiar with its inflammatory cousin arthritis. Arthralgia is simply joint pain without the associated swelling of arthritis.

All statins at all doses resulted in tachyphylaxis.[18] This term sounds serious enough but what exactly does it mean? Tachyphylaxis is the decreasing response to a drug or physiologically active agent. Basically, the same dosage of a drug that is taken initially can with time have a lessened effect with no dosage changes. One of the more significant implications here is not only that the effectiveness of a certain drug is decreased but potentially the effect of other agents as well. Cells can have a worsened response to hormones and other physiologic agents when statins are used.

Heart failure may occur in patients taking statin therapy. In some individuals, the myopathic (referring to muscular disease) effects of statins may impair the pumping function of the heart.[19] The incidence of congestive heart failure has tripled in the time that statins have been on the market.[20] Statins deplete coenzyme Q10 (CoQ10), which can contribute to heart disease. CoQ10 is located in most cells and is a part of the energy generation process through which most of the energy used by the human body is produced. Organs which require a great deal of energy, such as the heart, have the largest concentrations of CoQ10.

This depletion can contribute to heart disease. In 1990, Merck (a large pharmaceutical company) sought out and received a patent for *Mevacor* and other statin drugs in a formula with up to 1,000 mg of coenzyme Q10 to prevent or alleviate cardiomyopathy, which is a serious condition that can cause congestive heart failure. However, Merck has not put such a product on the market and has neglected to educate physicians on the importance of supplementing CoQ10 to offset the dangers of these drugs to the heart. Because they hold the patent, other drug companies cannot create such a combination statin/CoQ10 product. There is probably something witty and clever we could put here, but there isn't much that can portray such a move in a less negative light. It does the job well enough on its own.

Results of one study showed that statins reduce lipid levels but do not prevent restenosis after coronary angioplasty.[21] Restenosis is simply a reoccurrence of stenosis, which is a narrowing of blood vessels. A coronary angioplasty is a surgical procedure which widens such narrow blood vessels. Why is this interesting? The danger that atherosclerosis causes is a narrowing of the blood vessel due to the impediment of blood flow, and one of the possible causes of stenosis is indeed atherosclerosis. The administration of statins should theoretically have a benefit here but does not.

Various forms of myotoxicity (toxic effect on muscle) occur from statin use, ranging from mild and commonly occurring myopathy (muscular disease) and myalgia (simply muscle pain). Statins have a direct effect on the respiratory chain of the mitochondria (vital organelles in cells that generate most of the energy in cells). Mitochondrial impairment leads to a mitochondrial calcium leak and it may account for the apoptosis (quite literally the natural, programmed act of cell death) process, oxidative stress, and muscle remodeling and degeneration.[22,23]

CLD are associated with altered hormone levels. There is a possibility that CLD treatment is associated with hormonal perturbations.[24] A significant association between statin use and total testosterone was observed.[25] Mevastatin induced a profound concentration-dependent inhibition of DNA synthesis decreased production of progesterone (by up to 49%) and testosterone by up to 52%).[26] Clofibrate significantly reduced plasma levels of testosterone and cortisol.[27] As we will show shortly, hormone impact of CLD use is quite a bit more than a simple association.

Severe irritability may occur in statin users. Manifestations of severe irritability include homicidal impulses, threats to others, road rage, generation of fear in family members, and damage caused to property.[28] Cognitive impairment, dementia, memory loss, and peripheral neuropathy may occur with statin therapy.[29-33] Mild, transient restlessness, euphoria, and mental confusion are possible adverse events of statins.[34] Recall that 25% of the cholesterol in the body is localized within the brain, and that these symptoms are mirrored in some of our examples of variable cholesterol levels.

We mentioned earlier that animal tests performed in the pioneering days of cholesterol research were flawed, not only because of the way in which animals process cholesterol, but also due to the choice of animals (herbivores in that case). So, if animals that were fed excesses of cholesterol reacted in a certain way, how did they react to the statin drugs that lowered cholesterol? Animal studies showed possible significant hepatic action, testicular atrophy, neurological toxicity, hemorrhages in the gastrointestinal tract, bleeding in the brain stem, fibroid degeneration of vessel walls in the choroid plexus, and lens opacity.[35-37] All members of the two most popular classes of CLD (the fibrates and statins) cause cancer and toxic liver damage in rodents.[38] Those rabbits might be feeling a bit luckier now.

One statin in particular showed how bad side effects can be from CLD. Baycol® (cerivastatin) was pulled from the market in 2001 because of severe side effects such as serious injury, rhabdomyolysis, organ damage and death. Around the world, 100 deaths and 1,600 injuries have been linked to the drug.[39]

Rhabdomyolysis, as mentioned before, is the breakdown of skeletal muscle tissue. This sounds bad enough by itself, but isn't the entire sequence of events. When the skeletal muscle tissue is broken down, it releases myoglobin which results in myoglobinuria and kidney damage. Myoglobinuria is the presence of a large amount of myoglobin in the urine, which usually gets excreted out of the body. However, when there is too much of it in the urine, it can interfere with the filtration system which can cause serious problems. Myoglobin can also break down into potentially toxic compounds, which cause kidney failure.

Crush syndrome (also known as traumatic

rhabdomyolysis) is a serious medical condition which is characterized by major shock and renal failure following a crushing injury to skeletal muscle. The mechanism is the release into the bloodstream of muscle breakdown products – most notably myoglobin, potassium, and phosphorous – that are the products of rhabdomyolysis. For example, if a miner got his leg crushed by a cave in, this would occur in his leg. The products of the breakdown would go into his kidney filtration system and lead to renal failure.

Why are we talking about extreme physical trauma that can lead to death? We do so quite simply because this is the normal (certainly not normal for the poor miner with a crushed leg) occurrence that would lead to rhabdomyolysis. In other words, taking this particular statin could result in a reaction in the body that was equivalent to an event that occurs when severe physical trauma occurs, without said physical trauma actually occurring to bring about the rhabdomyolysis.

This reaction is not something one would prefer to occur. Some unfortunate people thought that they were doing a good job fighting that terrible cholesterol, only to die a death or suffer injuries that they could have never foreseen. Some serious thought needs to be put behind a decision made to release a product with such destructive potential. This line of thought needs to occur during testing and focus groups, not after it has spread on the market and killed or injured that many people.

Cholesterol Lowering Drugs and Cancer

CLD increase cancer occurrence at the expense of decreasing cardiovascular disease in certain populations, such as the elderly and those treated with immunotherapy for cancer.[40] A significant increase in the incidence of cancer, especially gastrointestinal, is observed in the CLD group.[41]

There are studies that suggest that statins may be used as effective anti-cancer drugs for cancers because this class of drugs has a high cytotoxic (simply the quality of being toxic to cells) potency.[42,43]

Now, ordinarily this would be good news. Cancer is no friend to mankind, and any new weapons against it are not bad news. However, the matter at hand is that chemotherapy is a very taxing and draining procedure. Cancer patients undergoing chemotherapy have extremely diminished quality of life and numerous side effects.

The fact that a statin drug can be potentially used in chemotherapy is a tad troubling, since people who are prescribed this drug take it every day, whereas chemotherapy only lasts for as long as it is needed. The fact that it can have a possible use as an anti-cancer medication might sound contradictory when groups of people who were studied who took statin drugs versus controls had more incidence of cancer, but it is more complex than simply x does y. From the viewpoint of chemotherapy, a statin drug can come in and kill off the cancer (as well as regular healthy cells). However, if there is no cancer, the body's physiology is altered due to decreased hormonal production (which stems out of cholesterol) and an overall weakened system develops. Cancer can then come out of such a weakened system and go about business as usual, wreaking havoc and acting as cancer is liable to do.

Putting side effects aside, not to imply that they are a walk in the park by any stretch what with simulated trauma leading to renal failure and all, it is interesting to notice what

CLD do as far as helping promote improved mortality. One would hope that after the trials and tribulations of all these side effects are negated by an overall improved mortality. The reduction of total cholesterol in the blood by these drugs is associated with a decrease in the incidence of CHD, which is certainly good. However, there is an increase in noncardiovascular mortality. CLD have also not been proven to extend a person's life span.[44-47]

A scientific statistical meta-analysis of six major primary prevention trials shows that the 15% decrease in deaths from heart disease in the cholesterol lowering treatment groups is offset by increased death from gallbladder disease, cancer, and injuries.[48] The lowering of cholesterol appears to increase the risk of cancer, accidental and violent death, stroke, and strangely enough CHD when certain medications are used.[49] Reduced serum cholesterol concentrations increase mortality from hemorrhagic strokes.[50] A meta-analysis of cholesterol-lowering trials demonstrated that coronary mortality was not decreased by the lowering of cholesterol, but total mortality was increased.[51,52] One of the most important things that we have to keep in mind is total mortality, at all times. It doesn't matter if death comes from CHD, cancer, or even appendicitis – the end result winds up being the same. The patients didn't die of a heart attack, but **dead is dead** whatever the cause. This is why it is very important to pay attention to any drugs that show an increase in total mortality.

Everything sounds like quite a mess at this point. Low cholesterol does not appear to be beneficial. High cholesterol is either a problem or a potential life saver, depending on the situation. CLD come into the picture and seem to cause side effects left and right, decreasing death from one source while increasing it from others. The field of cholesterol management seems to be a battle that anyone would be hard pressed to win no matter which direction is taken. To top it all off, there is that whole shady business of associations. Cholesterol is always "associated" with various conditions, and it seems like half the battle is in understanding what exactly the precise role of cholesterol is in all these events. Perhaps we can shed some light on all this.

CHAPTER 5

Cholesterol and Steroid Hormones

Why do cholesterol levels increase? What brings about hypercholesterolemia, the terrible enemy that puts millions at risk? We believe that it is a matter of cause and effect. The mysterious issues swirling about the ever enigmatic cholesterol are always an association. What is the association? How is it brought about?

The Body and Cholesterol

Recall that cholesterol is a most vital element in the body. It is the great progenitor, builder of cells and creator of hormones. Obviously, building cells and creating hormones can be considered a pretty good thing for the body, what with that being a necessary component of being defined as alive versus dead. Through long chains of conversions, cholesterol is ultimately responsible for creating more or less that which makes us run properly, as per the simplified chart below.

Biochemical Pathways of Steroid Hormones

Cholesterol
↓
pregnenolone → 17a-hydroxypregnenolone → DHEA → androstenediol
| | | |
progesterone → 17a-hydroxyprogesterone → androstenedione → testosterone
| | | |
11-deoxycorticosterone → 11-deoxycortisol → estrone ← estradiol
| | |
corticosterone → cortisol estriol
|
18-hydroxycorticosterone
|
aldosterone

Going back to the issues of cause and effect, we believe that by this rather simple reasoning (and with observational data) a hypothesis can be established regarding hypercholesterolemia. In our hormone deficit hypothesis of hypercholesterolemia, we state that hypercholesterolemia is the reactive consequence of enzyme-dependent down regulation (whenever a cell creates less of a certain component) of steroid hormone creation and their interconversion.[1] Simply put, the cholesterol level increases as a compensatory mechanism for the decreased production of steroid hormones. That is certainly a mouthful, but we can break it down quite easily.

Cholesterol creates hormones. What happens when hormone levels decrease, whether naturally via age or through other means? The said compensatory mechanism kicks in and the agent which is responsible for the formation of new hormones is created in greater numbers. Hormones fall, cholesterol production is increased to greater numbers to try and restore the balance. However, this is when the problem arises. The compensatory mechanism is unfortunately trying to fix the wrong thing. The compensatory mechanism has the right idea but is not working on fixing the actual problem. If increased cholesterol requirement to create more steroid hormones was the problem, then this would fix hormone levels. Unfortunately it does not, and steroid hormone levels remain low. Extra cholesterol production does not fix the malfunctioning enzymes.

The body can keep throwing cholesterol at the decreased hormone levels all day, but it is attempting to fix the problem with the wrong means. There isn't some magical point where suddenly cholesterol becomes less effective. Consider that an optimally balanced body has an optimum level of cholesterol and an optimum level of hormones, for the body in question (this is important, because the human body is not a statistical variable and everyone is unique). If the problem arose from an increased need of cholesterol, then logically the increased level of cholesterol would in turn raise hormones to an optimal level. This is not the case.

Cholesterol increases, but hormone levels stay low. The underlying fault working, or not working in this case, is the enzymes that are responsible for the myriad of interconversions through which cholesterol turns into hormones (which are converted into other hormones, also via enzymes). The building supplies are increased, but the problem is not a lack of supplies but instead the construction workers not putting the building supplies in their place via proper application. As a consequence, the body keeps the level of cholesterol elevated accordingly. In this sense, cholesterol takes on more than ever the function of a biological marker. The elevated level shows that the production of hormones is not optimized according to the needs of the body in regards to hormones.

From our point of view, in such a situation the most optimal steps to take would lead to the restoration of normal enzyme function, such as the enzyme that converts cholesterol into pregnenolone or the various enzymes that control other hormonal interconversions. In the case of an enzyme deficiency, they can be simply replaced or restored. This will allow for the restoration of normal physiological pathways instead of their suppression. We think that drug companies should focus on such an approach instead of trying to disrupt the body's normal physiology.

While speaking of cholesterol disorders, we can look at hypocholesterolemia. The work flow, so to speak, is reversed in this situation. While hypercholesterolemia is caused by low steroid hormone production, hypocholesterolemia causes low steroid hormone production. The hyper version sees a situation where the building blocks start to pile up because there is not enough builders to route them as needed, while the hypo version is a situation where there aren't enough building blocks in the first place.

In other words, there are many paths to a malfunctioning system. A very easy example would be a statin drug, which interferes with HMG-CoA reductase, which has the overall effect of disrupting cholesterol production. Thus, the level of hormones decreases due to the lower level of cholesterol. This happens because there is less of what we can describe as the steroid hormone building block to go around.

One could argue, however, that this is an artificially created impediment to the regular function of the system. If someone were to shoot you in the arm, then the movement of that arm will be impaired. Your arm now suffers a handicap that was not there initially due to this outside force. How does this take into account individuals who naturally have lower levels of cholesterol? Once again, the uniqueness of each human being must be pointed out. Many malfunctions can occur in the long pathway of conversion before cholesterol is even formed.

Cholesterol is not simply created as a whole particle and let loose upon the body. Bits and pieces join together and convert into other parts with the help of various agents. All it takes is just one of those steps or parts not working to their full potential to cause a cascading chain reaction of impaired production. Any factory assembly line operates under the same principles. If a car in the process of being constructed has one screw missing in the beginning of the process there is sure to be trouble with the finished project.

The Relationship Between Cholesterol Lowering Drugs and Hormones

It is important to understand where cholesterol lowering drugs come into the picture. Let's remember the key fact here.

Diminished hormone production -> increased cholesterol

Note the arrow, in this case we can determine it to be the "factor of causation." Now let's bring CLD into the mix.

Diminished hormone production -> increased cholesterol + CLD

Here we can let CLD stand for a negation factor for roughly all the increased cholesterol (though in most cases the CLD lowers the cholesterol level even lower than what it used to be originally under a fully optimal system). What do we have left?

Diminished hormone production

To sum up: the original problem remains in full swing, but the cholesterol has been decreased. But the cholesterol is not the cause, it is the effect.

Imagine a nice, relaxing day during a holiday. The mood is soured, however, by the beloved family pet leaving a "present" on the carpet. What would be the course of action? Sprinkle a bit of baking soda on top and call it a day? We would certainly hope not. A thorough cleaning, removal of excrement, and a wash of the carpet with an outside air dry would surely be the course of action. The only problem with this scenario is that it is a bit too lighthearted of a comparison. Let's consider instead a nuclear power plant. One of the reactors is acting up, and the problem appears to be a cooling rod, which if not eventually replaced will surely cause a meltdown. The temperature gauge has picked up the problem and the engineers wonder about a solution. They then get together and create some software to lower the temperature reading on the sensor, without replacing the cooling rod. The temperature now shows everything to be fine, and all is well – with the exception of that bothersome looming nuclear meltdown, that is.

These two scenarios seem quite illogical (and humorous if not for the implications). The truth of the matter is, it is the exact same concept with CLD. They are actively working to treat the effect rather than the cause, which doesn't make a whole lot of sense either way the matter is cut. A more practical real world application directly related to human health would be hyperthermia. A lesson taught in medical schools and institutes is that the temperature should be brought down somewhat to prevent seizures and denaturing of proteins, but it should still remain to carry out its purposes of killing off the invading microbes in the body.

Something else is amiss in all this. CLD often lower cholesterol past the point where it was originally under the optimal system. The implications here are not great. Going back to the nuclear reactor example, the temperature on the sensor would actually be lower than what it was before the cooling rod stopped performing at full capacity. Now, if something starts to malfunction further, it would have a greater capacity to cause harm because the system in place would not show the issue. This all goes without mentioning the studies showing that low cholesterol has more than its fair share of problems. Compounding this entire matter even further are the side effects and conditions associated with statin use, ranging from muscle ache and fatigue to cancer and rhabdomyolosis, as we well described earlier. Here our example takes a turn for the worse. Suddenly, the software used to lower the reactor temperature infects all vital systems in the power plant leading to various system failures, as well as randomly causing parts of the building to collapse.

There is another unintended side effect of statin drugs due to their method of effect. The chain of conversion for the creation of steroid hormones is quite lengthy, with many links of said chain. In fact, simply a chain would be an oversimplification because certain links branch off into other directions, while other links branch off only to rejoin at a certain point for a common goal. So, imagine, if you will, a chain that is also a giant spider web. When one of the links of the chain is broken, cholesterol production is increased in order to rectify the problem. Meanwhile, the other hormones are being produced at relatively regular rates. One condition here is that the hormones that have good levels are in the link prior to the malfunction in the chain.

This can all get terribly confusing when written out, so here is an example to illustrate this:

$$X \rightarrow A \rightarrow B \rightarrow C \rightarrow D \rightarrow E \rightarrow F$$

As it correlates to hormone conversions, this would be an oversimplified (and wrong) chain. Consider these units to be hormones being converted further along, with X being the progenitor (for our example cholesterol). Now let's say that unit D is malfunctioning, in this case we designate this condition with r.

$$X \rightarrow A \rightarrow B \rightarrow C \rightarrow Dr \rightarrow E \rightarrow F$$

Units A, B, and C are maintaining their status quo. Unit D is not. Units E and F are impaired in their production because their point of origin is a conversion from unit D. The chain can now be updated to reflect this.

$$X \rightarrow A \rightarrow B \rightarrow C \rightarrow Dr \rightarrow Er \rightarrow Fr$$

X is increased to repair the link of D. That is the situation as we know it currently. What happens when statins, in this case S, are introduced?

$$S + X \rightarrow Ar \rightarrow Br \rightarrow Cr \rightarrow Dr \rightarrow Er \rightarrow Fr$$

Suddenly, the entire chain is compromised. What happened exactly?

We stated earlier that statin drugs operate on the basis of treating the effect of actual raised cholesterol rather than the cause. Unfortunately, when dealing with the systems of the body, breaking anything down into a straight system of cause and effect is not the optimal method of observing or treating an issue. The processes of the human body are much too complex to be separated into two conceptual variables that can be applied across all systems. Perhaps a more appropriate phrase would be "sheltered cause and effect." Cause and effect is everywhere in the body, but it is hardly ever locked at the two variables it is in charge of. The effect stemming from one cause is the potential cause for a variety of other problems all leading out from the original cause.

In this case, the statin drugs do accomplish their objective of lowering cholesterol. As they do this, they are consequently lowering other hormone levels by removing large amounts of cholesterol from the equation. The hormones that were previously functioning at a normal level find their source of cholesterol to be impaired and are lowered as a result, not to mention the hormones with already impaired production. Not only are statin drugs trying to treat the effect rather than the cause, they are actually also contributing to a worse state of the cause. Again, since the levels of cholesterol are artificially decreased, the surface value shows that all is well while the reality is anything but.

We stress this point, that a system of cause and effect is insufficient in the realm of cholesterol and hormones, because it quite simply cannot be stressed enough. To add emphasis to this, let's observe precisely what occurs when our ever maligned cholesterol begins the journey of interconversion, what occurs along the paths, and where this system leads up to. So, we begin this climb of Everest. So, get your double insulated pants and supplemental oxygen on, because it is a rough hike up. We will try to keep this light.

The Birth of Cholesterol

Even before cholesterol becomes cholesterol, it goes through quite the ordeal to even achieve that status. Initially, Citrate and Acetate are floating along without a thought in the world (as well they should, since acids don't need to concern themselves with the world at large), before a reaction occurs through which they are transformed into Acetyl CoA (Coenzyme A). The grand schematic that leads to the creation of cholesterol is shown on the following page.

The regulation of these paths is controlled by the sterol regulatory element binding protein (SREBP). It would be heartening to know that we have been working on analyzing all these complex matters during the big push towards identifying precisely what it is cholesterol does, if not in the early 1900s then certainly by the 1950s. It certainly would, if this was actually the case. The truth is, SREBP was discovered in the early 1990s, 1993 to be precise.[2]

So, as of 2010, we have known about this protein for roughly 17 years. Individuals who have been around the bend for a while might remember that lovastatin was the first statin drug to go on the market under the name Mevacor, which occurred in 1987, some 6 years prior to the discovery of this vital part of the cholesterol creation process. This statin drug was placed on the market before a comprehensive flow of the pathways towards cholesterol creation was fully mapped.

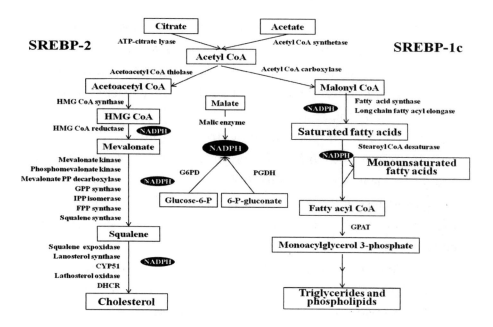

In regards to cholesterol, SREBP-2 is the one that we want to look at more closely. SREBP-1c controls the pathway of lipid creation, which begins when Acetyl CoA carboxylase acts upon Acetyl CoA. Ultimately, this leads to the creation of triglycerides and lipids, which in the grand scheme of things are relevant here because the cholesterol carriers are lipoproteins.

Mevalonate, which is part of the mevalonate pathway, is a vitally important compound that not only furthers the synthesis of cholesterol but is also responsible for its fair share of work. One such example is its role in N-glycosylation, which is a specific process related to amino acids, one of which is arginine. Arginine is also a precursor to creatine, and creatine has a vital role in the energy metabolism of muscle, nerves, and testes.[3] This is simply one of the roles that the mevalonate pathway is responsible for, amongst others.

Another agent on the pathway of conversion is squalene. What's so important about squalene? Nothing much, that is if anti-cancer properties can be put under the heading of "nothing much." Squalene has antioxidant properties and works with physiological functions as an anti-cancer agent.[4] Such functions are certainly good to have around, and the very least should not be robbed from the body.

The most important thing to get from all this is that nothing is cut and dry. It is certainly easy and convenient to think that HMG CoA leads to cholesterol, and suppressing HMG CoA reductase simply cuts the level of cholesterol production nice and proper. However, that's all that it is: easy and convenient.

We cannot expect to come in with a drug that sabotages this complex system and not expect other parts of the system to break. Hamstringing the actions of HMG CoA reductase naturally (in an unnatural way) reduces the levels of both mevalonate and squalene, these being just two examples. They are precursors to cholesterol but are also responsible for energy processes and anticancer properties.

It is very easy to tell an uniformed public that high cholesterol is bad and that we'll take care of it. People who question how will get an answer that it acts as an HMG CoA reductase suppressor, which is part of the cholesterol precursor chain and will think that that sounds pretty decent. But what if people were also told – "Oh yes, that mevalonate and squalene, nah those are fine. So what if you have a little bit less energy for nerves and muscle, and cancer isn't so bad right?"

This line of questioning quickly goes from comforting and reassuring to something which can best be said in the vernacular as "what the hell are you doing to me?"

Scientia potentia est

That old phrase *scientia potentia est*, or as we better know it - "knowledge is power," comes into play here. Consider a patient with an "elevated" level of cholesterol going to the doctor. He is given the option of taking a cholesterol lowering drug. As far as he's aware, the simple association is as such

Cholesterol = bad

We don't mean to imply that this poor consumer, or rather patient, is operating on troglodyte level intelligence (although we would hope that with the proper education, *Homo neanderthalensis* would make the informed decision as well). The problem is, once again, what we are bombarded with every day.

"Hey Johnny," says the energetic and upbeat 40 year old man to his downtrodden friend, "let's go jogging!"

"I can't Bobby," replies Johnny, "I have high cholesterol".

"Why that's easy," says Bobby, "*insert popular statin name here*, along with diet and regular exercise, will help you bring that cholesterol level down".

One month later.

Johnny and Bobby are jogging along a wooded path.

"So how do you feel now?" Bobby asks with a smile.

"I feel great!" Johnny replies, "Race you to the next bend!"

They race to the next bend with the sunset in front of them, and Johnny wins. They jump up in slow motion and high five each other, with a freeze frame. The name of the statin is flashed across the screen. Shortly after, time resumes and Johnny collapses to the ground, grasping his leg as severe myalgia overtakes him.

We don't mean to poke fun in an obvious way, but it gets to a point where certain things need to be said. If we went in and replaced "help lower your cholesterol" with "synthetically disrupt the mevalonate pathway to make a vital precursor to steroid hormone production go down which in this case is only a signifier of trouble instead of the actual problem," well we would assume there wouldn't be as much statin therapy going around. A commercial for a fast imported car, for example, is enticing with nice buzzwords, displays of high speed, and flashes of luxury. The issue here is why are there commercials for something like a statin drug in the first place?

Elevated cholesterol is a medical condition. Desire for a fast imported car is not. One of these belongs in a commercial. In an ideal setting, an individual would go in for a regular checkup and if the blood results call for it, the doctor can suggest the use of a drug to lower cholesterol. Then, doctor and patient would discuss why high cholesterol is bad, what is the data behind it, how does the drug work, and so on and so forth. As it stands now, the public is so inundated with anti-cholesterol propaganda that if the doctor suggested a statin for high cholesterol they would accept this as a fact of life and take it without question. The doctors are not at fault either.

The point of the healthcare industry lies in its name – to care for the health of people. It should not be about trying to disseminate as much of a product as possible and to build brand awareness. We aren't bombarded with commercials for morphine in the unfortunate event of traumatic injury, nor are we constantly seeing advertisements for chemotherapy drugs in case we get cancer. So why do we see so much focus on cholesterol?

Cholesterol is a pretty big deal right now. With a "normal" range that keeps fluctuating, more and more people are "eligible" for the use of cholesterol lowering drugs. Even products such as breakfast cereals and fiber supplements are getting in on it, proudly stating that they can make that terrible cholesterol go down. It is an unfortunate predicament we are currently in, where the powers of commerce have more of an influence on public health than actual medical science.

Let's go back to the individual considering the issue of high cholesterol with our "knowledge is power" notion. This person ordinarily would not know much and be guided by persuasion more than personal choice. Now let's think on how the situation would go down if this individual is aware fully of what is going on.

Beginning with the most basic level, we can keep moving up the stair of complexity until knowledge truly does become power, the power to make an informed decision. At the first steps, we will know that LDL and HDL are not cholesterol at all, but are carriers. As such, the scare words of "good cholesterol" and "bad cholesterol" do not have as much of an effect, if any. Next, we know that cholesterol is a precursor of steroid hormones. However, we are given information that high cholesterol can lead to issues, which leads to rationalizing and a consideration of the option of lowering cholesterol because atherosclerosis doesn't sound like a cheery day at the park. As we move higher up we know that cholesterol is vital for the body, and is even located in large quantities in the brain. Conflicts of interest arise, since how can something naturally in the body in such great quantities by definition be bad. Devil's advocate says that even a good thing not in moderation can cause issues. Overall, the desire to lower cholesterol, not necessarily normalize because few to none use that terminology, begins to win out because it appears to be the logical choice. The consideration of using a cholesterol lowering drug now becomes the primary point as we move further up the stairs.

The next step becomes quite a big leap, as it turns out. This is bridging the gap in understanding the effect that statin drugs have on the body. On the one side, a purely surface association is made with HMG CoA reductase and how it leads to cholesterol creation. On the other side is the vast array of reactions that occur after the activity of HMG CoA reductase. Compound all this with the potential side effects of cholesterol lowering drugs and the various studies performed about both high and low cholesterol. When all this information is laid out and an individual can use knowledge of the subject matter to make an informed decision, would the same choice to use CLD be reached?

One thing which doesn't help this situation is the overall attitude a patient might get when he goes to the doctor's office. An important job for any medical practitioner is not only to treat the patient but also for education. An individual who is given all the information about the treatment being suggested cannot have the benefit of comprehension but also of being aware of every option that is available. Unfortunately, knowledge is often replaced with fear. Going into the doctor's office and having atherosclerosis, cholesterol, and statin drugs all thrown at the face will elicit a knee jerk reaction based not on logical assessment but instead on fear.

However, the issue here isn't simply some doctors neglecting to mention all the facts to their patients. There is also the matter of the interpretation of scientific data. We can look at some examples that illustrate the disparity between that which is reported or given as opposed to that which is actually within the data.

First let's consider a study based on coronary heart disease from elderly people. In this analysis, all fatal coronary heart disease events are recorded. Elderly individuals with the lowest total cholesterol levels had the highest rate of death from coronary heart disease. Meanwhile, individuals with elevated total cholesterol levels appeared to have a lower risk from coronary heart disease.

The conclusion that you would gather from this is that it appears that the individuals with the higher levels of total cholesterol have the greatest rate of survival from coronary heart disease. This would seem like a logical conclusion, right? The authors of the study would disagree. According to the conclusion, elevated total cholesterol level is a risk factor for death from coronary heart disease in older adults. What happened?

Adjustments were made. What were these? Risk factors for coronary heart disease and markers of poor health are part of the list. Poor health markers included chronic conditions, low iron, and low albumin (protein) levels. 44 deaths from coronary heart disease itself were excluded because they occurred within the first year. After all these adjustments, elevated cholesterol levels predicted an increased risk for death from coronary heart disease.

Let's look at another example. Let's say that you are told that you will reduce the chance of dying from a heart attack by 50% if you take cholesterol lowering drugs for 10 years. That doesn't sound bad at all, surely those side effects can be worth it? However, then you hear a slight clarification on what 50% means. You are now told that you reduce the risk of a heart attack from 2 out of 1000 to 1 out of 1000. You might think – what the devil is this? A quick application of mathematics clearly shows that this is actually a 50% less chance. Both are the same exact thing, but one certainly sounds much better than the other.

This cherry picking of facts and phrases is somewhat rampant and is not a good thing, any way you cut it. The problem is clearly evident in various studies. You read the body of the text, which contains the actual observations and the scientific data. By focusing solely on the facts that are presented and as such are virgin territory not fouled by interpretation, you can make a deduction which focuses solely on the data and not an assumption. Then, when you look at the conclusions that are written, you become puzzled. This is where the magic happens.

Some of these conclusions and interpretations have language that looks like it isn't from a scientific paper, but would instead feel more at home at a complex and confusing document written by a king trying to rob the poor of their rights. The words written out look almost perfectly tailored not to give a clear analysis but instead to show whatever it is the researcher is trying to reinforce, whether the data supports it fully or not. This is the language part. An important part of this methodology includes statistics as well as the language.

The statistics is where it gets really harrowing. In some studies, the populations being studied are cut up and edited in a multitude of ways, none of which seems for the benefit of the reader or enlightenment. These statistical portions separate the subjects strategically to reinforce the original goal of the research more so than accurate representation of said research.

Far be it for us to imply that some of this data seems misrepresented for the furthering of various agendas, but some of these conclusions are more or less baffling based on the data that they are meant to represent. The point here is not furthering agendas (this happens everywhere, though it should have no place in scientific studies), but rather the occlusion of information. People aren't given a bulk amount of data to examine for themselves, they are given a filtered down version of whatever the conclusion is. Compound this with our earlier explanation on how information is held back from the general public and you have a bad day for cholesterol awareness.

Bearing all this in mind, we should now have a rough idea of what we can expect as far as pros and cons of lowering cholesterol via CLD. That would be jumping the gun, however. We have observed the pathways leading up to the creation of cholesterol, but we still haven't looked at the steroid hormones created by cholesterol in greater detail. They are another vital, and arguably greater, part of the equation when it comes to further understanding the impact of cholesterol.

CHAPTER 6

Age - Cholesterol – Hormones

One key aspect of steroid hormone production to keep in mind as we go along is that it declines with age. This goes with the fact that we are genetically programmed to die. Why is it, then, that everyone is not stricken down with a wealth of impairments and issues as they get older due to decreased hormone production? Once again, the uniqueness of each human body comes into play. To better understand cholesterol metabolism, you can refer back to page 16.

Steroid hormone production may decrease in certain individuals much faster than others, with variable rates that laugh in the face of any statistical analysis or the possibility of a unified formula. For example, the overall hormonal profiles of two men, one aged 74 and another aged 52, can be examined. If we were to ascribe to a generalized notion of decreased steroid hormone production solely on the basis of age, we would expect that by default the 52 year old man will have better hormone levels than the 74 year old. Upon examination, we may well find that it is actually the 74 year old who has a better hormonal profile.

The actual process where cholesterol begins hormone production is thankfully simple, and perhaps wrongfully so because once the chain of conversions kicks into high gear, it can get a little hard to keep up. Cytochrome P450scc, the enzyme with the sinister sounding name, is responsible for the process which leads to the synthesis of the first hormone from cholesterol. This hormone is pregnenolone. We can think of cholesterol as the precursor to all steroid hormones, but pregnenolone is the actual steroid hormone which is the precursor to all other steroid hormones.

The "Grandmother" of Steroids

Pregnenolone has more going for it than simply being the precursor to other steroid hormones. It belongs to a group of agents called neuroactive steroids (common name of neurosteroid). Neurosteroids are an important factor in the function of the nervous system due to their ability to modify the excitability of neurons.[1]

They aren't assigned only to this function however, and are responsible for the control of anything from sexual activity, anxiety, and even blood pressure, among others.[2] A study performed on patients with schizophrenia and schizoaffective disorders supplemented with pregnenolone showed that symptoms and memory function improved.[3] With this sort of information one can't help but think of the studies mentioned earlier on about statin users having such issues as cognitive impairment. Though there are various ways in which this can occur with the use of CLD, in this particular instance one of the links appears quite clear. If cholesterol is lowered, the precursor to pregnenolone is decreased, and there is less of this vital neurosteroid to go around. This, coupled with the natural decline of steroid hormone production with age can potentially lead to some dire straits.

Low levels of pregnenolone were observed in elderly

patients with dementia.[4] Such observations point to pregnenolone's function as a neuroprotective agent against such cognitive impairments as Alzheimer's. A study performed on adult men with generalized anxiety disorder pointed out that patients with this disorder have "significantly" lower levels of pregnenolone than their control group.[5] Decreased levels of pregnenolone were found in individuals with generalized social phobia.[6] Pregnenolone is also a factor in mood control.[7] Various studies have pointed out that a deficiency of pregnenolone is associated with depression.[8] The domain of pregnenolone does not lie solely in the mental realm, however.

Pregnenolone has been linked to improvements in arthritis. One study particularly noted the additional benefit of arthritis patients acquiring a "more cheerful psychological outlook".[9] Some studies show benefits associated with pregnenolone in arthritis patients.[10] One study shows that pregnenolone seems to play a vital part in stress response within the body, with beneficial improvements related to pregnenolone supplementation.[11] Pregnenolone can also improve heart health, protect against coronary artery disease, and boost the function of the immune system.

We can now move on further down the conversion pathways to see what can come out of pregnenolone. We will be looking at the more recognizable steroid hormones that should be at least somewhat familiar. Thus, the next ways in which pregnenolone can go is either into dehydroepiandrosterone (DHEA) or progesterone. For now, we will focus on DHEA.

The Standpoint of DHEA

To get to DHEA, we need to make another stop to do so since pregnenolone does not convert directly into DHEA. First, an enzyme called CYP17A1 converts pregnenolone into 17a-Hydroxypregnenolone. From this point onward we are going to neglect mentioning the enzymes to prevent the giant trail that this entails, and for our purposes here listing them all is not important. However, do remember that they are always there. A good rule is that when in doubt, always assume enzymes are carrying out the reaction. In fact, there can be no doubt, because nothing "just happens" in the body. 17a-Hydroxypregnenolone is then converted into DHEA.

When DHEA is mentioned, the name DHEA-Sulfate is often lurking near. DHEA-S is a metabolite of DHEA, and can convert back into DHEA. For the purpose of clinical testing, levels of DHEA-S are the more ideal ones to be observed since much more of it can be found in the blood. This in turn provides a more accurate gauge of how much DHEA is in the body.

A decline of DHEA levels with age is linked with atrophy of the zona reticularis in the adrenal cortex (illustrated here).[12]

Adrenal gland

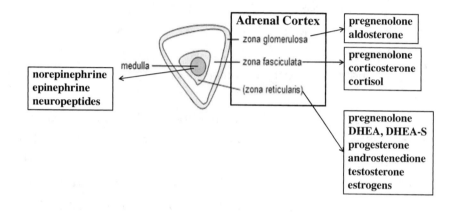

The adrenal cortex is located in the adrenal glands, which are responsible for a wealth of functions related to the release of hormones. The adrenal cortex itself is responsible for producing corticosteroids (the name given to steroids produced in the adrenal cortex, easily enough) from cholesterol. In short, it goes hand in hand that a production site for adrenals can diminish if said production is also lessened. If a factory starts creating fewer products, then parts of it will be shut down appropriately to save energy. As these levels drop with age, they may lead to decreased immune function, osteoporosis, and atherosclerosis. The decrease in DHEA production with age can decrease the production of all androgens (what could be called "male" hormones) by half.[13] In the 50- to 60-yr-old group, serum DHEA decreased by 74% and 70% from its peak values in 20- to 30-yr-old men and women, respectively.[14]

While a shrinking zona reticularis is no great thing, it is perhaps not so widely considered when speaking of health among the general population. Something which is well known is dying. A higher level of DHEA-S is associated with improved mortality and in particular improved mortality from cardiovascular disease.[15] Other studies also point to the simple fact that a higher level of DHEA-S is linked to improved mortality overall.[16] Not a bad day's work for DHEA in this regard. One of the best symptoms to always stay away from is death.

While on the subject of declines of DHEA with age and decreased function of adrenals, an observation of DHEA levels and how they interact with the elderly population would be ideal. Looking at a human's twilight years, one would imagine that they are times to look forward to, seeing the benefits of a life's work unfold and other great things which are seen in movies all the time. In reality, one fear that exists is the prospect of losing independence via various impairments that come with age, be they mental or physical. The lovely children looking through nursing home brochures certainly don't help. It was observed that women with significantly lower values of DHEA-S had more cases of "functional limitation," ranging from confinement (such as cases of being bed-ridden) to poor life satisfaction.[17] This same study pointed out that men with low DHEA-S had a significant association with short term mortality. The jury is still out on which gender wins that one. As far as actual causes of decreased mobility, older individuals who can be categorized as "frail" have lower levels of DHEA-S.[18]

There is a good amount of information regarding menopausal women and DHEA, and there is a good reason for that. In women, DHEA can contribute to up to 70% of estrogen via conversion before menopause, and close to 100% afterward. In this manner, it becomes apparent that DHEA can be seen almost as a replacement (though it is not by any means, simply a step in the conversion process) for estrogen for women, especially ones advanced in age. It has been shown that DHEA acts as a defense against osteoporosis in a specific way but ultimately because of the conversion of DHEA into estrogen.[19] DHEA-S levels were noted as being lower in women with osteoporosis versus those without it.[20,21] DHEA supplementation has even resulted in "significantly" higher pregnancy rates among older women.[22]

This particular point is a somewhat important one to stress if only for the popular preconceived notion of DHEA. Generally, when the word DHEA is heard it is in relation to how it is used for performance enhancement and is banned from use by athletes. This gives the impression that DHEA is some kind of steroid (or rather steroid hormone) that is useful only for specific physical activities. In fact, this is clearly far from the truth. Would a simple performance enhancer contribute in such large parts to estrogen? DHEA can even potentially act as a deterrent to flare ups of lupus.[23] DHEA, like pregnenolone, is also a potent neurosteroid. The phrase of don't judge a book by its cover is appropriate for a lot of the elements in the body, and this is especially true in the case of DHEA and all steroid hormones. No one trick ponies are in this stable.

DHEA supplementations can lead to improved memory and mood, as well as a decrease in cortisol (more on this later) levels.[24] DHEA has been shown as effective treatment for midlife-onset dysthymia (chronic depression). The response that the subjects experienced as far as improvements included better mood, motivation and energy among others. In fact, this course of treatment was comparable to treatment with antidepressants (without the side effects of such drugs, since DHEA is a natural product of the body and not an introduced artificial agent).[25] Older individuals suffering from major depression and low DHEA-S levels were given doses that would bring these levels in line with those of younger individuals. Both memory and depression improved in direct relation to the rise in DHEA and DHEA-S levels.[26] DHEA is even shown to be an effective treatment for depression in patients with HIV/AIDS (an affliction which will certainly turn anyone's prospects grim).[27]

Progesterone

With DHEA in the bag, we can look at progesterone next. Unlike the conversion process of pregnenolone to DHEA, there is no intermediate step like 17-Hydroxypregnenolone. Progesterone is a hormone that is labeled as a female hormone, although this is inappropriate. While it is true that females have a much greater production of progesterone than males, males do nonetheless have progesterone production in their bodies. It's all a matter of concentrations.

Progesterone in men is not, however, a useless hormone with nary a function. This "female" hormone is actually a part of the creation process of fully functional sperm, which superbly demonstrates the variance in this hormone's function (suffice to say, there's not a whole lot of this going on in the female body).[28] Progesterone is a natural antagonist to estrogen (more on this as we move along the pathways of conversion) and creates balance to offset the strong effects of estrogen. It isn't simply confined to such a limited function, however (here limited in the sense that this seems to be a single simple process, when in fact it is in charge of many processes in the tightrope act of balancing estrogen).

Progesterone fluctuates throughout the menstrual cycle (in males it remains stable to an extent). When taking into account a standardized cycle of 28 days between menses, the first half has estrogen dominance, while in the second half progesterone increases and then drops again at the onset of menses. Here it is important to make the distinction of "dominance." Having estrogen or progesterone dominance does not necessarily mean that either value is high, but instead that the relative amounts of either hormone are higher than the other. Both levels could be very low but if one of these hormones overshadows the other then dominance can exist.

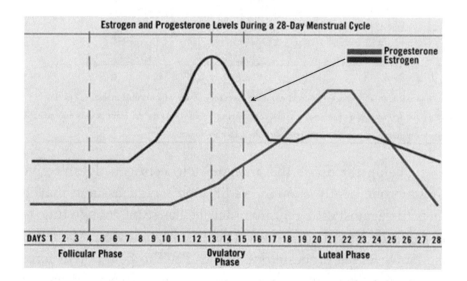

Another fluctuation in progesterone values comes with age. During the secretory phases of the normal menstrual cycle the ratio is balanced. However, once the body begins pre-menopausal cycles this ratio is greatly modified. At this point, the ratio of estrogen to progesterone leans heavily in favor of estrogen. Once full menopause is experienced, estrogen values also drop but the ratio remains in favor of estrogen. This can be easily summed up by the chart below.

Estrogen/progesterone ratio during aging

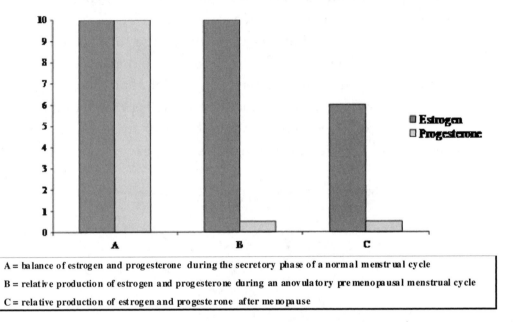

A = balance of estrogen and progesterone during the secretory phase of a normal menstrual cycle

B = relative production of estrogen and progesterone during an anovulatory premenopausal menstrual cycle

C = relative production of estrogen and progesterone after menopause

Being set up as the antagonist to estrogen doesn't give progesterone nearly enough credit. One would assume that in the battle against estrogen progesterone has scant enough time to do anything else in good form. That assumption would be a bad one, however, as progesterone proves itself to be a potent force with applications outside the realm normally associated with it (female hormone dealing with female physical symptoms and issues).

One of the primary problems in female health care today is the lack of knowledge about progesterone among the general public and medical professionals. Many physicians and pharmacists even go so far as to believe that women who have hysterectomies do not need progesterone. Clearly, progesterone is not just a hormone for the uterus.

The body needs progesterone for many reasons. It's almost something akin to saying that a man without testes does not need testosterone.

Natural and Synthetic Hormones

There is one important distinction that needs to be made before proceeding further: progesterone is not progestin. When we refer to progesterone we are speaking about the hormone in the body, not the synthetic product made to mimic the naturally occurring hormone. This muddles public perception of this hormone because the side effects which can occur with progestin are not indicative of progesterone.

To add to this confusion, there are different "kinds" of progestins, and they have variable effects instead of standardized ones across the board.[29] One of the major issues with progestins versus bioidentical hormones is cancer. Women who used estrogen in conjunction with progestin had a significantly increased risk of breast cancer, while women who used bioidentical progesterone had a significant decrease in breast cancer risk.[30]

Why, then, are progestins so widespread? A cynical individual might say that to create a new patent for a synthetic derivative of a natural hormone one would have to modify the formula somewhat, or else the patent couldn't be created. But surely health and well being are more important than patents and ludicrous amounts of money, as always. As you can see by the illustration below, it becomes immediately apparent that the chemically created hormone is not what belongs in the body.

Natural Hormone

A Drug

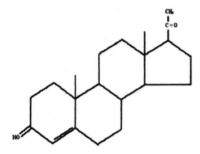

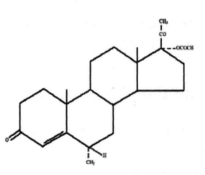

The Progesterone in YOUR BODY

A Drug used to replace Progesterone in your body

While those little lines and small additions may seem trivial on a diagram, they are very important on the molecular level. For example, sulfuric acid (H_2SO_4), is corrosive and not the best of things to be putting on human skin, but is nonflammable. Peroxymonosulfuric acid (H_2SO_5), on the other hand, is highly explosive with just the one additional oxygen molecule. There's obviously more to this with bonds and such, but this is a book about cholesterol, not which form of sulfuric acid blows up the best.

Progesterone and the Nervous System

Progesterone has the effect of calming the central nervous system, and boosting mental acuity and all manner of mental function. One study points out the "significantly improved cognitive performance" observed when subjects were given daily doses of progesterone. There is a bonus in this one, on top of all that. The main purpose of this study was to observe the effects of progesterone on individuals who ceased smoking, and the result showed that supplementation of this hormone actually decreased urges for smoking.[31]

A good amount of studies were done in regards to women with Parkinson's disease. An overall meta-analysis of these studies shows that symptoms of Parkinson's disease fluctuate based on which part of the menstrual cycle the subject was in. Observed differences were even established in women during times when they were pregnant and following childbirth.[32] It is vital to remember in these cases that progesterone is not the only actor in the theatre during the menstrual cycle, and that estrogen is just as important. The interplay of these two fluctuating levels with these symptoms shows that estrogen and progesterone concentrations have an impact on a serious neurodegenerative disease, which points to some measure of cognitive improvement from these agents.

Potential improvements in Parkinson's are certainly nice, but what about something with a bit more force? Evidence suggests that progesterone may be a factor in the clinical treatment of traumatic (is there any other kind?) brain injury with its wealth of neuroprotective functions.[33] Supplementation of progesterone shortly after injury to the brain and central nervous system has been shown to limit damage, loss of nervous tissue, and decrease in the time for recovery.[34] The measure of neuroprotective action added because of this hormone is evidently quite significant.

Progesterone and Estrogen

Having touched on the benefits to the nervous system, we can now delve further into the stereotypical function of progesterone, the antagonist of estrogen. Recall the previous mention of the monthly fluctuations in women of progesterone and estrogen, and how the ratios of each one are either balanced out, or more often than not unequal. Here the fluctuations of progesterone can lead to the well-known premenstrual syndrome (PMS). The wide array of symptoms of PMS range from cramping, breast tenderness, irritability, to bloating, rounded out by other symptoms that vary in each woman, with the overall connection being a terrible time for any woman who experiences these symptoms prior to menstruation. This is not the only time these symptoms have the potential to happen. Women going through menopause can get PMS like symptoms based on the same variables as actual PMS – the decrease of progesterone in comparison to estrogen. You can refer back to the chart on page 116.

There is a difference between the low levels associated with the natural fluctuations of progesterone on a monthly cycle as opposed to what can be termed as chronically low progesterone. This would be a situation where the progesterone level remains constantly low regardless of cycle, which can happen during a variety of scenarios. The most obvious one is the one already mentioned, which is during and post menopause, when the level of progesterone becomes low and stays low. There is then the case of low progesterone during a regular menstruation cycle which is caused by low production of progesterone, which can occur for a variety of reasons when speaking of women who have not yet experienced menopause.

Symptoms of this chronically low progesterone are worse than the regular dips of a normal cycle. Infertility is one such symptom, and is not just related to having trouble with conception, but with keeping pregnancies viable as well.

Depression can occur, much like with dips in the regular cycle but for a longer time. Another side effect of a low progesterone level is increased susceptibility to fibroids and cancer of the uterus, as well as cysts and cancer of the breast and ovaries.

Testosterone

Having taken care of one "female" hormone, we can switch gears and cover what can be described as the ultimate "male" hormone. Without much guesswork, this is of course testosterone. This hormone comes from DHEA, which converts to androstenediol, which then converts into testosterone. Whether it includes references to bodybuilders long past the point of proportion, "testosterone fueled rage," or a good old fashioned bout of male impotence, this hormone is called out frequently as the catalyst of all these "manly" events. And once again, the term "male" hormone is a misnomer since it is available in both men and women, in different amounts of course.

Then it gets even better. The chains of conversion stay steadfast, and testosterone is also created from the chain leading away from progesterone, one of the "female" hormones. To seal the deal, testosterone also converts into a major estrogen. In other words, female to male and then back to female shows exactly how pointless labels are when it comes to steroid hormones. Our body is certainly not a single celled organism with simplistic labels.

To get rid of this bothersome association, once again the gender barrier must be broken to show that testosterone is a vital component to both men and women. Cardiovascular health can be a good place to look for this, because after all, both men and women have hearts. A study which looked at men with heart failure found that up to 37% had low testosterone. Furthermore, such levels were in correlation to the severity of symptoms.[35] In other words, the lower the level of testosterone, the worse off the individuals were.

Testosterone and CHD

Men suffering from coronary artery disease fared worse in the correlation of values, where testosterone deficiency had a negative effect on survival.[36] A valid question can be asked regarding these results and examples, in that there are no women in this particular equation. One of the issues in testing of both "male" and "female" hormones is that they are often observed in the respective genders as opposed to as a sample of both genders. There are multiple factors at work here, from the preconceived notions of "male" and "female" hormones (in regards to importance) penetrating research to the fact that if a study is done on both male and female subjects, then the genders have to be divided into different populations anyway because of the disparity in standardized testosterone ranges in men and women.

This goes without mentioning a potential study with both genders where testosterone supplementation would have to be standardized, meaning that it would still be split into two genders to show accurate results. If this would not be done then the women might not be happy coming away with a light covering of facial hair and a deeper voice. However, there are still studies that are done with women where they are given testosterone dosages that not even men can dream to attain. Suffice to say, the results of such tests can be less than favorable with women coming away with clitorises enlarged to the point of being mistaken for small penises. The best part here is that such studies are often done to find out whether or not testosterone supplementation is safe while raising female testosterone values to superhuman levels. All is not lost, however. A study that was done solely on women with chronic heart failure showed testosterone supplementation to be an effective treatment for elderly women with this condition.[37]

Testosterone and ED

Testosterone is well known for its association with the male libido (or lack thereof). It is certainly not locked for this role in males, however. Menopausal women suffering from hypoactive sexual desire disorder (a rather long term for sexual dysfunction) who were given testosterone supplementation had improvements in their disorder and improved overall sexual function.[38] With this information in mind, it should be no small surprise that testosterone supplementation also improves the sexual function and viability of males.[39] Though there is more than one pathway to ED, the connection between it and low levels of testosterone is perhaps the most significant one. The upper limit of the normal testosterone range for men is more than 10 times that of females (based on the more regularly used values for the female version of the test).

Like estrogen and breast cancer, there is a public perception of testosterone being linked to prostate cancer. Fortunately, this is not quite accurate. Lower testosterone levels actually increase the risk of prostate cancer, and low testosterone levels are associated with more aggressive prostate cancer.[40,41] There is no scientific data that supports the concept that higher testosterone levels are associated with an increased risk of prostate cancer. In fact, not only was a higher testosterone level associated with less incidence of prostate cancer, but also with a longer lifespan as well.[42] Elevated levels of testosterone prior to the onset of prostate cancer increased survival rate.[43] Based on such results, it seems that while testosterone is a prostate growth factor, it does not promote prostate cancer.

Testosterone and Brain Function

Testosterone is not one to be outdone by the other hormones in its effect on the brain. Low levels of testosterone in the brain were observed in patients with full blown Alzheimer's disease. These levels were also decreased in individuals with the early symptoms of Alzheimer's disease.[44] Though Alzheimer's disease and Parkinson's affect those afflicted in different ways, individuals suffering from either of these conditions showed similar decreases in testosterone levels.[45]

Regimens of testosterone treatment can help neurons improve from impaired function. Low levels of testosterone have also been observed in individuals suffering from amyotrophic lateral sclerosis (more commonly known as Lou Gehrig's disease).[46] Lou Gehrig's disease is a condition where motor neurons (those nerve cells which control voluntary movement) degrade. The disease is progressive, getting worse over time and usually leading to death via respiratory failure. Testosterone supplementation has also been shown to increase the overall quality of life in patients suffering from Alzheimer's disease.[47]

These mental benefits and associations of hormones with the nervous system seem to keep crawling out of the woodwork. Anytime a hormone well known (or not so well known) for specific and seemingly strictly physical actions shows neuroprotective function, it appears to come out of left field. This is simply a by-product of the public perception that narrows them down into niche roles which hardly give them justice. This lack of readily available information to the general masses is one of the impediments in hormonal education. Odd as it may sound, but hormonal stereotypes set back public awareness and deny individuals information about these highly beneficial agents. This is compounded by the fact that hormone replacement therapy tends to involve strictly non-physiological compounds meant to mimic natural ones, throwing a great wrench in the gears of progress.

Even the mentioned studies and illuminations about testosterone don't give it justice. This section is meant to be a cursory glance at the functions of the more prominent hormones and their importance. Encyclopedias can be filled by the vast and varied functions of hormones, providing education and an insomnia aid. Testosterone can help control blood sugar as demonstrated in instances of higher insulin resistance in the presence of low testosterone levels. A deficiency of testosterone can even lead to insomnia.

Cortisol

Before covering the last major steroid hormone we will look at, we will make a short detour to look at cortisol. This hormone is created when progesterone converts to 11-Deoxycortisol which then converts into cortisol. Cortisol is often known as the "stress" hormone because secretion is increased in response to physical and psychological stress. This isn't to say that cortisol is slacking off when the body is not under stress. It helps regulate blood pressure and cardiovascular function, controls metabolism and the breakdown of proteins, carbohydrates, and fats, and has anti-inflammatory and immunosuppressive properties.

One important thing to remember when speaking of cortisol values is that the levels are higher in the morning in relation to the rest of the day. This is not what would be termed "high" cortisol, but rather just part of the daily cycle. Whenever side effects of high cortisol are mentioned, this is in reference to a high and prolonged level in the bloodstream.

One of the side effects of a high constant cortisol value is impaired cognitive performance. Though one would make the logical connection that being stressed out and in such a state of mind would certainly affect the thought process, this notion would be neglecting the actual physiological properties of this impairment. It is the high cortisol which plays a role in this, and not simply the mind's attempt at trying to reason while under a stressful state. A correlation exists with higher cortisol values during the day (when they should be lower) and with overall mental processing.[48] Memory formation is impaired when the process of memorization is performed under stress, pointing at cortisol's work here as well.[49]

The effects of high cortisol are not solely based around the feeling of mental and physical stress. Symptoms can range from increased abdominal fat to increased blood pressure. Another symptom of high cortisol is depression (which would go hand in hand with stress). So is low cortisol the way to go? Not quite.

In fact, depression has been noted in individuals with both high cortisol and low cortisol.[50] Low levels of cortisol actually share some symptoms such as depression and insomnia, even while introducing new ones such as chemical sensitivities and allergies. In this respect, the core concept behind an optimal level of cortisol is much like that of cholesterol. Neither high nor low is good, with a middle balance being the optimal situation as far as symptoms are concerned.

Estrogen and Unfavorable Misconceptions

We can now focus on the "hormone" which is perhaps the most misunderstood and has the most renown, usually of the negative variety. This is the other "female" hormone, "estrogen". There are some things to clear up before the effects of the hormone can be discussed. When estrogen is discussed, it is usually spoken of as thus when in reality the broad term should be estrogens.

Taking some time out of discussion here in regards to the natural estrogens found within the body to discuss some of the bad press that this hormone gets. Immediately, we can make the distinction in regards to the worst offender. If someone says estrogen, what is the first thing that pops into mind? If the natural hormone found within the body is that thing, then this would be a proper conclusion. If someone says that the first thing that comes to mind is an estrogen synthesized from the urine of horses, then one might rightfully wonder if that person is all proper in the head. Unfortunately, this is somewhat the thing that happens.

Premarin, that very infamous estrogen made from the urine of pregnant mares, is unfortunately the one that is jumbled in with estrogen. This is because Premarin is a large component of hormone replacement therapy (HRT), and as such when tests were accomplished they were haphazardly labeled as "estrogen" therapy. In other words, such studies were attempting to see what impact raising estrogen levels would have, but doing so with an estrogen that doesn't belong in the body. In fact, the major part of Premarin is estrone, which is actually present in very small quantities pre menopause, but as a dominant estrogen post menopause.

What is the big deal with non-bioidentical estrogens? In one particular study where women were given solely estrogen, specifically estrogen derived from horses, the risk of stroke was increased.[51] This is important because stroke isn't exactly one of the things associated with estrogen.

A certain large study in particular showed the pitfalls of HRT with non-bioidentical estrogens. This study employed HRT that included the use of estrogen on its own or the use of combined estrogen and progestin (a synthetic progesterone, because one non-bioidentical hormone sometimes just isn't enough). Some of the logic behind HRT with these estrogens is not only for the improvement of symptoms post menopause, but also for heart health since pre-menopausal women enjoy lower rates of heart attacks. Going with this thought process, restoration of estrogen would help with this. Unfortunately, the non-bioidentical estrogen and progestin combination actually caused the study to be halted ahead of schedule. This was not due to overwhelming success, but instead because heart attack rates actually increased, and as icing on what can only be described as a very bad cake, there was an increase in breast cancer.[52]

Estradiol, estrone, and estriol are the "main" estrogens, but are far from being the only ones. In fact, estradiol and estrone are converted into 40 metabolic products.[53] Another interesting fact is that estradiol can be made from a conversion of testosterone. This alone, without even bringing to mind all the other examples, shows how superficial the term "male" and "female" hormones is when the primary "male" hormone gives rise to what can be considered the primary "female" hormones.

We covered the bad reputation of estrogen from non-bioidentical estrogens, but the vast variety of estrogens themselves can lead to a bad reputation. How so? The main things to keep in mind are alpha and beta receptors in breast cells. These receptors are places where hormones can bind. When estrogens bind to alpha receptors, breast cell proliferation occurs, which can in fact lead to breast cancer. Meanwhile, estrogens that bind to beta receptors have the opposite effect and inhibit breast cell proliferation and prevent breast cancer.[54-59]

Estradiol and estrone are the ones which bind to alpha receptors, while estriol binds to beta receptors.[60,61] One long term study showed that women who had the highest levels of estriol actually had a lower risk of breast cancer.[62] So is there bad and good estrogen? Not quite. Breast cell proliferation is not a function that is dedicated to the creation of cancer. Cells need to proliferate, and balanced estrogen amounts, as well as the addition of progesterone's cancer controlling effects, create a healthy system where cells are created and proliferate in a healthy balance.

While this might make some individuals worry, they shouldn't, to put it bluntly. An optimally functioning system takes care of itself and has safeguards to prevent breakdown of normal action. Take the example of free radicals.

In the interest of not derailing this section on estrogen into an in-depth chemistry lecture, suffice it to say that free radicals are important "molecules" in many functions, the body's biochemistry being one of them. Some free radicals are actually vital to bodily function and have important functions. However, two important free radicals derived from oxygen also have a side effect of cell damage, which in excess amounts causes anything from cancer to stroke (antioxidants help protect against this function).

The point is, these free radicals are derived from oxygen. How could we stop them? Stop breathing. This doesn't sound particularly smart but illustrates the point well. The body is a well-designed system that utilizes the good and protects against the bad, but malfunctions can happen, as with any system. That isn't to say that there aren't extra steps that can be taken to help keep such functions at optimal levels (there are), but to worry about something which is as natural as breathing and happens constantly within the body is an easy way to worry your way to an early grave.

One of the more apparent effects of estrogen is the determination of the female physical appearance. While this would seem as a given reached by any shred of common sense, it is not a simply cut and dry "female appearance" toggle. Varying levels of estrogen during the development of the female secondary sex characteristics also account for variables such as breast and hip size. In fact, judging such characteristics can be a good marker for issues such as estrogen dominance because they guide the development of the body.

Estrogen is not solely a sculptor of the female form, of course. Like all other hormones, estrogen plays an important role in many processes. Estrogen is responsible for the process of ovulation, releasing ova from the ovaries. The next logical step here is estrogen's role in the menstrual cycle. Variable levels of estrogen are responsible for differences in the menstrual cycle. A good balance of estrogen and progesterone leads to the "normal" monthly cycle with roughly 28 days in between menstruations, which last approximately 3-4 days.

Estrogen dominance can lead to shorter intervals between menstruations as well as a longer duration of the actual menstruation. If progesterone is dominant, then the opposite is true. The interval between menstruations becomes longer and menstruations become shorter (or possibly not happen on some occasions). Another benefit of estrogen is relief from menopausal symptoms such as hot flashes. This actually goes hand in hand with progesterone, since both levels drop during this time.

Estrogens, Bone, and Skin Health

It seems that whenever a commercial comes on about a drug or extremely large calcium supplement for osteoporosis the subject is invariably older women. At first glance, it would seem a strange bit of focus, since men can also be afflicted with this condition. An important part of this issue is that estrogen has beneficial effects on both bones and joints.[63] Since these levels drop off post menopause, elderly women find themselves at a higher risk than men. One would certainly wonder why all men aren't brittle boned then, due to their naturally low levels of estrogen. This is because in men testosterone has this bone protective function (although to a much lesser extent than the association estrogen has with bone health in women).

Products such as wrinkle creams that are made to combat aging tend to work on a surface level, but this method of attack doesn't fully cover everything that goes along with aging. For example, there is a 30% loss in skin collagen in the first five years of menopause. The benefits of estrogen for the condition and health of skin seem rather obvious here.

Estrogens and Neural Function

Estrogen, not wanting to break the trend, also has neuroprotective functions like the other steroid hormones. It is interesting to note that women who had "estrogen therapy" at time of menopause and from then on had the best results as far as the protective benefits of estrogen against Alzheimer's Disease are concerned in relation to women not taking such preventative measures.[64] This correlates to the drop off in estrogen at the time of menopause, and the additional estrogen supplementation shows the benefit that this hormone has on the brain.

Stepping away from the blanket term estrogen, by which we are always referring to the estrogens as a whole, we can take a look at one of the estrogens in particular: estradiol. Not content to let testosterone take all the credit for improving blood sugar levels, estradiol also takes a swing at this and can improve insulin sensitivity.[65] Estradiol has been shown to lower blood pressure in postmenopausal women.[66] Estradiol even inhibits the oxidation of LDL, which is an initiating event in atherosclerosis.[67] Estradiol is not a lone wolf war hero by any means, and the most optimal outcomes come out from a balance of estrogens and other hormones.

One benefit of estrogen that immediately seems to stand above other benefits of the hormone is increased female life expectancy. Although it would certainly be a happy event if estrogen simply increased the longevity of women, many more factors go into this than simply prolonged life. Life expectancy is an overall measure of the average age that a person can expect to live. As such, events like premature death can push the life expectancy down. Therefore, a good estrogen level provides the protection that makes a woman less susceptible to risks that can increase overall mortality.

Unfinished Story

And that wraps up steroid hormones! But, not really. Our friends allo-tetrahydrocortisol, 11-hydroxyetiocholanolone, and 11-OH-androstenedione are feeling left out. At this point it might seem like we are just name dropping, but this is not the case. We just want to keep on our promise of not putting you to sleep, and we still feel bad about that whole introduction to the synthesis of cholesterol affair. Just because we listed the "main" steroid hormones does not mean that they are collectively in charge of everything.

We mentioned androstenediol but did not mention androstanediol, not because lack of importance but to simply keep with the more known and recognizable steroid hormones. We also didn't mention it because there is exactly one letter of difference, and this steroid hormone web can be a chore to memorize as it is without two hormones which look like typos of each other. If we had continued from a certain pathway of conversion stemming from progesterone, going through deoxycorticosterone and then corticosterone, we would have arrived at aldosterone, a steroid hormone which is extremely important in regulating blood pressure. The body uses over sixty different steroids derived from cholesterol, but we just presented the basic "bricks" to show how complex this chain is.

Vitamin D-3

At this point we can sneak in something that will probably not come to mind immediately when we are speaking about the products of cholesterol. Vitamin D-3 is this particular item. How is a vitamin created from cholesterol, and how does that even work? As you might know by that famous phrase – "getting in all of your vitamins and minerals," vitamins are something that the body needs but the method of procurement is from sources outside the body such as food.

Why do we make this distinction? Because according to the definition of a vitamin, vitamin D-3 is actually not a vitamin. When the first vitamins were scientifically discovered in the 1900s, the scientists doing the discovering were on a roll.

Unfortunately, in their quest to find out more and more about the body, they found a new agent and labeled it vitamin D-3 based on their experience with other vitamins. The problem here is that vitamin D-3 is what is termed a secosteroid and is produced within the body from cholesterol via a reaction from sunlight.

One might argue that since sunlight is something taken in from outside of the body then vitamin D-3 might tentatively be labeled a vitamin. They would of course be wrong. We aren't talking about "vitamin sunlight," but rather an item that is produced in the body. Furthermore, since vitamin D-3 is a product of cholesterol, it can also affect cholesterol levels if there is a deficiency of it (increased production of cholesterol to make up for vitamin D-3 deficiency).

Quite simply put, the amount of steroid hormones in our body is as vast as it is vitally important in controlling the day to day functions of the body. The main objective to take away from all of this is the origin of all these vital components: cholesterol. Oh that cholesterol, trying to confuse us by giving the body the functions it needs to perform to keep us alive.

CHAPTER 7

A New Hypothesis of Hypercholesterolemia

Now we can come to the part where we describe what we do. Our hypothesis on hypercholesterolemia was explained earlier but we'd like to reiterate the core concept.[1] Cholesterol levels are high when there is an issue with lowered steroid hormone production. Going by that whole "logic" thing we keep on mentioning, with our friends cause and effect, we will now explain how our method works to lower cholesterol.

The most important thing to remember about this hypothesis is that it follows the principles of causation. Cholesterol is the precursor of all steroid hormones and as such is a very important signifier of what is going on. As the body ages and enzyme reactions start to malfunction and break down, the amount of steroid hormones decreases. Thus, the amount of cholesterol is increased to try and make up for this shortfall. Unfortunately, the amount of cholesterol is not the problem but rather the vast chain of further interconversions. The body is attempting to fix the broken supply line by increasing the supply line and not being able to fix the machinery.

Though biologically speaking this issue is extremely complex, from a standardized analysis it can be broken down quite easily. Steroid hormone levels fall, which leads to increased cholesterol production. If steroid hormone levels are normalized, then the level of cholesterol has no reason to be elevated. This reasoning is what we base our method of cholesterol normalization on.

Furthermore, we believe that due to all of these factors, seeing the trend of cholesterol elevation over an individual's lifetime is much more important than seeing an isolated level with little context. Seeing how steroid hormone levels decline over time can show the risk for disease in a better fashion than a test for cholesterol value.

Practical Application

Before we get into our method, we must clarify the "lowering" of cholesterol. This isn't a speeding train with no brakes with the final destination of low cholesterol. Low cholesterol as a static variable is not something that we want to achieve. Rather, we want to reach a level of cholesterol which is "normalized." In the case of our method, this normalization is achieved when steroid hormone and cholesterol levels are in the same range as they were during the age interval of 20 to 29 years. This interval is chosen because at this point in a person's life the production of steroid hormones and cholesterol is the most stable and at peak levels. The latter part of that statement shows one of the benefits of using the age range (other than the benefit of it making sense). It wouldn't be a bad guess to think that the highest hormone numbers occur during 10-19, better known as those years that we want to forget because of how insufferable we were. However, other than not being the peak of hormone production, there is that pesky fluctuation on account of puberty and the process of maturation into adulthood.

Why do we make the distinction then, when a lowered level of cholesterol is something that would be ideal to achieve precisely if hypercholesterolemia is present? This is in part because of our multimodal and specified approach that targets each person as an individual and not as a unit broken down into variables and statistics. The ideal cholesterol level of one person is not going to be identical to another's, and approaching both individuals with a factory line program is never the optimal solution.

We mentioned earlier that one of the issues with scientific testing for studies regarding something like steroid hormone supplementation is the static approach. As a hypothetical example which is actually not hypothetical at all and happens all the time, let's imagine a study where all participants are given 200 mg or 20 mg of a certain agent regardless of their condition or pre-existing levels. People with the lowest levels of a hormone being tested might get the 20 mg while those with near peak levels might take the 200 mg.

What would happen? The people who took the 20 mg say, hey nothing is going on, and the people who took the 200 mg say the exact same thing. The test concludes and the researchers deduce that a grand total of nothing happened.

If a different path was selected and the individuals with low levels got the high dose, then they would see an appropriate response, but the ones with the normally high levels would receive the small dose, and once again see no change. This hypothetical example is not even taking into account a third group (which of course would normally be there) that is in between the naturally low levels and high levels. These individuals could be given either the high or low doses, and have variable changes.

All in all, this would create a big mess with hard to follow results due to initial assessment of values. This example is why it is extremely important to match up the people who actually need it as opposed to those who don't. Otherwise, some will see a beneficial difference, others won't, and science will suffer defeat by being performed poorly.

It is perfectly understandable that during clinical trials there needs to be a measure of static variables. For example, a new blood pressure drug needs to be tested, so everyone is given either the drug or a placebo, with a control group and all the required goods. However, the reason that this can work is because humans are not born with a synthetic substance to control our blood pressure floating about inside of us. This drug with a single act is being tested to see how it will work across a wide range of people who have no exposure to such a thing. Hormones are in an entirely different league. We do have pre-existing levels of these agents in our bodies and adding on top of these levels without adequately or at all checking them prior to the fact is not the best of ideas if accurate results are the goal of the day.

Our approach takes into account all the variables that are necessary to create an individualized program. We employ both a standardized blood test for steroid hormone levels and a questionnaire which when filled out gives a person's clinical history. Here we must clarify that the standardized blood test is only called that because we are looking for all the values of the steroid hormones that we need to observe. The test is standardized, but the program created from it is far from that.

One of the other reasons that we use the term normalization and not lowering is because not all cholesterol levels need to be lowered. Recall that our hypothesis of hypercholesterolemia can be turned around into a hypothesis of hypocholesterolemia. In the latter, the low level of cholesterol is the cause of low steroid hormone production. In this case, we would certainly not want to lower cholesterol. However, here is the good part. We can't. In both cases we are restoring steroid hormones to their optimal levels. In other words, restoring steroid hormone levels in the case of hypercholesterolemia lowers the level of cholesterol because there is no need for extra cholesterol production. In the case of hypocholesterolemia, we are restoring the steroid hormone levels which are low and are the underlying causes of the issues at hand. To use the analogy again, the cholesterol is in both cases a thermostat, and we work to fix the temperature and not break the thermostat to show what we want.

As far as optimized cholesterol levels are concerned, what are some of the results that happen? They vary by each individual person and it is difficult to predict precisely where the total cholesterol value will wind up when the optimization of steroid hormones occurs. However, we must reiterate that our method is not a break neck race to lower cholesterol to as low a number as possible or to any preset values. To illustrate these points we can briefly mention two results from our program (the way in which our results are achieved will be explained in due time). In one instance a 63 year old man came on the program with a total cholesterol value of 349 (all cholesterol values in these examples are mg/dL). At the follow up blood test, this value was 128. In another instance a 39 year old woman came on the program with a total cholesterol value of 202 and had a value of 164 at the follow up blood test.

What's important to remember here is that we simply chose those two individual instances for the sake of demonstrating what kind of difference can occur. We'd also be lying if we said we didn't specifically pick out the 349 to 128, just because it's not a bad day's work considering no cholesterol lowering drugs of any kind were used, as in all of our examples. Other values can range from 232 to 198 for a 53 year old female to 221 to 190 for an 82 year old male. Does this mean that some of these are more successful than others? Not necessarily.

Once again, we will fall back on the fact that everyone has an individualized physiology. If individual A's cholesterol is lowered by 80, and individual B's cholesterol is lowered by 30, it in no way means that A has better results than B. In fact, from a viewpoint strictly observing lab data, individual B might actually have a better hormonal profile than A. Cholesterol can in no way have a static association with steroid hormone production if considering some kind of unified formula. It is not logical, for example, to say that a decrease in cholesterol of 5 mg/dL is equivalent to increases in 3 different steroid hormones at certain rates, because such a decrease in another individual could lead to an entirely different outcome in steroid hormone levels.

Going back to the original examples that we gave out, you might wonder at something, and rightfully so. A red flag should come up at this point with the value for the 63 year old man whose total cholesterol value went down to 128. After all, did we not mention that low cholesterol is not all it's cracked up to be (increased mortality and all)?

It is here that a distinction must be made. A low level of cholesterol by default is bad because it is a marker for low steroid hormone levels. If low steroid hormone levels are optimized, then the root issue of the variety of problems and malaise associated with low cholesterol are in turn rectified (because they are actually the outcome of low steroid hormones). As such, the new low level of cholesterol is associated with healthy and optimal steroid hormone production which mirrors the values that were present during the 20 to 29 age bracket. This is in direct opposition to the low levels attained by cholesterol lowering drugs, which lower the cholesterol but keep the steroid hormone production low. In fact, since they lower cholesterol even further they exacerbate the low steroid hormone issue as well.

Relative Hypercholesterolemia

Before we proceed into the workings of our program there is another hypothesis that we have formed due to test results that we have observed. We have termed this "relative hypercholesterolemia." Consider a 54 year old woman with initial total cholesterol of 170. After a follow up blood test this value had dropped down to 140. In the beginning of this particular program, this value was not qualified to be labeled as hypercholesterolemia and was quite far from the lowest range to qualify for this distinction. However, steroid hormone levels were not yet optimized. After the optimization of steroid hormones this new level was achieved. In short, even though the initial level of cholesterol was normal, it was "high" in relation to the level of cholesterol which was present at a youthful age of optimal steroid hormone production. The relative part of the hypothesis is key, since it is relative to the original amount and cannot be considered hypercholesterolemia. We can all agree that the scientific votes have brought down the range for hypercholesterolemia as far down as it should go. Not to mention the fact that if CLD were given in such a situation then steroid hormones would drop even further with no benefit.

The table below shows a good example in the difference between relative hypercholesterolemia and regular hypercholesterolemia.

Age	25	40
Patient 1 (nl <200 mg/dL)	130	190
Patient 2 (nl <200 mg/dL)	180	240

The first patient is relative hypercholesterolemia, while the second is regular hypercholesterolemia. Life cycle elevation of total cholesterol is a vital component in understanding what is going on with cholesterol and steroid metabolism.

Physiology Optimization

The actual program that we use begins with the two fundamental cores: a client history and an initial blood test. The client history contains a wide variety of questions, with different areas for men and women where applicable that allows a person to write out their health history and current issues. This information allows us to get a gauge on what kind of program should be recommended in broad scopes in certain areas while precise in other areas.

For example, the initial history might give a clear indication that progesterone supplementation is advisable, but it is not until we observe the precise progesterone value in the blood test that we can make a recommendation to the precise dose of progesterone.

An examination of the clinical symptoms could have indications in the world, but an accurate dosage would usually be extremely hard (although in some cases easier than others). For example, recall our previous explanation of estrogen or progesterone dominance, which can occur even at low levels. A woman might be experiencing all the symptoms of estrogen dominance but it would still not give accurate dose information for us because the level of estrogen could be relatively low or relatively high. There are some slight variations of symptoms between estrogen dominance and an actual high level of estrogen, but then even this can be completely variable according to the estrogen antagonist actions of progesterone. Regardless, the most precise information for dosage recommendations comes from observing the exact values on the blood test.

Blood Tests

As far as the blood test goes, we have a baseline of tests that we request for program creation:

- Complete Blood Count (CBC) – this test gives important information about the kinds and numbers of cells in the blood. A CBC helps diagnose different conditions and allows us to see if there are any issues with the immune system and some factors such as coagulation. This test covers the scope of blood function and content with tests for such things as erythrocytes (red blood cells that are the most common type of blood cell and responsible for the delivery oxygen to the body tissues), lymphocytes (a type of white blood cell that increases in number in response to viral infections), platelets (cell fragments which are responsible for clotting action), hemoglobin (iron carrying proteins), etc.

- Comprehensive Metabolic Panel (CMP) – a range of tests

that helps with an overview of an individual's physiology. There are general tests such as glucose and calcium, as well as tests for electrolytes such as sodium and potassium. A large part of this test has signifiers for kidney and liver function. Examples of these tests are creatinine (a breakdown product in muscle which is filtered through the kidneys) and ALT (an enzyme that is found in the highest amounts in the liver and which is released into the blood when damage to the liver occurs).

- Lipid Profile – how could we do without our friend cholesterol? This test includes the overall cholesterol value, LDL, HDL, and Triglycerides (depending on the lab used it can also include VLDL).

- Pregnenolone – as the precursor of the other steroid hormones this test cannot be overlooked.

- DHEA-Sulfate – we ask for a DHEA-Sulfate because it provides a much more precise value for DHEA in the body overall than just a DHEA test.

- Total Testosterone – the total in this instance is because a test like Free Testosterone can provide values which are in no way indicative of actual testosterone production. Free testosterone is available and unbound, which does not take into consideration the testosterone that is chemically bound and therefore not freely floating about. Total testosterone takes all these numbers into consideration and is the more accurate test. Free testosterone numbers may actually be normal or high while total testosterone levels are low.

- PSA – this is prostate-specific antigen, an important protein produced within the prostate that is necessary for optimal function. However, elevated levels of this protein can signify prostate malfunctions or cancer.

- Total Estrogen – as we mentioned previously, there are many estrogens in the body and focusing on only one or three of them would not be an efficient method of gauging estrogen production. The usual course of action in a blood test for "estrogen" is to test for estriol, estradiol, and estrone, while a test for total estrogen takes into account the broad scope of all estrogens. For women who are still menstruating, the ideal time to take the test is 3-7 days prior to the beginning of menses and the fluctuating nature of this level is always considered.

- Progesterone – the test for progesterone is thankfully simple, with no total or free versions floating around. The time in the menstruating cycle (if applicable) that the test was taken is also considered here.

- Cortisol – as mentioned previously, this "stress hormone" is an important value to know. Knowing if the level is too low or too high is vital.

- Aldosterone – this hormone helps the body regulate blood pressure and can help identify issues with such symptoms as dizziness, headaches, hearing loss, tinnitus, etc.

- Vitamin D-3 – Why did we include a vitamin in this list? Poor vitamin D-3 suffers from a bit of a crisis in public perception. It was discovered as the fourth "vitamin", in the early 1900s. Unfortunately, vitamin D-3 is actually a secosteroid (a molecule that is similar to steroids) and is created in the human body. By definition, a vitamin is an organic compound which cannot be created in enough quantities by an organism and requires outside supplementation. Since vitamin D-3 does not fit this criterion, it is actually not a vitamin at all. We ask for this test because vitamin D-3 has an impact on cholesterol values due to the creation of vitamin D-3 from cholesterol through the action of ultraviolet radiation.

- Serotonin – an important neurotransmitter. Numerous drugs used for treating depression utilize this agent within the body (unfortunately this often leads to extremely low serotonin levels as they are depleted).

- Homocysteine – an amino acid which can serve as a marker for cardiovascular disease if levels are high. However, if levels are low this is not optimal either.

- Prolactin – has a deep relationship with serotonin, dopamine, thyroid hormone, estrogen, progesterone etc., and various functions such as lactation. It is equally important in both men and women.

- C-reactive protein – the level of this protein is elevated when inflammation is present in the body. This test, serotonin, homocysteine, and prolactin do not have a direct association with the normalization of cholesterol, but are good to know as they are useful in the optimization of physiology.

- Thyroid Panel – this is a series of tests which measures the levels of thyroid hormones as a gauge of thyroid function. The thyroid is a large endocrine gland and is important in controlling the body's sensitivity to hormone levels. We ask for tests for thyroid-stimulating hormone (TSH), thyroxine (T4), and triiodothyronine (T3). TSH can show if the thyroid is creating an excess of thyroid hormones (known as hyperthyroidism) or is experiencing a lack (known as hypothyroidism). For T3 and T4, we prefer to use the tests of total T3 and total T4, rather than free T3 and free T4, because of the reasons we have already listed when considering the disparity of actual levels when speaking of total and free hormone values.

These tests allow us to individualize the program to the best of our abilities. There is no such thing as a "standardized" program. There are certainly standardized agents and hormones for the associated issues, but the dose for each one is tailored for each person.

For example, two individuals may have the same tests in their blood results (which isn't exactly going to happen), but based on all the factors that we take into account they would not receive the same program.

Hormonorestorative Therapy

In 1996 we employed the term hormonorestorative therapy (HT) into our practice for the regimen that was used for our patients. Hormonorestorative therapy was defined as multi-hormonal therapy with the use of a chemically identical formula to human hormones (anthropo-identical) and is administered in physiologic ratios with dose schedules intended to simulate the natural human production cycle and allows to restore the optimal level of hormones.[2]

For the sake of ease of recognition with convention, we have been referring to the non-synthetic variety of hormonal supplementation as bioidentical. However, in our efforts we prefer to use the term anthropo-identical, specifically to designate the hormones as the bioidentical variety that is found in the human body. As we mentioned previously, whenever we refer to the optimal range of hormones we are referring to the upper one third of the normal range for individuals aged 20-29. This is due to hormone levels being the highest during life at this particular time range.

All the hormones utilized by our program are bioidentical. They are exactly the ones that are found within the human body. As we mentioned previously, the negative press associated with hormones is linked to the synthetic hormones, which would make sense with something artificial synthesized from the urine of pregnant horses used as a replacement for human hormones. Another issue is in the name, HRT – hormone replacement therapy. What we aim to do is hormone restoration and not replacement.

Testosterone, progesterone, and estrogens are offered in gel forms, as well as drops in much rarer cases. These methods of application allow modifications to be made as needed based on various factors. Something like a hormone "patch" delivers a steady amount of hormone that eventually decreases as the hormone begins to run out, making this an inadequate choice. The other option that is sometimes offered is a hormone injection, which is also not an ideal method of delivery.

An injection provides a large (overly so) amount of hormones in the beginning and begins to quickly drop down in levels as the body takes care of it. Patches and injections also in no way take into account the daily fluctuation of hormones as well as monthly fluctuation for other hormones. A large part of an optimized physiology in regards to certain hormones is a cyclical fluctuation, which does not happen when a static dose of hormones is introduced. The estrogens gel is actually Triest, which is a combination of Estriol, Estradiol, and Estrone in a 90:7:3 ratio, respectively. In our experience this formula and ratio is a very good one.

The program is not solely based on hormone application and utilization, however. There are various supplements and agents that are utilized to help the activities of hormones in some ways. Take testosterone, for example, which has three agents that can affect its metabolism. One of these is zinc, which is also responsible for a variety of reactions within the body. Progesterone is another, but that is usually part of the suggested regimen already.

The last that is employed is saw palmetto, which helps prevent the conversion of testosterone into dihydrotestosterone, or DHT. DHT is a much more powerful form of testosterone and as such can also have side effects, such as acne and hair loss. As men age and their default level of testosterone decreases, the body can go into semi-emergency mode and attempt to correct for this deficiency by converting more testosterone into DHT. Technically speaking, this accomplishes the goal of improving the decreased testosterone level, but the side effects of DHT are less than favorable.

Though triglyceride and cholesterol levels do not have a 1:1 correlation (or should we say a 5:1 correlation with a transport), it is not uncommon to have elevated triglycerides in conjunction with elevated cholesterol. An elevated amount of triglycerides in the blood is certainly no friend to man, and can be taken care of quite easily. Omega 3-fatty acids, perhaps more commonly known through fish oil (though we prefer to use krill oil because it contains a phospholipid complex that increases absorption), can help lower triglyceride levels. Another important thing is that whenever we talk about triglycerides we must remember what affects lipase (which is the enzyme that controls the conversion of triglycerides into free fatty acids and glycerol). The diagram below shows agents that can work on this reaction.

Effect of various hormones on lipase

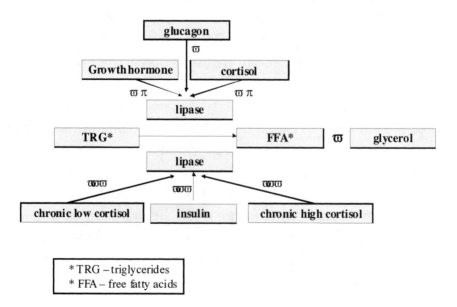

Lipase per se, as a part of the majority of digestive enzyme formulations, can help normalize triglyceride levels when they are elevated.

We don't stray out of the bounds of absolutely necessary, however. It would certainly be very convenient to suggest 40 different agents, collect the income, and call it a day, but this is not how we operate. The initial program is meant to be as inclusive for symptoms while focusing on hormone restoration as possible and at the same time having a minimalist approach for convenience. The previous mention of "calling it a day" after assigning the program brings us to another main tenant of our program: support.

Once an individual of the program receives their full program and begins taking it, we monitor the entire process in the form of updates. Individuals are encouraged to update as much as needed so that we can modify the program accordingly. The initial program is an optimal effort on our part to create a good program based on the information available but to get the best results we work with feedback to optimize the program further based on the needs and issues of each individual person. We ask for, at the very least, weekly updates so that we can make adjustments to the program as needed. It would be quite an arrogant move on our part to think that the initial program that we create is fully optimized and perfect for the individual in question, which is why we work with the client to get the greatest result.

Each program is created from the ground up with a multimodal approach in mind. All the agents of the program are meant to be adjusted if the need calls for it with ease. All hormones that are in capsule form are suggested in such a way that if they need to be decreased or increased this can be done without simply putting the agent on hold. The hormonal gels are in easy to use applicators with measurements built in. We can also use hypo allergic base for gels in case a person has any skin irritation after program initiation. We do not use any bloated multi supplement formulas due to the inherent difficulty in obtaining specific results that can also be gauged properly. For example, consider a supplement which has 10 different agents in each pill. If just one of those agents causes some kind of issue, then the entire formula needs to be put on hold until the situation is rectified. Our approach of individualized agents allows us to pinpoint any issues and modify the single item that is causing the problem. This works both ways, and not just for possible decreases. If a symptom arises that can be fully controlled by an increase in one of the agents in the multi supplement formula then another dosage of the entire formula would have to be taken, which is extremely unwise since it can raise the levels of the other agents above the recommended values. Furthermore, the additional agents would also increase cost when there is no need.

Follow Up Blood Test

Another important factor in creating the best program possible as time goes on is our use of standardized follow up blood tests. The general rule of "do no harm" is quite important. We must be sure that major program modifications with time are not done blindly, but are based on lab value results (minor modifications are built in as part of the initial program with dosage variations, but for larger changes it is best to go with blood test results). We ask for a retest of the values initially tested so that we can see in great detail what modifications can be made to further optimize the program. The three month mark was chosen because it is a good period of time to allow for the optimization of physiology. When we observe the values of this first follow up blood test, we use two factors as gauges in terms of how the body is operating. These are the cholesterol value and overall steroid hormone values, and including vitamin D-3 values. Due to the relationship between steroid hormone production and cholesterol values, this is almost always the time when we begin to see either a normalization of cholesterol or progress in such a direction.

Follow up blood tests are also important because of an effect that can occur over time. As time progresses, the same amount of a steroid hormone that led to a good increase in the first place creates a level that is too high. When this occurs, a possibly much smaller dose of the hormone is enough to create the same optimal results that were achieved in the beginning with the larger amount. Such cases point to both an improved physiology through better absorption and utilization of hormone supplementation as well as improved production of the body's own hormones.

A sizeable amount of improved numbers is always nice if data collection is the goal, but what is the practical application here? This question is valid, as it always should be whenever programs or agents that affect the body are concerned. We can start off by using the general logic employed by some drugs: preventative. Consider any type of statin drug. The condition in this instance is increased cholesterol, which is purported to be bad with nary a distinction of whether cholesterol is associated with "bad things" or if it is the direct causation. In the case of our program, this "bad thing" is impaired steroid hormone production, which causes increased cholesterol production. We are out to fix the core issue. Our program helps make the house resistant to incidences of fire whereas a statin functions somewhat akin to removing all the smoke alarms in the house. In the latter situation, that bad boy will still light up but at least it won't make all that horrible loud and blaring noise in the meantime.

Preventative is not the only tier of the program, of course. The program is designed from the ground up to restore hormone levels to the ranges experienced by 20-29 year olds. It isn't a numbers game, of course. Something that those crafty 20-29 year olds also experience is the feeling of being, for lack of a better word, young. Full of energy, riding on bikes to their local coffee shops throughout the day and going to obscure musical concerts at night, they have the energy and drive to actually do all of that. Meanwhile, we all get older and suffer the ravages of age and declined hormone production. The younger generation has the benefit of peak hormone production. When this state of optimal hormonal levels is mirrored in older individuals, the natural response is a renewed vigor. That injury from carrying concrete both ways up a hill in the snow will still be there, but the feeling of a youthful constitution is well within reach.

Energy may seem like an obvious one, but it isn't confined to this general description. The application of the program is as far reaching in scope as hormones allow. Which is to say, quite far. Recall the mention of the benefits of pregnenolone (and many steroid hormones) on overall bone health, and the benefit that it produces in arthritis. DHEA and testosterone in particular have a good effect on libido, and supplementation of these hormones can help with this issue. Libido might be a bit of a given for these two powerful hormones, so let's throw in benefits such as improved fertility for DHEA and improved heart health in men for testosterone. Consider the wide set of symptoms associated with PMS, which are associated with an imbalance of progesterone and estrogen. If these two hormones are supplemented in a way so that balance is created, then PMS symptoms can greatly abate and even disappear completely. When considering the application of hormone supplementation, you can simply go over their natural function. If the values of these hormones decline, then their effectiveness in performing their job will follow suit because there won't be enough to go around and perform at full power.

Hormone restoration is so versatile it is hard to describe an all encompassing term. It is a multi-front war against the ravages of age related or physiologically impaired hormone decline, but this action is at all times performed by surgical strikes which go after specific targets. In fact, any kind of "war" scenario more or less falls flat because hormone restoration is not waging war on our own bodies. Instead, it can be considered as reinforcing that which the body already has. The blueprints, the plans, they are all there for the body to function properly and through whatever circumstances are applicable it finds itself short on manpower. Our program seeks to reinforce this depleted garrison so that the body can operate to the best of its ability without any kind of unnatural help or forced acceptance.

Now we can describe the process behind the creation of a sample program. But in this hypothetical sample there will be no specifics. The reason for this is simple. A hypothetical program that we are creating out of thin air is certainly based on what we do every day but is not real itself. This goes hand in hand with a lack of specifics because we do not want any preconceived notions of templates to enter into the mind. This might sound odd but consider this other hypothetical scenario – a person, perhaps you, crafty reader, who is going through this part of the book, looks at a sample program with dosages for an individual with specific afflictions and then enters the program. Lo and behold, the program that they get is not like the program that he or she saw described here even though the symptoms appear quite similar. This goes with our individualized approach to all cases. A small snippet of information on one part of a health history can be an indication or contra-indication for the use of an agent. This will help prevent confusion and more confusion.

Recall the list written out on a prior page about the tests that we require for the creation of a program. These tests are what can be considered "no-brainers." What we mean by this is if a person is lacking in pregnenolone, then we would recommend pregnenolone as part of the program. Out of all the tests that we ask for, these have a 1:1 correlation for the item being tested to the hormone or supplement: pregnenolone, DHEA-Sulfate, testosterone, total estrogen, progesterone, cortisol, aldosterone, and vitamin D-3.

CBC and CMP can have indications for the use of certain agents or holding them back (in conjunction with information from the health history), but overall they serve as a beneficial marker for overall health in various areas of the body. The lipid profile is our biological marker test for steroid hormone production. We never suggest any kind of supplement that claims to lower LDL or raise HDL, because that goes against what we are trying to do. We simply aim to normalize cholesterol through the supplementation of steroid hormones. In fact, some tests with drugs that attempt to raise solely HDL have met with unfavorable results, one of said results being increased mortality.

Testing results for a new type of drug (Torcetrapib) from Pfizer (of Lipitor and Viagra fame) that focused solely on raising HDL showed some rather unfortunate results. The risk of death was increased by 59% and the risk of heart problems increased by 25%. It appeared that the elevated HDL was stealing the supply of cholesterol from the "production plants" that are in charge of hormone production.

This is a very good example of the effect of a great marketing campaign that makes up for any shortfalls of questionable logic with science in the other parts. That sounds slightly confusing so let us explain. According to all those great commercials on the television and radio, there are certain rules to be followed. Water is wet, death kills, and cholesterol is bad. But not good cholesterol, because HDL is great, so levels of the good should by logic be elevated as much as possible. Then we have test results where elevation of HDL has quite simply catastrophic results. These are the kind of results that throw the backbone of the entire anti-cholesterol campaign right out the window.

But the commercials on TV keep going, cholesterol "medicine" keeps being sold, and not much has changed. It seems that if enough money is thrown at an obstacle, then everything is good and well in the world. If the levels of total cholesterol are normalized, what reason would exist for the production of extra HDL? If there is nothing to transport back to the liver, then what is the purpose of the extra carrier. By this logic, the level of HDL should decrease as a sign of improved function.

Another reason why we want to shy away from concrete examples with specific dosages is variability in absorption. Weight is another important factor when considering the dosages for each program. Logic would dictate that the same dose would have a lessened effect on an individual weighing 250 pounds than it would have on an individual weighing 120 pounds. That would certainly sound logical, and make our job a lot easier. If only it were so. The truth of the matter is that the great thing that makes us all unique and requires different approaches also dictates how said approaches work. In fact, a small dose of a hormone on the 250 pound individual could actually have a greater effect in raising levels than the same dose on the 120 pound individual.

To spice up the mix this is in no way constant across the board for agents either. A small dose of DHEA can have a ridiculously good effect on the heavier person while a large dose of pregnenolone can have a very small effect. Meanwhile these same hormones can have the opposite effects in terms of the strength of the impact on a lighter person. To top it all off there are random variables that can occur such as tachyphylaxis due to the use of pharmaceutical drugs, which can lessen the effect of any other agent.

One aspect of the program is more constant regardless of tests and histories. The main hormone doses are clustered in the morning, to simulate the natural time of peak hormone production in the human body. Note the use of main, since there are indications to use some hormones at other times in addition to the morning dose. Why use hormones at other times as well when we just stated that the peak production is in the morning? Consider an optimum production of one hormone. The largest production occurs in the morning, with less throughout the day and towards the night. Now consider a scenario where hormone production is already well below optimum. Small-scale and ineffective production of hormones in the morning means that there are even less for the rest of the day.

To sum up, the program that we employ is a multimodal approach to the restoration of optimal physiology by using bioidentical hormones and natural supplements. The primary concept to remember is that in the grand scheme of events, the normalization of cholesterol can be seen as far from the primary goal. The optimization of steroid hormones leads to the optimization of cholesterol. It is the optimization of the hormones which provides the benefits that are evident in a fully functional human body. A simple observation of the studies that we mentioned earlier shows a great correlation with the numerous impairments to overall health due to decreased steroid hormone levels.

Based on all this, we can make an order of sorts to describe the associations:

- Decreased steroid hormone production leads to increased cholesterol

- Health issues that appear to be related to high cholesterol can in large part be associated with lowered steroid hormone production

- Optimization and restoration of steroid hormone levels helps with optimal function

- Because of optimized steroid hormone levels, there is no need for extra cholesterol to be created to pick up the slack

- Cholesterol levels are optimized

Thus goes this little bit of logical progression. We go after the cause, not the effect. By doing so, the effect is taken care of quite well because the cause is of course responsible for the effect. At the end of all this we must always remember the slippery slope associated with this "cause" and "effect" by breaking through what can be easily considered a popular culture viewpoint instead of a scientific one. The house is on fire (steroid hormone production) and the smoke alarm (cholesterol) is going full blast. Seems pretty obvious right? The fire needs to be put out and then we can turn off the smoke alarm. For some reason, the popular notion wants to turn off the smoke alarm and expect the fire to be put out. By this logic, the effect would be the root of the cause (this doesn't quite make sense with the rules set upon us with the English language and the core concept of cause and effect).

We can of course go on for days with fiendish and cleverly crafted metaphors and analogies about the broken status of public perception towards our good old friend cholesterol. However, a large amount of rhetoric can wind up being a bunch of hot air when there is nothing to back it up. Fortunately for us, we have a hot air balloon handy so that said air can be put to good use. This comes in the form of scientific data to back up our claims. We wouldn't have gone on for so many pages to pull a bait and switch at this point and not provide any data to back up what we are saying, after all.

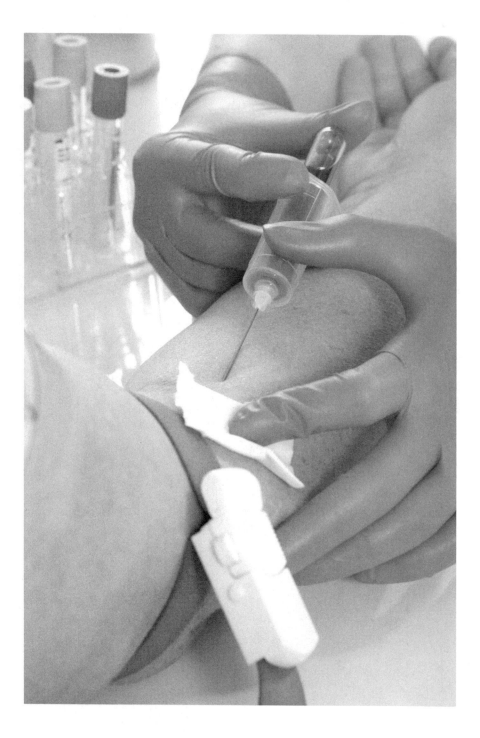

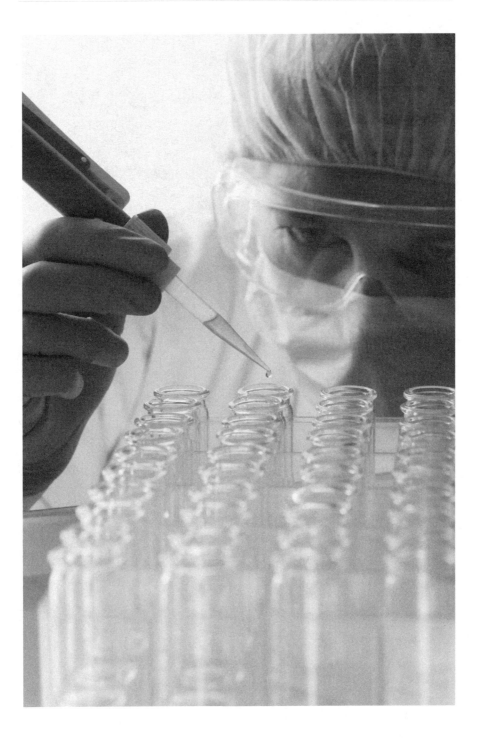

CHAPTER 8

Clinical Evidence

Here we will present two studies that we performed which back up our hypothesis. This book is for laypeople and physicians, and we try to present the information in a way that is beneficial for doctors while at the same time being understandable to lay people. They have been edited for clarity's sake, because as a rule such medical articles submitted to medical science journals are written in concise way that also assumes that everyone reading it has at least a somewhat advanced knowledge of medical terminology (as well as a doctorate in statistics and a master in obfuscation). They deal with the correction of hypercholesterolemia with the use of hormonorestorative therapy. The first one is named, appropriately enough, "Hormonorestorative Therapy is a Promising Method for Hypercholesterolemia Management".[1] The second one is called "Correction of Steroidopenia as a New Method of Hypercholesterolemia Treatment".[2]

Publication One

Abstract

Cardiovascular disease (involving not only the heart but also the veins and arteries) is a leading cause of death and impairment in the United States. Hypercholesterolemia is associated with a high risk of coronary artery disease and the treatment of hypercholesterolemia is still a controversial issue. We investigated the role of hormonorestorative therapy in the management of hypercholesterolemia. We performed a retrospective analysis of 112 patients that were treated for hypercholesterolemia. The population group consisted of 34 male and 78 female patients, with an average age of 54.2 years. Blood test values of the lipid profile, serum pregnenolone, DHEA-S, progesterone, total estrogen, total testosterone, cortisol, and vitamin D-3 were measured.

Hormonorestorative therapy was used with bioidentical hormones which included oral pregnenolone, DHEA-S, hydrocortisone, vitamin D-3, topical or oral triest (a combination of 3 major estrogens), progesterone, and testosterone. The follow up period ranged from 3 months to 12 years and cholesterol levels decreased in all patients treated with HT. The mean total cholesterol level was 252.9 mg/dL before and 190.7 mg/dl after treatment. Total cholesterol levels normalized in 63.4% of patients and forty one patients still had a minimal elevation of total cholesterol. No side effects or complications related to HT were recorded. This study shows that hormone restoration can decrease total cholesterol levels significantly without side effects and be a viable recommendation for clinical use.

Introduction

Each year, twelve million people around the world die from cardiovascular disease, and around 50% of deaths in the United States are caused by this disease.[3-5] Irregularities in lipid levels are a large factor in ischemic heart disease. Ischemic heart disease refers to decreased blood supply to the heart, which damages heart muscle tissue (much in the concept that ischemic stroke damages neurons due to decreased blood supply to the brain). Elevation of total cholesterol has an association with an increased risk of atherosclerosis and cardiovascular disease.[6-8] A decreased level of cholesterol is associated with a regression of atherosclerosis in patients with coronary heart disease.[9]

In the population of high risk, middle aged people, the treatment of hypercholesterolemia has been recognized for a long time as the most effective intervention therapy for primary and secondary prevention of atherosclerotic cardiovascular disease.[10] Primary and secondary prevention refers to the different routes of attack against disease. These two strategies are just half of the overall defense against disease.

Primary prevention deals with actually preventing the disease from ever appearing. In other words, this is measures taken towards a healthy individual who has no disease so that said disease never occurs or has little chance thereof. Secondary prevention refers to treatment strategies for a disease which is present but is still in the very early stages. This treatment is meant to prevent the disease from proceeding any further in severity. Tertiary prevention refers to a time when the disease is already well established at which point treatment seeks to restore bodily function and reduce any potential complications from the disease.

Quaternary prevention is somewhat odd in this scheme

because it isn't the expected strategy just by analyzing the previous three. Quaternary prevention refers not so much to treatment but rather an overabundance of treatment. Overmedication or unnecessary or excessive procedures are advised against in this strategy to prevent further damage.

There is a multitude of pharmaceutical and treatment regimens in both North America and Europe.[11] Drugs that work to lower lipid levels reduce atherosclerotic cardiovascular disease, but are associated with a decrease in quality of life, which shows the necessity of looking for treatment options for hypercholesterolemia that do not have as many side effects and decreases in quality of life.[12,13]

There is a new concept called "quality of life adjusted survival" that has developed in numerous areas of medical treatment that stresses that survival from disease should not be the sole determining factor. While it is easy to measure (being a true or false question linked to patient life status), it does not take into account which preventative therapies are better overall. In other words, staying alive just to keep living in a bad state is not an optimal approach to treatment. There is still a good amount of disagreement surrounding precise triggers for intervention treatment and ideal pharmaceutical approaches.

The effect of "estrogens and androgens" on the functions of the body was first looked at in the early 1900s. Estrogens were first artificially created in the 1920s, when they were observed for their use to alleviate menopausal symptoms and even reduce the previously mentioned ischemic cardiovascular disease. Androgens have been written about in medical works since 1936, when Mocquot and Moricard described their use in the relief of vasomotor (referring to the widening and narrowing of blood vessels) symptoms in postmenopausal women. Recently performed studies show that a combination androgen and estrogen therapy was able to reduce serum levels of total cholesterol, LDL, HDL, and triglycerides.[14,15] Application of DHEA supplementation has been observed to lower both total cholesterol and LDL.[16] However, other studies have failed to confirm such observations.[17-19]

Through our reviews of the available medical literature, we did not succeed in finding a connection between the restoration of youthful levels of steroid hormones with the normalization of total cholesterol. The American Academy of Anti-Aging Medicine believes that when hormone intervention is performed (in other words, the supplementation of hormone therapy), the levels that should be aimed at are the ones around the age of 25, which is a time in life when hormone levels are highest. This view is not shared with the American Geriatric Association. General belief states that high levels of cholesterol are a result of genetic factors and diets that are high in fat. Both patients and doctors have had a hard time trying to establish a way to decrease levels of cholesterol with the use of drugs and the modification of diet.

Our hypothesis is that steroidopenia (literally the deficiency of steroids) is a result of aging and is a primary mechanism of hypercholesterolemia. This hypothesis identifies hypercholesterolemia as a consequence of age-related, enzyme-dependent down regulation (decrease of cellular components) of steroid hormone biosynthesis and their interconversions. Using this hypothesis, we attempted to cement the vital part that hormone restoration plays in the treatment of hypercholesterolemia.

Material and Method

The patients that are described in this study were not specifically selected based on strict criteria or previously known lipid disorders. The patients were either looking for anti-aging management or were seen to require anti-aging intervention as part of cancer treatment. Measurements were taken for levels of the lipid profile, serum pregnenolone, DHEA-S, progesterone, total estrogen, total testosterone, cortisol, and vitamin D-3. Again, 112 patients with hypercholesterolemia were treated, 34 of which were male and 78 female, with an average age of 54.2 years. The patients all received hormone restoration with bioidentical hormones.

We define hormonorestorative therapy as a multi-hormonal therapy that uses formulas which are chemically identical to human hormones. These hormones are applied in physiologic ratios with a schedule that is meant to mirror the pre-existing natural production cycle of hormones allowing for the restoration of optimal levels of hormones. This optimal level was established as hormone levels in the upper one third of the standard laboratory range for individuals in the age bracket of 20-30 with optimal health. This range is for all steroid hormone levels with the exception of estradiol or total estrogen levels for men.

The actual hormonorestorative therapy includes oral pregnenolone (doses between 15-300 mg), DHEA (15-200 mg), hydrocortisone (5-10 mg), and vitamin D-3 (1000-5000 IU). The triest, progesterone, and testosterone were applied in gel or drop form. The triest gel used [a ratio of 90:7:3 for E3:E2:E1 (Estriol:Estradiol:Estrone) respectively] was 1.25 mg/ml or 2.5 mg/ml, progesterone in 5% gel (which is 50 mg/ml), and testosterone gel of 5% at 50 mg/ml. Triest drops were used as 5 mg/ml (ratio of 80:10:10 of E3:E2:E1). Progesterone and testosterone drops were used in doses of 50 mg/ml.

Certain patients in the group were already taking steroid hormones that were not bioidentical (such as conjugated equine estrogens, medroxyprogesterone acetate, methyltestosterone, and others). Those names alone sound sinister enough without the knowledge that they completely don't belong in a human body (but one does belong in a horse's body, but that is the problem isn't it). All of these patients were switched over to bioidentical hormone formulations. The monitoring follow up period ranged from 3 months (the standard time for the first follow up blood test) to 12 years.

Results

The actual age range of the patients was 22 up to 81 years. All patients (at a 100% rate) responded to the therapy. The average total cholesterol prior to treatment was 252.9 mg/dL and dropped to 190.7 mg/dL for an average reduction of 24.6%. In men, the drop was from 268.3 mg/dL to 188.6 mg/dL (an average change of 29.7%). In women, this drop was 246.1 mg/dL to 191.6 mg/dL (an average change of 23.6%) as seen in Graph 1 on the next page.

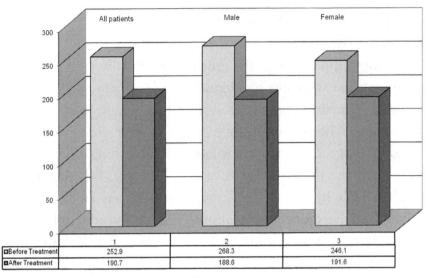

	All patients	Male	Female
	1	2	3
□Before Treatment	252.9	268.3	246.1
▣After Treatment	190.7	188.6	191.6

Graph 1

Serial HDL levels decreased from 62.7 mg/dL to 50.1 mg/dL (a 20.1% drop), but remained much higher than the minimal normal level in all cases. The levels of HDL decreased by 3.5% in men and 23.3% in women, as seen in Graph 2.

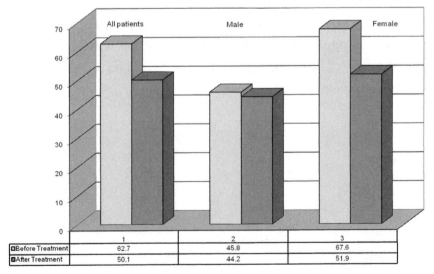

	All patients	Male	Female
	1	2	3
□Before Treatment	62.7	45.8	67.6
▣After Treatment	50.1	44.2	51.9

Graph 2

LDL levels showed a drop from 154 mg/dL to 118.6 mg/dL (23.4%). LDL decreased by 32.7% in men and 20.1% in women, as seen in Graph 3.

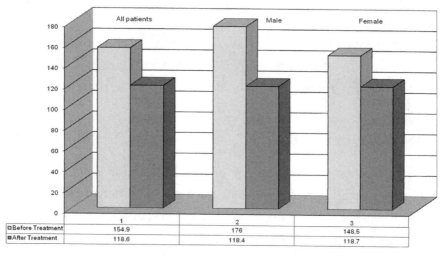

	All patients	Male	Female
	1	2	3
□Before Treatment	154.9	176	148.5
▣After Treatment	118.6	118.4	118.7

Graph 3

Triglycerides dropped from 197.3 mg/dL to 114.8 mg/dL (41.8%). A much higher drop of triglycerides was noted in men (58.9%) than in women (27. 3%), as seen in Graph 4.

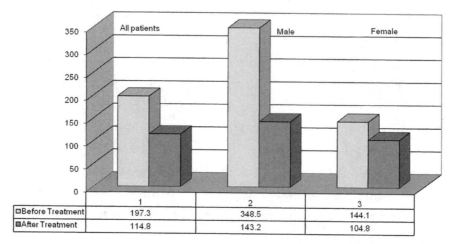

	All patients	Male	Female
	1	2	3
□Before Treatment	197.3	348.5	144.1
▣After Treatment	114.8	143.2	104.8

Graph 4

During the follow up period no patients showed adverse complications related to hormonorestorative therapy and most described an overall improvement in quality of life. The acute morbidity of this therapy was zero. Serum total cholesterol levels normalized in 71 patients (63.4%). 41 patients (36.6%) still had total cholesterol levels that were slightly higher than normal because of the difficulty associated in optimizing the levels of DHEA and pregnenolone in the majority of those patients.

Discussion

The most powerful risk factor of cardiovascular disease is age. Andropause and menopause in men and women, respectively, mark the end of the normal cycle of gonad function which marks the end of the natural protection functions against coronary heart disease. Since coronary heart disease is a rare occurrence prior to these age related changes, cardiovascular protection may be given by steroid hormones. Data collected from more than 30 epidemiologic studies (those focusing on the study of disease) showed that postmenopausal women on hormone replacement therapy (HRT, stressing this because it is hormone replacement therapy and not hormone restoration therapy) have their risk of coronary heart disease reduced by 50%.[20,21] A recent finding of the Heart and Estrogen/Progestin Replacement Study trial did not succeed in confirming this link.[22] Testosterone or other steroid hormones show no clear role in andropausal men in regards to coronary heart disease.[23] One of the issues with andropause is that it is not as well established as menopause.

Steroid hormones are created through conversions from cholesterol, which is the building block of steroid hormones. Various enzyme processes initially convert cholesterol into pregnenolone, which then leads off into all other steroid hormones, as per this simplified flow chart.

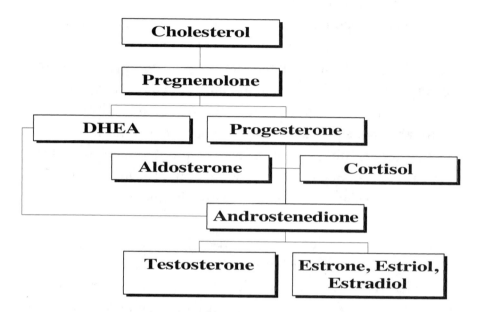

The production of steroid hormones greatly decreases around 40 years of age. Aging is also associated with the dangerous lipid disorders. Creation of new proteins, which includes the creation of new proteins that function in enzyme systems, appears to decrease with age as well. As the construction of enzymes failure in conjunction with failure of lipid breakdown become more widespread, cholesterol can begin to accumulate in the body. With age, all break-down processes overtake the construction processes (catabolic events overtake anabolic events, respectively).

This imbalance increases the rate at which most diseases that are associated with advanced age progress. Cardiovascular disease is one such disease. This shift in the human metabolism with age could be a primary agent in the natural deterioration seen in the body in later years. Consequently, a restoration of the anabolic construction processes can help slow down this process of continuing decline.

Our proposed hypothesis for hypercholesterolemia and its treatment is called the hormonodeficit hypothesis of hypercholesterolemia. Taking into account our hypothesis, the majority of hypercholesterolemia and the consequences of this occur as more or less a reaction to the age related decline of steroid hormone production. The primary role in this reactionary mechanism is under control of the pituitary-hepato-adreno-ovarian axis (an overly complex word that takes into account the primary systems associated with hormone production). According to our hypothesis, hypercholesterolemia is the compensatory reaction for decreased steroidogenesis (literally decreased steroid production). At the same rate, if an individual had what can be considered a low level of total cholesterol at a young age, at the middle and advanced age he or she can have what can be referred to as "relative or functional hypercholesterolemia" with total cholesterol levels that are "normal" according to the standard laboratory values. Based on our observations and opinion, the change of total cholesterol over the course of an individual's life is more vital than the absolute values of total cholesterol. The information about changing levels of total cholesterol could help give the possibility of decreasing vascular damage before the collapse of this compensatory mechanism.

This approach is in particular important for individuals with "normal" total cholesterol (because if we focus on absolute values and not changes over a lifetime then we get a very skewed result) and can be a great help to doctors who treat arteriosclerosis and coronary heart disease.

Our hypothesis implies that a therapeutic treatment strategy which centers around the change of total cholesterol can potentially be a viable cost effective method to assess high atherogenic (plaque forming) risk. It is not an optimal approach to focus solely on cholesterol lowering drugs. Strategies that reduce risk need to be looked at in regard to the treatment of arteriosclerosis, with one such possible strategy being hormonorestorative treatment. One of the issues with cholesterol lowering drugs is that they are not made to address the reason why the liver is producing more cholesterol in the first place. In our view, other than the age related increase in cholesterol levels (which includes relative hypercholesterolemia), pregnancy may be a good event for studying cholesterol disorders. In both pregnancy (when a woman's body requires more hormones) and age related hormone decline, hypercholesterolemia operates as compensation for the increased demand for hormonal production.[24,25] When this compensatory mechanism fails to optimally operate and the elevated level of total cholesterol is not kept up, women usually experience an abortion.[26] Increased levels of cholesterol can actually result in optimized delivery of lipids to cells during responses of the immune system or repair of damaged tissue and enhanced protection against endotoxins and viruses.[27]

Lowered hormone production affects the compensatory mechanism to increase production of cholesterol through multiple feedback actions, which try through a combined effort to restore normal homeostasis by increasing production of the precursor (cholesterol). Unfortunately, cholesterol lowering drugs inhibit the natural production of cholesterol and can be a cause of multiple unwanted health consequences since the sole focus is on the elevated level of total cholesterol and not the reason of elevation. Decreased production of steroid hormones can be expected as a result of such drug use.[28,29] The inhibition of extra cholesterol synthesis, which is meant to offset failing steroid hormone production during deterioration of these production pathways during aging, leads to somatic, psychological, and immune impairment. This includes decreased defense against cancer and infections as well as speeding up of aging processes with various noncardiovascular disorders.[30,31] The most frequent complaints for patients withdrawing from cholesterol lowering drug treatment included musculoskeletal pain, elevations in liver transaminase levels (an enzyme involved in reactions with amino acids, the elevation of which indicates liver damage), rashes, and gastrointestinal complaints.[32,33] The negative consequences would be expected to be equally as detrimental when cholesterol is leeched out of the gut by agents that bind cholesterol as opposed to being recycled for production of steroid hormones as per the natural chain of events.

We attempted to figure out the clinical problems of hypercholesterolemia by not approaching it traditionally. Hormonorestorative therapy appears to be a much safer treatment option in comparison to the standard method of blocking cholesterol production with pharmaceutical means. This therapy is also frequently associated with a significant boost in quality of life.

These assumptions of ours were confirmed by decreases in cholesterol levels in conjunction with a significantly improved quality of life during hormone restoration therapy.

Some studies looked at in retrospect show that patients with normal levels of cholesterol have the same frequency of myocardial infarctions as the patients with hypercholesterolemia. 45-60% of patients who were admitted for myocardial infarction had "normal" levels of cholesterol.[34,35] A possible reason for these observations can be seen via our hypothesis. Nearly every individual after the age of 40 undergoes an elevation of cholesterol levels (barring those who have congenital enzyme issues). This elevation occurs due to the decline in steroid hormone production even while taking into account the mechanism trying to compensate for this issue. We believe that total cholesterol elevation over time is a much more important factor in the assessment of cardiovascular disease risk than a simple analysis of absolute total cholesterol at one time. Such observations can explain the high percent of patients with normal cholesterol levels who experience heart attacks, at an almost equal number to patients who have hypercholesterolemia.

Cholesterol lowering drugs decrease atherosclerotic damage but as mentioned before the quality of life suffers for this. Side effects of fatigue, cognitive clouding, anxiety, depression, insomnia, obesity, and impotence may be linked to related declines in pregnenolone, DHEA, and sex hormones.[36,37] In the study that we conducted, we introduced a new reason behind hypercholesterolemia and looked at a unique approach of pharmacologic intervention. We believe that changing cholesterol levels can be looked at as an optimal marker of the aging process and can be utilized as a good tool to approximate the best time when a patient needs to initiate hormonorestorative therapy.

The presence of hypercholesterolemia is evidence for the malfunction of our homeostasis. We believe that elevated levels of total cholesterol (including relative hypercholesterolemia), in particular when they are joined by steroidopenia, are a good enough sign for the restoration of hormone levels that existed in youth. Optimal levels of steroid hormones like pregnenolone, DHEA, progesterone, estrogens, vitamin D-3, cortisol, and testosterone in the correct ratios are needed for the maintenance of an optimal health profile in both women and men. These hormones are responsible for a wide variety of vital physiological function and the alteration of these levels plays an important part in age related changes.

In our study, patients received hormonorestorative therapy with bioidentical hormones, with no use of synthetic hormones. The body already has all the parts in place for the assimilation of natural hormones in the proper proportions, while the use of synthetic hormones is done with much less effectiveness. In our opinion, an insufficient rejuvenation of hormonal levels in one or more steroid hormones can be cause enough for an inadequate restoration of cholesterol values. We believe that the large amount of controversy in the medical literature is due to hormone replacement therapy, which does not achieve adequate enough levels of hormones and does not utilize bioidentical hormones in their proper physiological doses. This can be a primary cause for the controversial results stemming from the use of estrogens, progesterone, androgens, and DHEA for the correction of lipid disorders.[38,39] In most cases, hormone use in hormone replacement therapy (in particular estrogen replacement) follows regimens with one or two standardized doses given to all women following the treatment procedure without taking into account the very significant differences in absorption rates, metabolism, and pre-existing hormone levels. We believe that the majority of failed treatments of hypercholesterolemia by hormone replacement therapy is due to the wide array of complex interactions between many hormones, and not just the one or two that are administered in such studies. Sending in one or two hormones to make up for the lack of many more is not an adequate approach. To bring back normal function to a level where cholesterol production is normalized is a task where multiple bioidentical hormones need to be employed.

We did not use a standardized treatment approach in regards to dosages and necessary hormones because the best method of treatment takes into account variable levels and factors in different individuals. An excellent treatment regimen for one patient can be completely ineffective for another. The safe correction of hypercholesterolemia was obtainable if the restoration of youthful hormone levels was focused upon. The primary difference between hormonorestorative therapy and other conventional treatment methods for elevated cholesterol is that we did not attempt to directly decrease the level of cholesterol. This decrease is achieved through a multitude of feedback mechanisms related to youthful hormone levels for the basic steroid hormones, in an indirect fashion (steroid hormones are increased while cholesterol decreases). We are not suggesting a cure-all for all manner of hypercholesterolemia, but our approach towards the matter can be a useful additional treatment option in a large variety of situations.

Summary

Cholesterol lowering drugs are not economically feasible for the healthcare systems of most countries, being too expensive for the majority of individual citizens. Consequently, if resources are not adequate, then effective alternative means of controlling cholesterol levels are necessary. In our study, hormonorestorative therapy was an effective method of controlling hypercholesterolemia. The use of this therapy can help create a better understanding of cholesterol disorders, establish methods of control without resorting to drug use, and provide an inexpensive resource for the healthcare industry.

Publication Two

Our second publication that described another study was titled "Correction of Steroidopenia as a New Method of Hypercholesterolemia Treatment" Once again, steroidopenia means deficiency of steroid hormones.

Abstract

In 2002 we proposed a new hypothesis regarding the causation of hypercholesterolemia. There is a scant amount of data in regards to the association of steroidopenia and hypercholesterolemia. Our primary goal was to establish if the treatment of steroidopenia with hormonorestorative therapy to levels that were present at a young age brings about a normalization of total cholesterol levels.

We retrospectively analyzed 43 patients with hypercholesterolemia who were treated with hormonorestorative therapy. Laboratory testing included the lipid profile, serum pregnenolone, DHEA-S, progesterone, total estrogen, cortisol, total testosterone, and vitamin D-3 levels at program initiation and during follow up blood tests (which ranged from 3 to 9 months after beginning therapy).

The results showed that hormonorestorative therapy lowered average total cholesterol from 228.8 mg/dL to 183.7 mg/dL (a change of 19.7%) in all patients. In 12 men with an average age of 62.3, hormonorestorative therapy statistically significantly lowered total cholesterol from 227.9 mg/dL to 177.1 mg/dL (22.3%). This appeared to occur mostly by the decrease of LDL without a significant change in HDL. In women with an average age of 57.0, total cholesterol declined from 229.2 mg/dL to 186.3 mg/dL (18.7%). HDL, LDL, and triglycerides were also decreased to a statistically significant degree. Such decreased results were in turn associated with statistically significant elevations in pregnenolone, DHEA-S, testosterone, progesterone, but not total estrogen, cortisol, or vitamin D-3 in both men and women.

From this we concluded that correction of steroidopenia with the use of hormonorestorative therapy is an effective method for the normalization and maintenance of cholesterol homeostasis.

Introduction

There is a great deal of debate and discussion on the subject of hypercholesterolemia in the medical literature. Various ways are put forward to treat hypercholesterolemia, ranging from diet and exercise to the use of drugs.[40-42] Unfortunately, one of the main issues here is that the mechanisms that actually cause hypercholesterolemia are still uncertain.

There is no information in medical literature concerning the connection between hypercholesterolemia and low levels of steroid hormones except in a few studies.[43-48] A ground breaking study in 2002 of the hormonodeficit hypothesis of hypercholesterolemia showed the link between steroidopenia and hypercholesterolemia.[43,44] This study proposed that elevated levels of cholesterol are a reactionary compensation mechanism for decreased steroid hormone levels.

The purpose of this study was to test a hypothesis regarding the connection of steroidopenia and hypercholesterolemia by analyzing the influence of hormone restoration in the treatment of hypercholesterolemia.

Methodology

This study is a retrospective chart analysis of 43 patients who were treated with hormonorestorative therapy due to hypercholesterolemia after the failure of conventional treatment for high cholesterol or the side effects from cholesterol lowering drugs. The population included 12 males and 31 females. The overall average age was 58.4 years, with a female average of 57.0 years and a male average of 62.3 years. All members of this population received hormonorestorative therapy. Since 1996, we have used the term hormonorestorative therapy in our practice for the regimen used for our patients. This therapy was described as a multi-hormonal approach with the use of hormones that are chemically identical to human hormones (anthropo-identical) in physiologic ratios and dosing schedules that are meant to simulate the human production cycle (such as majority production in the morning or cyclical schedules based on menstrual cycles). Hormonorestoration relies on a multiple approach that includes various agents such as pregnenolone, DHEA, triestrogen, progesterone, testosterone, hydrocortisone, and vitamin D-3. The blood tests that were looked at were the lipid profile, serum pregnenolone, DHEA-S, progesterone, total estrogen, cortisol, total testosterone, and vitamin D-3. These were checked at program initiation and 3 month intervals, with a follow up period of 3 to 9 months.

One of the most important events due to aging is the

change in abundance and the pattern of variable levels of hormonal release.[49] The goal of hormone restoration is to help establish a hormonal profile that is found in a normally functioning physiology. The application of the estrogen, progesterone, and testosterone was done primarily by gels because of the good absorption via skin and the ease of dose modifications due to the gel being in a syringe so that precise doses are easily squeezed out. The basic formulations were 1.25-2.5 mg/mL (at a ratio of 90:7:3 for E3:E2:E1) for Triest, 50 mg/mL at 5% or 100 mg/mL at 10% for progesterone, and 50 mg/mL at 5% or 100 mg/mL at 10% for testosterone. In scenarios where the absorption was not optimal via skin the addition of drops was utilized. The drop formulations were 5 mg/mL (at a ratio of 80:10:10 for E3:E2:E1) for Triest, 50 mg/mL for progesterone, and 50 mg/mL for testosterone. The application of pregnenolone, DHEA, and hydrocortisone was done via oral forms (tablets or capsules). The doses of pregnenolone ranged from 15 to 300 mg for pregnenolone, 15 mg to 200 mg for DHEA, and 2.5 mg to 10 mg for hydrocortisone. Vitamin D-3 was employed at doses ranging from 1000 IU to 5000 IU.

Three criteria were followed to establish dosages for the individuals during hormonorestorative therapy.

- Recommended dosages for the various individuals undergoing hormonorestorative therapy differed significantly based on each individual case and were determined by clinical data and hormone levels obtained from testing.
- The doses were specifically selected for each individual to optimize levels which are standard for healthy

individuals between the ages of 20 and 30.

- The doses were also selected in amounts adequate enough to elevate hormone levels to the optimal range which is defined as the upper one third of the normal range from laboratory testing.

The following rules were followed with the use of hormones:
- bioidentical (anthropo-identical) structure of hormones
- doses modified for each individual
- cyclical dosing schedule where applicable
- larger doses in the mornings
- control of the treatment regimen based on hormone level tests
- therapy with just one or two hormones is not adequate
- optimal therapy is achieved with the use of multiple hormones

Results

All of the patients responded favorably to hormonorestorative therapy (as seen in the adjacent figure), with no adverse effects.

The student T test (simply a type of statistical hypothesis test) was chosen to evaluate the results found in the program. The average level of total cholesterol dropped from 228.8 mg/dL to 183.7 mg/dL (a change of 19.7%). Seven individuals had levels that ranged between 202 mg/dL to 211 mg/dL, but even these showed a beneficial drop in total cholesterol. These individuals required further treatment and continuing optimization of steroid hormone levels. Average total cholesterol decreased from 229.2 mg/dL to 186.3 mg/dL (18.7%) in women and 227.9 mg/dL to 177.1 mg/dL (22.3%) in men. Total cholesterol decreased by an average of 51 points in men and 43 points in women, with 45 points in all patients. These decreased levels were statistically significant (p<0.05) in men despite the small sample size and also in women (p<0.05) in women, as well as the entire population of patients.

Total Cholesterol Before and After Hormonorestorative Therapy

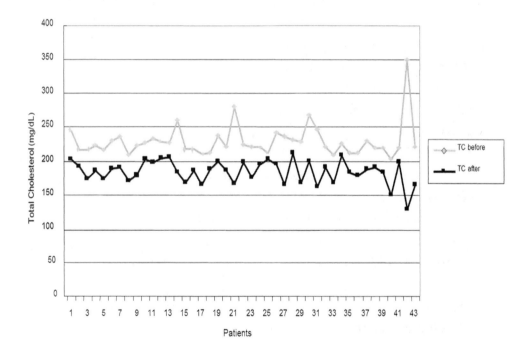

Average HDL dropped from 65.0 mg/dL to 53.8 mg/dL. In women, the average HDL decreased from 73.3 mg/dL to 59.5 mg/dL (p<0.05). The average HDL in men declined from 43.6 mg/dL to 38.8 mg/dL, but was not statistically significant like the change in women. Average LDL overall dropped from 137.4 mg/dL to 110.2 mg/dL (p<0.05). Average LDL in men decreased from 149.3 mg/dL to 112.5 mg/dL (p<0.05), while the average LDL in women decreased from 132.8 mg/dL to 109.3 mg/dL (p<0.05).

What's important to remember here is that the total cholesterol value is the combined values of LDL and HDL, and triglycerides divided by 5. Based on this equation, it was expected that LDL levels were found to decline in all patients at statistically high (p<0.05) levels that are consistent with total cholesterol changes. However, HDL is a carrier that brings back substances to the liver and was not found to have significantly changed (p=0.09) in men, but did decline in both women (p<0.05) and all patients (p<0.05) at a statistically significant level. Average triglyceride values dropped from 132.7 mg/dL to 100.3 mg/dL (24%). The average triglycerides in women declined from 115.0 mg/dL to 86.7 mg/dL (p<0.05) and 178.7 mg/dL to 135.6 mg/dL (p<0.05) in men. Triglycerides levels thus declined statistically significantly in men, women, and all patients.

For steroid hormone levels, some hormones had more significant changes than others. This is not due to overdosing in those steroid hormones but rather simply those steroid hormones which seemed to be consistently lower with a higher range, thus leading to a greater change overall. The following two charts illustrate this well.

The first one is for men:

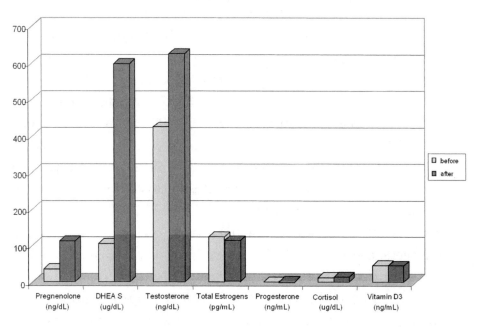

The second one is for women:

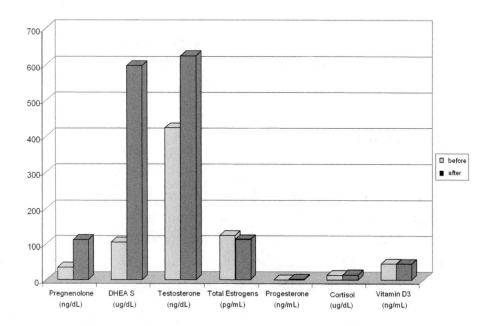

Average pregnenolone levels increased from 53.9 ng/dL to 172.1 ng/dL. The average pregnenolone elevation was 61.2 ng/dL to 193.5 ng/dL for women and 35 ng/dL to 112 ng/dL for men. Pregnenolone levels were found to be significantly elevated ($p < 0.05$) in men, women, and all patients. Average DHEA-S increased from 92.8 ug/dL to 457.0 ug/dL. The average DHEA-S increased from 88.3 ug/dL to 408.5 ug/dL for women and 104.4 ug/dL to 597.3 ug/dL for men. Like pregnenolone, DHEA-S levels were elevated in a statistically significant ($p < 0.05$) for men, women, and all patients. Testosterone levels were elevated on average from 424.0 ng/dL to 625.1 ng/dL in men, for a statistically significant ($p < 0.05$) change. Testosterone changed on average from 37.6 ng/dL to 63.2 ng/dl ($p < 0.05$) in women. Total estrogen did not change statistically in men and did not have significant changes for women either. Progesterone levels increased in women on average from 3.2 ng/mL to 7.5 ng/mL ($p < 0.05$). There was also an increase in men, from 0.4 ng/mL to 2.5 ng/mL. Average cortisol levels in all patients were elevated from 13.8 ug/dL to 14.1 ug/dL. This change in average levels did not lead to a statistically significant change in men or women. Average levels of Vitamin D-3 increased from 44.8 ng/mL to 46.3 ng/mL for all patients, with no statistically significant elevation.

Discussions

Hormonorestorative therapy in men lowered total cholesterol seemingly by lowering LDL and triglycerides but without an appreciable change in HDL. Based on this observation, the steroid hormone level changes that were connected to the changes in LDL and cholesterol were DHEA-S, pregnenolone, testosterone, and progesterone. There was no significant change in levels of vitamin D-3, cortisol, or total estrogen to explain these results. Total cholesterol in women was accompanied by decreases in HDL, LDL, and triglycerides, all to a statistically significant degree. Much like in men, steroid hormone elevations were statistically significant for pregnenolone, DHEA-S, testosterone, progesterone, with no statistically significant changes in total estrogens, cortisol, or vitamin D-3.

We believe that HDL level decreases during hormonorestorative therapy are a good marker of our intervention if HDL levels were not low initially. If the level of total cholesterol is normalized, then logically there is no reason for the excess production of HDL. If there is nothing to transport back to the liver, there is no need to produce the extra carrier and as such the amount of HDL should decrease. The odd lack of significant changes in total estrogen for women can be attributed to the fact that estrone and estradiol were the only ones used for the calculation of total estrogen. Though laboratory blood test values of total estrogen did not change significantly, the patients all had clinical resolutions of menopausal symptoms. Average levels of vitamin D-3 were not elevated significantly because more than 80% of patients were already taking some manner of vitamin D-3 supplements before initiating hormonorestorative therapy, showing an explanation for the small changes in vitamin D-3 in this study.

Cholesterol is the precursor for basic steroid hormones such as pregnenolone, DHEA, progesterone, cortisol, aldosterone, estrogen, testosterone, and others. A natural decline of these steroid hormones occurs with age.

We propose that the human physiology is wired to increase cholesterol production in an attempt to balance or reverse declining levels of hormones, since cholesterol is vital for the creation of steroid hormones in the first place. The rising cholesterol levels do so due to negative feedback loop mechanisms to make up for low steroid hormone levels. However, the problem at hand is that as the body advances in age, enzyme systems are not as effective and cannot completely restore the youthful levels of hormones. It is due to these factors that we see the connection between hypercholesterolemia and steroidopenia, which makes elevated levels of cholesterol a signifier of steroid hormone deficit.

The normalization of these steroid hormones to optimal levels corrects the issue that the over-production of cholesterol is trying to fix. Normalization of steroid hormone levels leads to the completion of the feedback loop, which in turn allows cholesterol levels to normalize due to the body approaching closer to equilibrium. This study reinforces our hypothesis regarding the link between steroidopenia and hypercholesterolemia due to their actions on one another. This revelation strongly suggests that the optimization of the body's natural physiology via a natural approach should come before intervention with pharmacologic means. Pharmacologic medicine that tries to fix the issue of cholesterol elevation does so in a way that interferes with normal body functions and is associated with many side effects. Our approach seeks to gently guide the body towards optimization while the conventional approach seeks to combat the body directly with drugs.

Conclusion

Our study confirms the validity of an interconnection between steroidopenia and hypercholesterolemia. Based on our observations, we believe that the resolution of steroidopenia with the use of anthropo-identical hormones can serve as an inexpensive and efficient method of hypercholesterolemia treatment in the healthcare system.

A Few Remarks

From our point of view, hormonorestorative therapy restores the normal conditions of all 3 regulatory mechanisms of HMG CoA Reductase:

- Negative feedback regulation, which is restored via the youthful levels of steroid hormones.
- Hormonal regulation, which is accomplished via progesterone and a balance between insulin and glucagon. Insulin and glucagon are hormones created in the pancreas that are responsible for lowering blood glucose and increasing blood glucose, respectively.
- Transcriptional regulation, which is done via the improvement of anabolic reactions on the transcription of HMG CoA mRNA.

Something that becomes evident is that the contents of these articles simply repeat what we have been repeating ourselves this entire time. Except now, we have our own scientific backing that reinforces our hypothesis. We not only have words and references, but we have words, references, and scientific data.

The first article is more focused on the observation of the hypothesis while the second one has a focus on application of the hypothesis. The method of hormonorestorative therapy described in the second is exactly what we mentioned earlier when speaking of our program. Everyone took individualized doses of bioidentical steroid hormones based on the myriad factors that modify them such as age, weight, history, and initial blood tests. To save on some words, we can simply say that the results speak for themselves.

One important aspect of this type of approach is that this is what can be termed physiologic medicine. Physiologic medicine simply refers to the concentration on the causes of physiology malfunctions and does not attempt to treat the disease, but rather the patient. There are several points towards the benefit of this type of approach:

- we know that when a person suffers from any disease our body makes an effort to restore normal physiology and struggles to restore vital equilibrium
- the luck of equilibrium leads to the development of different symptoms and diseases; disease is the final result of a chronic lack of equilibrium when the body reserves for balance maintenance run low or become completely exhausted
- it leads to the derangement of various body functions and natural defenses finally can be broken down
- disease is not the beginning of a destructive process, but rather the end of it
- thus, disease is not a primary object of our management manipulations.

A possible question, a very valid one at that, arises at this point. We have the description of human biology which cannot be refuted (in that cholesterol is the precursor of all of these steroid hormones). We have our hypothesis which works from these seemingly simple assumptions. We have our data which reinforces our hypothesis. So why, then, do we not have citations and links to studies of the same nature?

The answer to this is simple. There is a reason why we keep calling our hypothesis, "our" hypothesis. This is because we have established it, and through "experimentation" we have the evidence that it has a valid application. In other words, the reason we don't have any references to work like ours is because such references do not exist. There are certainly studies here and there that point that one or two steroid hormones can have an impact on cholesterol, but what they lack is the unified framework that we have created for a valid application to the process of normalization of cholesterol.

The fact of the matter is, when all the evidence is considered our hypothesis seems almost like common sense. We simply examined the biological processes in the body and saw that the potential was there for the correction of cholesterol production via strictly natural means, by reinforcing the agents of the body that already served this purpose but were in some way deficient. We do this without resorting to a synthetic agent which sabotages cholesterol production and is liable to do more harm than good. It seems almost frustratingly simple when all the data is laid out. Why did nobody else come up with our findings when it seems so obvious when all the data is put together?

We can try to answer this question from several viewpoints. The first viewpoint is that the development of this hypothesis is truly somewhat revolutionary and that we have created a major breakthrough in the understanding and treatment of a very wide ranging issue. We can file that viewpoint under "a bit arrogant, but correct."

The other viewpoint can seem cynical at first but with

enough time spent thinking will appear quite pragmatic. All those associations and tests with high cholesterol and that pesky atherosclerosis seem to tell us that cholesterol is no good. Then we find out that by altering a pathway with a drug, we can say that we have lowered cholesterol and everyone is safe and sound. Meanwhile, we make ludicrous amounts of money by proliferation of our treatment to as large a population as we can. What's that you say? There are hundreds of studies out there that show that what we use to lower cholesterol can be somewhat bad? Why, increase the advertising budget and join us for cognac and cigars in the antechamber you silly man!

There are some very interesting figures floating about in regards to articles about statin drugs and cholesterol and how they are utilized as references, or not utilized as the case may be. Thousands of studies that are not in favor of the "mainstream" hypothesis are neglected and ignored. Articles that are unsupportive of said hypothesis are not cited properly after 1970, even though their number is almost equal to the number of articles that are supportive.[50] Furthermore, when it's time to choose articles as references, a very small amount of articles dealing with randomized studies of cholesterol lowering trials with negative outcomes are cited, while a large amount of non-randomized (emphasis on this) trials with positive outcomes are chosen as support.[51]

One element which we mentioned briefly at the end of the article is the potential savings to healthcare costs. This notion is quite simple in practice and has more than one application. Many health insurance plans cover prescription drug costs because those can take a good chunk out of the old coin purse. After all, the price has to be at a good level to keep profit margins high and the advertising budget well stocked.

Meanwhile, agents such as DHEA and pregnenolone can be found in many locations for a variety of prices.

The other aspect of savings is one not directly tied into something like prescription drug costs and is rather more considerable in terms of monetary costs. Consider all the benefits shown through optimal hormone levels versus the large amount of problems associated with low levels of hormones. Many of these problems can lead to health care costs such as medical assistance and patient care. With optimal levels of hormones, many of these issues can be potentially averted. Take for example the studies that show an association with good hormone levels in afflictions of the elderly such as dementia and Alzheimer's. These two conditions with time necessitate constant care. If good hormone levels are kept up such conditions can be potentially held at bay or even averted completely.

This latter approach accumulates quite a bit of savings in the long run and has the capacity to greatly increase quality of life. Saving money and living better should be some of those desirable human rights that everyone has a chance for. After all, living well is always nice when there's some spare money lying about.

CHAPTER 9

Covering Other Hypotheses

Relative Hypercholesterolemia

Having covered what can be considered some of the main tenets of our points, we can move on to cover some odds and ends. Although, in this case said odds and ends lend themselves to being important reinforcement of our hypotheses. Everything goes back to the point that we always try to reiterate that nothing in the body happens as a localized event separated from any other systems. Recall our mention of the blood brain barrier earlier and its seeming impervious nature. On paper, anyway. As we quickly found out, the blood brain barrier is open to certain agents (or violated through brute force by certain pathogens), and this is just one example of the vast interconnected pathways of the body. Connections are everywhere in the body, which is why we can use cholesterol as such a good biomarker.

Relative hypercholesterolemia is one issue that we can focus a bit more on. For example, seemingly one of the greatest marks against cholesterol is the association with coronary heart disease. However, it is vital to remember that cholesterol increases with age, as does the incidence of coronary heart disease. In other words, the binding factor here, without any further investigation, could well be age just as cholesterol.

Something of interest (though certainly not to the individuals who experience it) is that myocardial infarctions occur in patients who have what are considered "normal" total cholesterol level.[1] Furthermore, the average total cholesterol levels did not differ between the patients who experienced myocardial infarction and the normal population.[2] So how can we explain that up to 70% of patients with coronary heart disease and myocardial infarction have what is documented as the "normal" level?

As we've been going on for quite a while already about the subject, it should be apparent that cholesterol elevation isn't the only thing that happens with age. Many important protective functions which are vital to optimal health are associated with hormones, and of course these functions are just as connected to an optimal level of hormones as well. The age-related decline of steroid hormone production is a key factor here.

Though the total cholesterol value may appear to be "normal," it is not normal when previous levels from earlier on in the life cycle are considered. Again, we must stress that the more important variables to keep track of are cholesterol values throughout life. Seeing what can be seen as a somewhat lower level earlier in life increase to what can be considered a normal level would immediately show that the age-related cholesterol increase did in fact happen. If a single isolated test is taken later on in life, the all clear can sound if the cholesterol level is normal. Unfortunately, this would not provide an accurate risk assessment.

Consider an individual who has body temperature elevation to such a point where enzymes denature and a great deal of damage occurs. However, the fever is brought down. If someone were to check the temperature right there, and base the wellness of the individual on that one factor alone, well they would be in for quite a surprise when the patient dies the next day.

How would cholesterol that is at a normal level later in life be defined as relative hypercholesterolemia if no prior information exists about decline or lack thereof over time? This occurs in our experience through hormonorestorative therapy, in cases where upon initiation of the program the total cholesterol level appears within the normal range. When a follow up blood test is performed, a moderate to large total cholesterol drop can be observed upon restoration of optimal hormone levels.

Take the example of these two individuals:

Patient 1	Age 25	Age 40
TC (nl<200 mg/dL)	120	195

Patient 2	Age 25	Age 40
TC (nl<200 mg/dL)	170	245

The life cycle related elevation of total cholesterol in both cases is 75 mg/dL. We hypothesize that the elevation of total cholesterol over time is a critical determining factor for the risk of coronary heart disease or myocardial infarction. We decided to investigate our hypothesis and study the results of treatment on a small group with "normal" cholesterol.

The results are shown below.

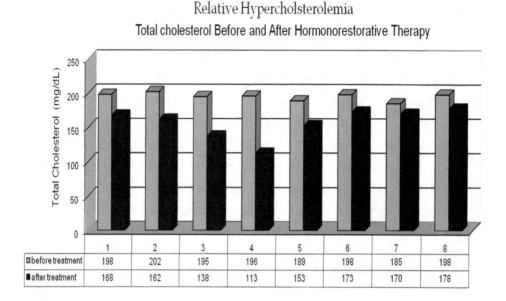

Relative Hypercholsterolemia
Total cholesterol Before and After Hormonorestorative Therapy

	1	2	3	4	5	6	7	8
□ before treatment	198	202	195	196	189	198	185	198
■ after treatment	168	162	138	113	153	173	170	178

This chart shows an example of the variety that can be seen in relative hypercholesterolemia. While in some examples the decrease can be as little as 15 mg/dL to as much as 83 mg/dL. This study showed how hormonorestorative therapy decreased cholesterol. The latter example is very important because it shows how well the true decline in optimal physiology can be obfuscated if only the total cholesterol value is taken into consideration at one time.

If the total cholesterol level was well above 200 mg/dL, such as at 250 mg/dL or so, then an 83 mg/dL decrease in cholesterol would be seen as quite a good day's work. An individual with a total cholesterol level this high above 200 mg/dL would well expect that something such as hormonorestorative therapy would normalize the cholesterol level, and an individual test would show that physiology is not optimal. However, an individual who has had total cholesterol values that have risen over time but never reached "high" levels would not be aware that physiology is not optimal based on just a total cholesterol test.

This hypothesis of relative hypercholesterolemia is important because based on the collected data it shows that hypercholesterolemia is not necessarily defined by predetermined values of "high," but more so through the elevation of cholesterol over time. Furthermore, it reinforces the point that a simple test for total cholesterol is an inadequate measurement of risk assessment.

Familial Hypercholesterolemia

Another "type" of hypercholesterolemia that we can briefly touch upon is familial hypercholesterolemia.

Familial hypercholesterolemia (FHC) is a frequent, inherited disorder which is characterized by elevated levels of total cholesterol and LDL. The widely accepted point of view states that individuals with FHC have mutations in the gene coding for the LDL receptor protein.[3] These people lack the LDL receptors or molecules which can identify cholesterol. With a decreased amount of these receptors, cells cannot get all the cholesterol out of the blood as needed, which causes cholesterol levels to increase. FHC is actually quite widespread, affecting one in every 500 people.[4]

It occurs much more frequently in certain groups of people such as Afrikaners, Christian Lebanese, French Canadians, and Ashkenazi Jews because certain individuals from these groups migrated and founded new colonies, where the founder population married within the group.[5,6] To put it simply, certain groups which tend to marry and reproduce within the same group leads to situations where gene mutations are more frequent. These groups have a high proportion of individuals who are carrying the genes which lead to the development of FHC. FHC actually has strong ties to environmental factors as well, and not just genetics.[7]

There is no doubt that FHC is a health risk factor, since it is associated with an increased frequency of coronary heart disease with one of the worst outcomes possible (this being a heart attack at an early age and premature death).[8] Life expectancy of individuals with FHC is reduced by 15-30 years unless they are treated with therapy to lower lipid levels.[9] This is why any individual with a family history of significantly elevated cholesterol, FHC, or heart disease should be tested to see if FHC is present.

A standard physical examination can reveal these details:
- Xanthomas, which are yellowish firm nodules in the skin lesions caused by cholesterol rich lipoprotein deposits.
- Xanthelasmas, which are very small (1-2 mm) yellowish plaques that are slightly raised on the skin surface of the upper or lower eyelids.
- Arcus senilis cornea, which is a whitish discoloration of the iris.

Meanwhile, laboratory testing may show these details:
- Total plasma cholesterol that is greater than 300 mg/cc in adults.
- Total plasma cholesterol that is greater than 250 mg/cc in children.
- An LDL level that is higher than 200, as well as elevated triglycerides.

- Protein electrophoresis (a process to determine protein amounts) may show abnormal results.
- Special studies of patient cells (fibroblasts) may show an update of LDL cholesterol. Fibroblasts are the most common types of connective tissue in the body and play vital roles in processes such as wound healing. LDL receptor gene defects can be identified with genetic testing.

Even though billions of dollars have been invested into the research and development of many cholesterol lowering drugs, coronary heart disease is still a leading cause of death in developed countries and FHC is a major contributing factor to this deadly killer.

The management of FHC includes a variety of options such as a diet low in saturated fat, cholesterol lowering medications, daily exercise, weight control, and cessation of smoking. Such management options can assist with the prevention of complications like lipid deposits in the skin, thickening of the Achilles tendon, atherosclerosis, and premature death. Other than the management options previously listed, there are also various medications available. In 1985, Brown and Goldstein were awarded the Nobel Prize in Physiology and Medicine for explaining the regulation of cholesterol metabolism.[10] This led to the development of statin drugs.

Since the introduction of statin drugs, the treatment of FHC has improved. However, despite the response of FHC patients to statin drugs, they nonetheless quite often needed additional treatment in addition to the statin drugs. New lipid lowering agents are currently being developed for clinical use, with the latest new drug (Vytorin) being approved by the FDA in

July of 2004. This drug was advertised as a compounded formula specifically targeting FHC. Vytorin is a combination of ezetimibe (which inhibits cholesterol absorption) and simvastatin (which inhibits the creation of cholesterol), thus operating on the basis of a two front attack.

Unfortunately, there are a few problems with using cholesterol lowering drugs (which isn't hard to see coming at this point). The long term use of statin drugs in children with FHC has not been established. Long term exposure of these drugs might affect growth and sexual development because statins decrease cholesterol biosynthesis. One study showed that DHEA sulfate levels were reduced in both boys and girls who were treated by statins as opposed to those treated with the placebo.[11] We know that any small change in the production of hormones at a young age can lead to major problems in adult life. The long term effects of ezetimibe are unknown in regards to FHC cardiovascular morbidity and mortality.[12] Of course, as we have previously discussed on multiple occasions, statin drugs are associated with many serious side effects such as poor quality of life, severe rhabdomyolysis, renal failure, and death.[13-16]

We already mentioned this situation, but it is a good example and important to repeat that during pregnancy cholesterol levels are increased significantly.[17-19] This is due to the increased need for hormones for both the woman and her baby. Nobody would ever consider treating a pregnant woman with cholesterol lowering drugs, however. This reflects the body's sensitivity in reacting by increasing the production of cholesterol when there is an increased demand for hormones.

We have had very good success with patients who have elevated levels of cholesterol, but how do those with FHC factor into this? If we agree that individuals who suffer from FHC lack the LDL receptors due to gene mutations, then what can we do? If looking at it in this cut and dry fashion, there is practically nothing that can be done except the direct lowering of cholesterol production or blocking the absorption of cholesterol in the intestinal tract. Or so it would seem, anyway.

Based on our clinical experience, we believe that FHC works on the same mechanism as does age related cholesterol elevation. We have an impression that FHC should not be viewed as purely a primary disease (in that the main method of action is the increased production of cholesterol), but rather as a secondary disorder associated with a hormonal imbalance. So, instead of it being familial hypercholesterolemia, it would instead be familial low hormone production. If we are right and our hypothesis is correct, then what would happen to an individual with FHC who underwent hormonorestoration? Logically, we would expect to see a normalization of total cholesterol and LDL.

In our experience with FHC we have observed that a medication free approach could actually produce superior results than if prescription drugs were used. This was done by observing the actions of hormones on the body and looking at how altering these levels to bring them back into the range of a normally functioning body can affect those suffering from FHC and high cholesterol in general. These results have been promising and we avoid dangerous side effects that are prevalent with prescription drug use.

We suggest that individuals with FHC should take a first step of a blood test for the determination of steroid hormone levels. Before beginning any regimen of strong cholesterol lowering drugs, hormone levels should be maintained at a youthful, optimal level. Any deficient or suboptimal levels should be corrected to the optimal and youthful level. We have had several patients with FHC whose cholesterol levels were normalized after they began to do hormonorestorative therapy. We would like to describe two interesting cases of FHC that illustrate this point.

Case 1

In one instance, a 38 year old patient (height of 5'11" and a weight of 255 pounds) suffered from a high total cholesterol level over 500 mg/dL and triglycerides over 1500 mg/dL. This was a man who ate no red meat, eggs, and everything was fat free. His wife understood that he had a need for statin drugs to get the values down, but was worried that the side effects could kill him. After all, not everyone with this condition dies of a heart attack and can lead a long and healthy life too. This man's father had this condition and in his 70s was still a very active fully practicing lawyer. This patient's family wanted to work with natural supplementation and hormone modification to reduce his cholesterol, but he was quite skeptical. His doctor was skeptical as well because he was not familiar with the use of hormones for the natural decrease of cholesterol and did not see the need in the first place since statin drugs work well for FHC.

When this man saw an ophthalmologist, he was told that his blood vessels appeared as if they belonged in a man twice his age. This convinced him to take supplements, but he refused to observe the base line for his hormone levels despite it being highly recommended. He started to take 50 mg of DHEA, 100 mg of pregnenolone, and 100 mg of coenzyme Q10 daily. In just 3 months his cholesterol had decreased down to 350 mg/dL, but further effort had to be taken to achieve optimal health. After he stopped taking the supplements regularly, he had a setback and his cholesterol went back up to 400 mg/dL.

After this happened, the pregnenolone was increased to 300 mg, the DHEA to 100 mg, and 600 mg of N-acetyl cysteine (to support healthy liver function) were added to his regimen. After 11 months, his cholesterol was down to 210 mg/dL and his triglycerides were down to 518 mg/dL. Also at this time, his hormones were finally tested and showed these results:

> total testosterone was at 274 ng/dL (with the normal range being 241-827 and optimal levels at 650-827);
> estradiol was at 55 pg/ml (normal range being 0-53 and optimal being 15-30;
> DHEA sulfate was at 919 ug/dL (normal range being 280-640, with an optimal at 500-640);
> pregnenolone was at 113 ng/dL (normal range being 10-200, with an optimal at 180-200).

As can be seen, a small modification of the regimen is still necessary due to the low level of testosterone, the sub-optimal levels of pregnenolone, and the high levels of estradiol and DHEA sulfate. In this case, a decreased dose of DHEA and an increased dose of pregnenolone would be required, as well as a prescription from his doctor for micronized testosterone gel. Vitamin D-3 supplementation is also advisable as well as a supplement to block the enzyme aromatase which controls the eventual conversion of DHEA and testosterone into estradiol. After hormone levels are normalized, we can expect a complete normalization of cholesterol.

Case 2

The second case describes a patient who was a 50 year old male (height 5'7", 168 pounds) on statin drugs since the age of 36. Before taking statin drugs, his total cholesterol was consistently over 350 mg/dL and his triglycerides of over 900 mg/dL. Even though he was taking multiple statin drugs (such as Zocor and Crestor), he was never able to decrease cholesterol levels below 240 mg/dL or his triglycerides below 350 mg/dL. The patient decided to try out 50 mg of DHEA, 100 mg of pregnenolone, and 4000 mg of EPA/DHA each day. After 8 months of this, he tested his lipids and found out that his total cholesterol had decreased to 187 mg/dL and his triglycerides to 113 mg/dL. His doctor was fearful of DHEA and did not know what pregnenolone was, so he asked him to stop the hormones and retest lipid levels. The doctor was sure that the hormones had nothing to do with cholesterol.

The patient listened to the doctor and discontinued the three agents for two weeks. A follow up blood test showed that total cholesterol had increased by 10 mg/dL and triglycerides by 20 mg/dL. Suffice it to say, the patient resumed his previous regimen of hormones. This case got us thinking that it isn't so much familial hypercholesterolemia as it is familial decreased hormone production. Our experience shows that FHC can be looked at in this fashion, because this is a closer description of the root of the problem and showing new avenues for treatment.

Based on this idea several years ago we suggested a new hypothesis of familial hypercholesterolemia. This hypothesis implies that familial hypercholesterolemia is a compensatory reaction of low steroid hormone production due to a congenital defect of the enzyme system which is responsible for the regulation of steroid hormone biosynthesis or their interconversions. In other words, patients with FHC have the same defects in enzymatic system that control cholesterol metabolism starting from birth similar to what our bodies gain during aging.

This malfunction of enzyme systems leads to a diminished ability to produce basic steroid hormones, regardless of the large overproduction of cholesterol. Thus, the body cannot produce enough hormones due to a congenital shortage in enzyme production. In these situations, hypercholesterolemia develops as a normal response of feedback mechanisms where the hormone deficiency serves as a starting point for the overproduction of cholesterol.

When there is a high synthesis of cholesterol, then an excess of LDL is required in the blood. There is no need for an increase in the number of LDL receptors on cell surfaces with a low ability for hormone production. This leads to an excess flow of LDL in the blood. It appears that the body creates a defense against high cholesterol by producing less LDL receptors. If this did not happen, then LDL will attach to LDL receptors, which will release cholesterol to the cells. However, this will deposit a large amount of cholesterol without the ability to utilize it for hormonal production because the enzymes are malfunctioning. This in turn may block normal cell function. We believe that keeping a low number of functioning LDL receptors is one of the possible defensive mechanisms to prevent overflow of cholesterol into cells.

The results of two described cases were significant and offered some interesting information. Familial hypercholesterolemia is thought of as a malfunction where an excess of cholesterol is created. It is, but these cases showed that hormonorestorative therapy helped decrease total cholesterol levels. Thus familial hypercholesterolemia can be more appropriately thought of as familial low hormone production.

We believe that hormonorestorative therapy can be a novel, effective and inexpensive way of FHC management beyond the use of cholesterol-lowering drugs.

A Few Observations on Atherosclerosis and Cholesterol

We would like to remind you that in 1858 Virchow clearly showed that cholesterol does not *start* the process but that it is the *end* product of degeneration. Damage to the tissue became evident first, and then came an accumulation of fat, and finally, as the scar tissue was formed, a high content of cholesterol appeared. It was part of the healing process of a wound from damage caused by something else.

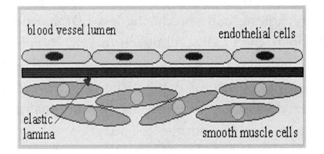

Atherosclerosis is a disease primarily involving four cell types, i.e., endothelial, vascular smooth muscle cells, monocytes, and platelets.[20] Arterial plaque contains a complex mixture of cholesterol, calcium, lipoproteins, mutated arterial cells, and fibrin. It is well know that the composition of the atheroma is the same as for many granulation tissues which are interpreted as a healing process.[21]

Earlier on we mentioned that a misconception about atherosclerotic plaque is the actual composition and that cholesterol is only part of the process. Of course, just like anything in the body it is never the whole story. Cholesterol is important in the process of normal repair of tissues because every cell membrane and organelles within the cells are rich in cholesterol.

Cholesterol is present along with fibrin, collagen, and elastin as a part of the repair process of lesions. Fibrin, in conjunction with platelets, works to clog wounds. Collagen and elastin are types of connective tissues. Arterial plaque begins as mutations to smooth muscle cells in the arteries, which can then proliferate, become fibrous, and eventually even create their own cholesterol.

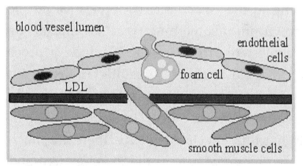

Anabolic influences within the human metabolism decline with age. Age related weaknesses of smooth muscle cells or infections can lead to endothelial injury. This type of injury refers to the thin layer of cells on the inside of blood vessels. This process may be followed by incomplete healing, which can in turn lead to permanent damage to the arterial wall. The endothelial cells are more easily impaired because of weaker arterial muscular responses under normal or elevated blood pressure due to increased peripheral vascular resistance (resistance to blood flow that helps regulate blood pressure) and increased arterial wall stiffness because of aging.

Based on all this information, we have several ideas about atherosclerosis.

- Cholesterol is a key component of the repair process
- Atherosclerosis is a consequence of the age-related metabolic shift from anabolic (creation) to catabolic (break down) process, which leads to tissue degeneration
- The healing of endothelial and smooth muscle cell microtrauma due to physical or chemical injuries is a cause of atherosclerosis
- Atherosclerosis is thus a physiologic adaptation to vascular injury and is a part of failed healing.

As with anything in the body, atherosclerosis cannot be simply broken down into something that is caused by elevated levels of cholesterol. In fact, there is a lack of proof that decreasing blood cholesterol levels resulted in decreased atherosclerosis risks.[22] Like any product of bodily metabolism, cholesterol can be overproduced or underutilized with harmful effects. However, there are much more agents that play a crucial role in the development and progression of atherosclerosis.

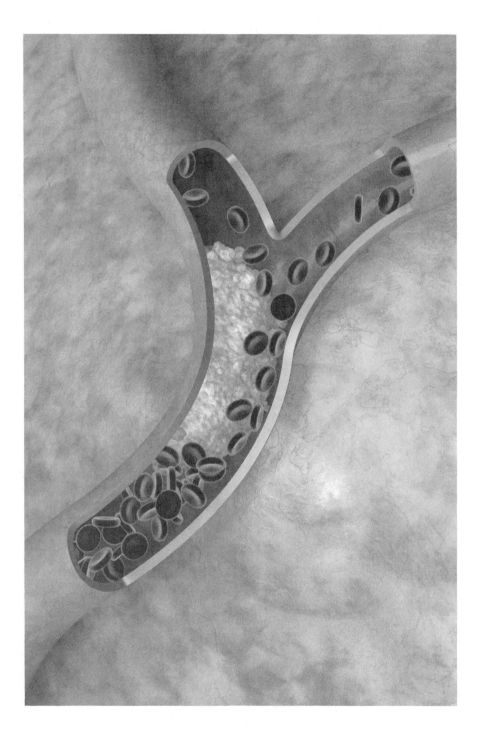

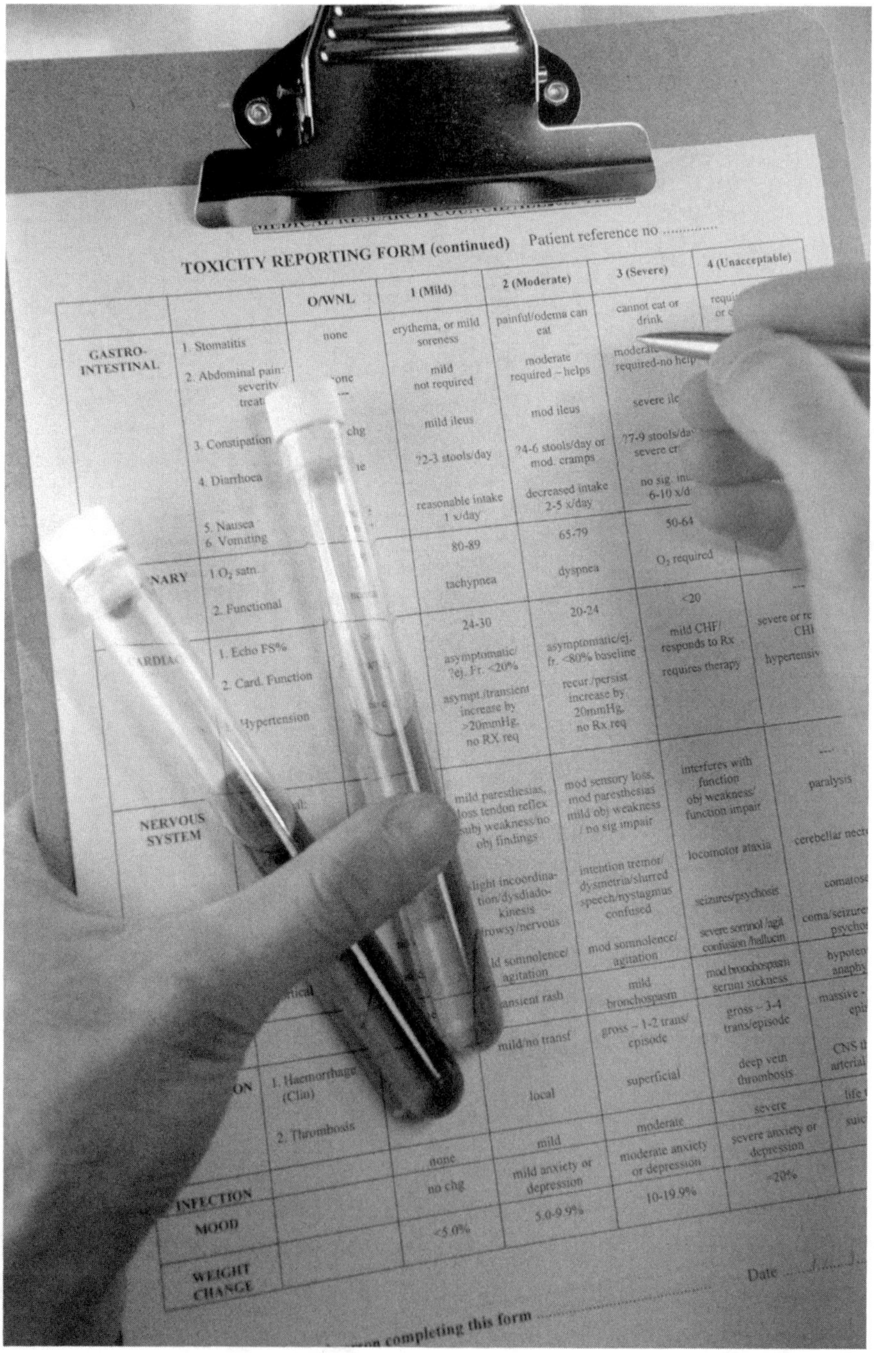
TOXICITY REPORTING FORM (continued)
Patient reference no
O/WNL
1 (Mild)
2 (Moderate)
3 (Severe)
4 (Unacceptable)
GASTRO-INTESTINAL
1. Stomatitis
2. Abdominal pain:
3. Constipation
4. Diarrhoea
5. Nausea
6. Vomiting
1. Echo FS%
2. Card. Function
NERVOUS SYSTEM
1. Haemorrhage (Clin)
2. Thrombosis
INFECTION
MOOD
WEIGHT CHANGE
Date

CHAPTER 10

Case Reports

Now we can observe some case studies of hormonorestorative therapy and how normalizations of cholesterol values are related to steroid hormone levels. We will also look at values in certain extreme cases and how hormone levels are affected. For clarification, here are the meanings of some of the abbreviations:

TC – Total Cholesterol
TRG – Triglycerides
Preg – Pregnenolone
Progest – Progesterone
Test – Testosterone
GLU - glucose

1. Case Study (Hypercholesterolemia)

57 Year old Male
Diagnosis – hypercholesterolemia, impotence, depression, insomnia.
Complaints – hypercholesterolemia, severe erectile dysfunction (since age 39), fatigue, depression, insomnia, short-term memory problems.

	TC	TRG	HDL	LDL	VLDL	TC/HDL
08/31/00	330	216	54	233	43	6.1
09/09/03	187	138	40	119	28	4.7

	DHEA-S	Preg	Estradiol	Progest	Test	Cortisol
nl – age 20-29	(280-640)	(10-200)	(0-53)	(0.3-1.2)	(241-827)	(4.3-22.4)
08/31/00	93	24	56	0.3	186	0.9
09/09/03	540	159	30	1.3	496	15.6

At the follow up on 09/09/03 there were no complaints.

2. Case Study (Hypercholesterolemia)

51 Year old Female

Diagnosis – hypercholesterolemia, anxiety, depression, arthritis, fatigue, insomnia, Crohn's disease, Irritable bowel syndrome, menopause, sarcoidosis, skin problems.

Drugs – Asacol (10+ years) – for Crohn's disease, Astelin - nasal spray – for allergies, Zegerid and carafate – for acid reflux and stomach pain, Xanax - for depression.

	TC	TRG	HDL	LDL
07/13/10	254	98	62	172
09/09/10	183	81	60	107

	DHEA-S	Preg	Total Estrogen	Progest	Test	Cortisol	Vit D-3
nl – age 20-29	(65-380)	(10-230)	(61-437)	(0.2-28)	(14-76)	(4.3-22.4)	(30-100)
07/13/10	24	46	<50	0.5	17	20.8	25
09/09/10	329	181	276	9.1	43	18.8	44

At the follow up on 01/06/11 no drugs were being used and there were no complaints.

3. Case Study (Hypercholesterolemia)

61 Year old Female

Diagnosis – hypercholesterolemia, depression, insomnia, arrhythmia, constipation.

Complaints – hypercholesterolemia, fatigue, depression, insomnia, arrhythmia, hot flashes, vaginal dryness, no libido, poor sex drive, constipation, leg cramps, short-term memory problems, frequent bladder infections, incontinence.

	TC	TRG	HDL	LDL	VLDL	TC/HDL
12/17/02	278	124	74	180	25	3.8
02/28/03	191	63	48	130	13	4.0

	DHEA-S	Preg	Total Estrogen	Progest	Test
nl – age 20-29	(65-380)	(10-230)	(61-437)	(0.2-28)	(14-76)
12/17/02	<30	75	121	0.8	17
02/28/03	269	149	124	3.0	n/a

At the follow up on 02/28/03 still had complaints of bladder infections.

At the follow up on 04/30/03 there were no complaints.

4. Case Study (Hypercholesterolemia)

58 Year old Female

Diagnosis – hypercholesterolemia, migraine (a 38 year history), chronic fatigue syndrome (CFS), depression, insomnia.

Complaints – daily migraine, hypercholesterolemia, CFS, depression, body aches, insomnia, constipation, hot flashes, vaginal dryness, no libido, poor sex drive, short-term memory problems.

	TC	DHEA-S	Preg	Estradiol	Progest	Test
nl – age 20-29	<200	(65-380)	(10-230)	(19-528)	(0.2-28)	(14-76)
01/07/05	300	86	<10	19	0.4	51
09/12/05	195	340	190	217	5.9	61

Follow ups on 09/12/05 and 12/12/07, no complaints at both times.

5. Case Study (Hypercholesterolemia)

24 Year old Female

Diagnosis – hypercholesterolemia, obesity, depression, polycystic ovary syndrome (PCOS), hypoglycemia (low glucose level).

Complaints – overweight, fatigue, depression, anxiety, irregular menstrual cycle, short-term memory problems, high cholesterol, hair loss, ovarian cysts, bruises, facial hair.

Weight – 252 pounds. Height 6'1".

	TC	TRG	HDL	LDL	VLDL	TC/HDL	GLU
11/22/02	210	171	34	141	34	6.3	54
03/05/03	150	107	32	97	21	4.7	95

	DHEA-S	Preg	Total Estrogen	Progest	Test
nl – age 20-29	(65-380)	(10-230)	(61-437)	(0.2-28)	(14-76)
11/22/02	233	44	168	0.8	61
03/05/03	312	178	356	9.4	59

(Blood was drawn on the 15th day of the menstrual cycle in both cases)

Follow up on 03/05/03 had complaint of overweight (at 228 lb; patient lost 24 lb) with no other complaints.

6. Case Study (Hypercholesterolemia)

34 Year old Female

Diagnosis – hypercholesterolemia, migraine, premenstrual syndrome (PMS), depression, insomnia, constipation.

Complaints – migraine (2-3 times a week) since age 15, fatigue, insomnia, constipation, PMS, no libido, poor sex drive, overweight, hypercholesterolemia.

	TC	DHEA-S	Preg	Total Estrogen	Progest	Test
nl – age 20-29	<200	(65-380)	(10-230)	(61-437)	(0.2-28)	(14-76)
11/22/02	207	81	87	128	0.8	42
03/05/03	178	205	172	274	17.7	47

(Blood was drawn on the 21 day of the menstrual cycle in both cases)

Follow ups performed on 10/18/04 and 01/17/08 – no complaints.

7. Case Study (Hypercholesterolemia)

54 Year old Female

Diagnosis – hypercholesterolemia, hypertension, migraine, fatigue, depression, insomnia, arthritis.

Complaints – high blood pressure that was poorly controlled with prescription drugs, high cholesterol, migraine, depression, severe anxiety, irritability, fatigue, poor libido, low sex drive, genital herpes, poor short-term memory, trouble falling asleep, weight gain, arthritis, and irregular menstrual cycles.

	TC	DHEA-S	Preg	Total Estrogen	Progest	Test	IGF-1
nl – age 20-29	<200	(65-380)	(10-230)	(61-437)	(0.2-28)	(14-76)	>300
04/13/99	241	66	50	643	0.7	29	90
09/16/03	182	350	182	315	14.4	49	250

(Blood was drawn on day 19 of the menstrual cycle)

Follow up on 09/16/2003 had a complaint of occasional, minimal neck stiffness.

8. Case Study (Relative Hypercholesterolemia)

24 Year old Male

Diagnosis – attention deficit hyperactivity disorder (ADHD), social anxiety disorder, major depression, insomnia.

Complaints – ADHD and social anxiety disorder, no energy, tiredness, severe depression (despite the use of Paxil), severe anxiety, no libido, erection problems, poor sex drive, decreased appetite, poor short-term memory, sleeping problem, frequent sinus infection and sore throat. Total cholesterol was 140 mg/dL in 2000. ADHD was diagnosed around age 7 and social anxiety disorder at age 14. Patient had been using Ritalin for several years. He was also on different drugs for depression during the last 10 years.

	TC	DHEA-S	Preg	Test
nl – age 20-29	<200	(280-640)	(10-200)	(241-827)
12/10/02	195	79	56	678
08/14/03	152	456	162	730

Follow up at 08/14/03 with no complaints.

9. Case Study (Hypocholesterolemia)

6 Year old Boy

We must remember that imbalance of hormones produced by our glands can occur at any age. Hormones are extremely important for mental health.

We want to stress the importance of the blood test by this demonstration of laboratory result assessment of a 6 year old boy with severe ADHD (this was diagnosed at age 4).

TC	DHEA-S	Preg	Estradiol	Progest	Test
(100-169)	<186	(10-200)	(0-53)	(0.3-1.2)	(0-20)
108	<15	41	<10	0.4	16

This test revealed that total cholesterol was on the low side as well as significantly decreased production of basic steroid hormones. We can make a conclusion based on this information that there are no "cooling/calming" effects on testosterone in matters of aggression and hyperactivity.

10. Case Study (Hypocholesterolemia)

29 Year old Female

Diagnosis – hypocholesterolemia, obesity, depression, menstrual disorder.

Complaints – overweight, fatigue, no energy, depression, anxiety, panic attacks, no libido, poor sex drive, irregular menstrual cycle, very poor short-term memory.

Weight – 242 pounds, Height – 5'5".

Body Fat Percentage (BFP) - 58% (nl 17-24%).

	TC	DHEA-S	Preg	Total Estrogen	Progest	Test
nl – age 20-29	<200	(65-380)	(10-230)	(61-437)	(0.2-28)	(14-76)
07/23/99	130	87	30	87	0.4	33
12/20/01	126	360	157	454	1.8	61

Follow up at 12/20/01, no complaints and weight at 146 lb with a BFP of 18%.

11. Case Study (Hypocholesterolemia and Cancer)

38 Year old Male

Diagnosis – small cell lung cancer with multiple metastases.

	TC	HDL	Progest	Test	DHEA-S
nl – age 20-29	<200	>35	(0.3-1.2)	(241-827)	(280-640)
12/05/02	70	45	<0.2	90	<30

As you can see, there are not enough building blocks (cholesterol) for the production of basic hormones. His body practically does not produce hormones. HDL is at a good level, but it is a bad sign because HDL returns almost all cholesterol back to the liver. Patient died quickly due to an inability to support a normal function of immune system, anabolic reactions, and malnutrition.

12. Case Study (Congenital Hypocholesterolemia)

38 Year old Female
Diagnosis – congenital hypocholesterolemia, depression, alcoholism, menstrual disorder, hepatitis C, hepatomegaly (liver enlargement).
Complaints – fatigue, no energy, depression, insomnia, headaches, suicidal attempts, no libido, poor sex drive, memory loss, irregular menstrual cycle.

	TC	TRG	HDL	LDL	VLDL	TC/HDL
02/26/03	80	66	23	44	13	3.5

As we previously discussed, a low level of cholesterol can significantly affect quality of life in a negative fashion. We presented a few cases with hypocholesterolemia because we want to raise awareness about serious health problems related to low cholesterol production. Multiple serious illnesses in this case could be explained by the body's inability to produce enough hormones for the normal function of physiology.

13. Case Study (Hypercholesterolemia)

61 Year old Male
Diagnosis – hypercholesterolemia, diabetes type II, hypertension (high blood pressure), chronic lymphocytic leukemia (WBC >60000), erectile dysfunction, obesity (280 lb), depression,

fatigue, insomnia, short-term memory problems, high PSA (18 ng/mL).

Total cholesterol was 310 mg/dL before the patient started to take statins. TC decreased on Lipitor at first to 114 mg/dL (TRG 102, HDL 39, and LDL 55), and then to 102 mg/dL (TRG 173, HDL 29, and LDL 38). He was told by his cardiologist that he had "two years to live". He was on 18 drugs before hormonorestoration.

	DHEA-S	Preg	E2/Total Estrogen	Progest	Test	Vit D-3	Cortisol
nl – age 20-29	(280-640)	(10-200)	0-53 <130	(0.3-1.2)	(241-827)	(30-100)	(4.3-22.4)
2004	40	10	56 (E2)	0.2	166	19	11.7
04/02/10	543	148	<50	1.8	462	41	20

In October 2010 the patient had a dramatic improvement in quality of life. Weight was decreased and fluctuated around 178-183 lb. PSA was at 8.1. WBC 23500; hormonal profile was improved. At this time the patient was on one drug for diabetes type II. His latest Lipid profiles are satisfactory.

	TC	TRG	HDL	LDL
04/02/2010	207	117	36	148
10/26/2010	181	153	25	125

CONCLUSION

So what can we gather from all this information? The most vitally important concept is first and foremost redemption of cholesterol in the public eye. We hope that with the information presented here we have at the very least adequately shown that there is no logical sense to bring out the pitchforks and torches to go after a vital component of the body. Information cannot be kept hidden or mired by popular consensus, locked from seeing the light of day.

Cholesterol is just as important as the steroid hormones that it is responsible for. The complex web of conversions that is linked to these agents is necessary for human life and is an irreplaceable part of our biological functions. By using this knowledge, it is possible to repair the function of the body without the use of non-physiological synthetic agents and to normalize the level of cholesterol. Steroid hormones themselves are a valuable tool that demonstrates how resilient the body can be to disease and even the ravages of time.

Having said all this, we would like to end with some truths. The body should not be considered so foolish as to manufacture a detrimental substance as long as a human draws breath. Deficiencies of the body can be resolved with the use of that which the body already creates. Planet Earth revolves around the sun and cholesterol is essential for life. These are all facts.

References

Introduction

1. Starfield B. Is US health really the best in the world? *JAMA*. 2000;284(4):483-5.

2. Smith D. Cardiovascular disease: a historic perspective. *Jpn J Vet Res*. 2000;48(2-3):147-66.

3. Jacobson TA. Clinical context: current concepts of coronary heart disease management. *Am J Med*. 2001;110 Suppl 6A:3S-11S.

4. Bostom AG, Cupples LA, Jenner JL, Ordovas JM, Seman LJ, Wilson PW, et al. Lipoprotein(a)-cholesterol and coronary heart disease in the Framingham Heart Study. *Clin Chem*. 1999;45(7):1039-46.

5. Samanek M, Urbanova Z. Cholesterol and triglyceride levels and their development from 2 to 17 years of age. *Cas Lek Cesk*. 1997;136(12):380-5.

6. Yang YH, Kao SM, Chan KW. A retrospective drug utilization evaluation of antihyperlipidaemic agents in a medical centre in Taiwan. *J Clin Pharm Ther*. 1997;22(4):291-9.

7. Okada T, Murata M, Yamauchi K, Harada K. New criteria of normal serum lipid levels in Japanese children: The nationwide study. *Pediatr Int*. 2002;44(6):596-601.

8. Suthutvoravut U, Charoenkiatkul S, Chitchumroonchokchai C, Kosulwat V, Mahachoklertwattana P, Rojroongwasinkul N. Elevated serum cholesterol levels in Bangkok children and adolescents. *J Med Assoc Thai*. 1999;82 Suppl 1:S117-21.

9. Gaist D, Jeppesen U, Andersen M, García Rodríguez LA, Hallas J, Sindrup SH. Statins and risk of polyneuropathy: a case-control study. *Neurology*. 2002;58(9):1333-7.

10. Schuff-Werner P, Kohlschein P. Current therapy of hypercholesterolemia. How much statin does your patient need? *MMW Fortschr Med*. 2002;144(31-32):24-6.

11. Papassotiropoulos A, Hawellek B, Frahnert C, Ra GS, Rao ML. The risk of acute suicidality in psychiatric inpatients increases with low plasma cholesterol. *Pharmacopsychiatry.* 1999;32(1):1-4.

12. Papassotiropoulos A, Hawellek B, Frahnert C, Rao GS, Rao ML. Cholesterol reduction yields clinical benefit. A new look at old data. *Circulation.* 1995;91(8):2274-82.

13. Bzduch V, Behulova D, Kajaba I. A new approach to cholesterol. *Cas Lek Cesk.* 2001;140(22):685-7.

14. Law MR, Thompson SG, Wald NJ. Assessing possible hazards of reducing serum cholesterol. *BMJ.* 1994;308(6925):373-9.

15. Law MR, Wald NJ, Thompson SG. By how much and how quickly does reduction in serum cholesterol concentration lower risk of ischaemic heart disease? *BMJ.* 1994;308(6925):367-72.

16. Hawthon K, Cowen P, Owens D, Bond A, Elliott M. Low serum cholesterol and suicide. *Br J Psychiatry.* 1993;162:818-25.

17. Chung N, Cho SY, Choi DH, Zhu JR, Lee K, Lee PY, et al. STATT: a titrate-to-goal study of simvastatin in Asian patients with coronary heart disease. Simvastatin Treats Asians to Target. *Clin Ther.* 2001;23(6):858-70.

18. Scheen AJ. Fatal rhabdomyolysis caused by cerivastatin. *Rev Med Liege.* 2001;56(8):592-4.

19. Muldoon MF, Manuck SB, Matthews KA. Lowering cholesterol concentrations and mortality: a quantitative review of primary prevention trials. *BMJ.* 1990;301(6747):309-14.

20. McKenney JM. New guidelines for managing hypercholesterolemia. *J Am Pharm Assoc (Wash).* 2001 Jul-Aug;41(4):596-607.

21. Simons LA, Levis G, Simons J. Apparent discontinuation rates in patients prescribed lipid-lowering drugs. *Med J Aust.* 1996 Feb 19;164(4):208-11.

22. Banga JD. Myotoxicity and rhabdomyolisis due to statins. *Ned Tijdschr Geneeskd.* 2001;145(49):2371-6.

23. Scheen AJ. Fatal rhabdomyolysis caused by cerivastatin. *Rev Med Liege.* 2001;56(8):592-4.

Chapter 1

1. Bjorkhem I, Meaney S. Brain cholesterol: long secret life behind a barrier. *Arterioscler Thromb Vasc Biol.* 2004 May;24(5):806-15. Epub 2004 Feb.

2. Vance JE, Hayashi H, Karten B. Cholesterol homeostasis in neurons and glial cells. *Semin Cell Dev Biol.* 2005 Apr;16(2):193-212.

3. Available at: http://www.sigmaaldrich.com/Area_of_Interest/Biochemicals/Enzyme_Explorer/Key_Resources/Plasma_Blood_Protein/Lipoprotein_Function.html Accessed February 28, 2008.

Chapter 2

1. Virchow, Rudolph (1856). Phlogose und Thrombose im Gefässystem. In: Gesammelte Abhandlungen zurwissenschaftlichen Medizin. Germany: Staatsdruckerei Frankfurt.

2. Clarkson S, Newburgh LH. The relation between Atherosclerosis and Ingested cholesterol in the rabbit. *J Exp Med.* 1926 Apr 30;43(5):595-612.

3. Duff GL, McMillan GC. Pathology of atherosclerosis. *Am J Med.* 1951 Jul;11(1):92-108.

4. Keys A. Atherosclerosis: a problem in newer public health. *J Mt Sinai Hosp N Y.* 1953 Jul-Aug;20(2):118-39.

5. Ravnskov U. The Cholesterol Myths. Washington, DC, USA;2000;56-60.

6. Goldberg B. Atherosclerosis and oxidized cholesterol. In: Alternative Medicine. The definitive Guide. Berkeley, CA, USA; 2002:754-5.

7. Ganong WF. Factors influencing plasma cholesterol levels. In: Review of medical physiology. Los Altos, CA, USA;1971:224.

8. Ingram DM, Bennett FC, Willcox D, de Klerk N. Effect of low-fat diet on female sex hormone levels. *J Natl Cancer Inst.* 1987 Dec;79(6):1225-9.

9. Available at: http://www.jsdstat.com/Statblog/wpimages/Cholesterol%20Myth%20A%20Journalistic%20Failure.pdf Accessed February 28, 2008.

10. Castleman B, McNeely BU. Case records of the Massachusetts General Hospital. Weekly clinicopathological exercises. Normal laboratory values. *N Engl J Med.* 1970 Dec 3;283(23):1276-85.

11. Van De Graaff KM, Fox SI. Some laboratory tests of clinical importance. In: Concepts of human anatomy and physiology. Dubuque, IA, USA; 1995:941.

12. Kuhar MB. Update on managing hypercholesterolemia. The new NCEP guidelines. *AAOHN J.* 2002 Aug;50(8):360-4.

13. Available at: http://www.pharmacy.umn.edu/img/assets/10745/Hypercholesterolemia%20Care%20Plan.pdf Accessed February 19, 2008.

Chapter 3

1. Martin U, Davies C, Hayavi S, Hartland A, Dunne F. Is normal pregnancy atherogenic? *Clin Sci (Lond).* 1999 Apr;96(4):421-5.

2. Warth MR, Arky RA, Knopp RH. Lipid metabolism in pregnancy. II. Altered lipid composition in intermediage, very low, low and high-density lipoprotein fractions. *J Clin Endocrinol Metab.* 1975 Oct;41(4):649-55.

3. Sitadevi C, Patrudu MB, Kumar YM, Raju GR, Suryaprabha K. Longitudinal study of serum lipids and lipoproteins in normal pregnancy and puerperium. *Trop Geogr Med.* 1981 Sep;33(3):219-23.

4. Brizzi P, Tonolo G, Esposito F, Puddu L, Dessole S, Maioli M, et al. Lipoprotein metabolism during normal pregnancy. *Am J Obstet Gynecol.* 1999 Aug;181(2):430-4.

5. Troisi A, Moles A, Panepuccia L, Lo Russo D, Palla G, Scucchi S. Serum cholesterol levels and mood symptoms in the postpartum period. *Psychiatry Res.* 2002 Apr 15;109(3):213-9.

6. Mizuno O, Yokoyama T, Tsutsumi N. The changes of serum total cholesterol, HDL-cholesterol and atherogenic index in postpartum. *Nippon Sanka Fujinka Gakkai Zasshi.* 1984 Dec;36(12):2593-7.

7. Erkkola R, Viikari J, Irjala K, Solakivi-Jaakkola T. One-year follow-up of lipoprotein metabolism after pregnancy. *Biol Res Pregnancy Perinatol.* 1986;7(2):47-51.

8. Smolarczyk R, Romejko E, Wójcicka-Jagodzińska J, Czajkowski K, Teliga-Czajkowska J, Piekarski P. Lipid metabolism in women with threatened abortion. *Ginekol Pol.* 1996 Oct;67(10):481-7.

9. Samánek M, Urbanová Z. Cholesterol and triglyceride levels and their development from 2 to 17 years of age. *Cas Lek Cesk.* 1997 Jun 12;136(12):380-5.

10. Rodkiewicz B, Szotowa W, Woynarowska B, Cerańska-Goszczyńska H, Ignar-Golinowska B, Pułtorak M. Serum cholesterol levels in children aged 4-14 years. *Probl Med Wieku Rozwoj.* 1984;13:95-102.

11. Lin CC, Lai MM, Liu CS, Li TC. Serum cholesterol levels and prevalence of hypercholesterolemia in school-aged Taiwanese children and adolescents: the Taichung Study. *Zhonghua Yi Xue Za Zhi (Taipei).* 1999 Nov;62(11):787-94.

12. Lerman-Garber I, Sepúlveda-Amor JA, Tapia-Conyer R, Magos-López C, Cardoso-Saldaña G, Zamora-González J, et al. Cholesterol levels and prevalence of hypercholesterolemia in Mexican children and teenagers. *Atherosclerosis*. 1993 Nov;103(2):195-203.

13. Suthutvoravut U, Charoenkiatkul S, Chitchumroonchokchai C, Kosulwat V, Mahachoklertwattana P, Rojroongwasinkul N. Elevated serum cholesterol levels in Bangkok children and adolescents. *J Med Assoc Thai*. 1999 Nov;82 Suppl 1:S117-21.

14. Rose G, Kumlin L, Dimberg L, Bengtsson C, Orth-Gomer K, Cai X. Work-related life events, psychological well-being and cardiovascular risk factors in male Swedish automotive workers. *Occup Med (Lond)*. 2006 Sep;56(6):386-92. Epub 2006 Jun 16.

15. Jacobs DR Jr, Iribarren C. Invited commentary: low cholesterol and nonatherosclerotic disease risk: a persistently perplexing question. *Am J Epidemiol*. 2000 Apr 15;151(8):748-51.

16. Wilson RF, Barletta JF, Tyburski JG. Hypocholesterolemia in sepsis and critically ill or injured patients. *Crit Care*. 2003 Dec;7(6):413-4. Epub 2003 Oct 6.

17. Dunham CM, Fealk MH, Sever WE 3rd. Following severe injury, hypocholesterolemia improves with convalescence but persists with organ failure or onset of infection. *Crit Care*. 2003 Dec;7(6):R145-53. Epub 2003 Oct 1.

18. Swaner JC, Connor WE. Hypercholesterolemia of total starvation: its mechanism via tissue mobilization of cholesterol. *Am J Physiol*. 1975 Aug;229(2):365-9

19. Lehtonen A, Viikari J. Serum lipids in soccer and ice-hockey players. *Metabolism*. 1980 Jan;29(1):36-9.

20. Boston PF, Dursun SM, Reveley MA. Cholesterol and mental disorder. *Br J Psychiatry*. 1996 Dec;169(6):682-9.

21. Jakovljević M, Reiner Z, Milicić D. Mental disorders, treatment response, mortality and serum cholesterol: a new holistic look at old data. *Psychiatr Danub*. 2007 Dec;19(4):270-81.

22. Tierney E, Bukelis I, Thompson RE, Ahmed K, Aneja A, Kratz L, Kelley RI. Abnormalities of cholesterol metabolism in autism spectrum disorders. *Am J Med Genet B Neuropsychiatr Genet.* 2006 Sep 5;141B(6):666-8.

23. Atmaca M, Kuloglu M, Tezcan E, Ustundag B, Bayik Y. Serum leptin and cholesterol levels in patients with bipolar disorder. *Neuropsychobiology.* 2002;46(4):176-9.

24. Cassidy F, Carroll BJ. Hypocholesterolemia during mixed manic episodes. *Eur Arch Psychiatry Clin Neurosci.* 2002 Jun;252(3):110-4.

25. Jakovljević M, Reiner Z, Milicić D. Mental disorders, treatment response, mortality and serum cholesterol: a new holistic look at old data. *Psychiatr Danub.* 2007 Dec;19(4):270-81.

26. Golomb BA, Stattin H, Mednick S. Low cholesterol and violent crime. *J Psychiatr Res.* 2000 Jul-Oct;34(4-5):301-9.

27. Steegmans PH, Hoes AW, Bak AA, van der Does E, Grobbee DE. Higher prevalence of depressive symptoms in middle-aged men with low serum cholesterol levels. *Psychosom Med.* 2000 Mar-Apr;62(2):205-11.

28. Hawthon K, Cowen P, Owens D, Bond A, Elliott M. Low serum cholesterol and suicide. *Br J Psychiatry.* 1993 Jun;162:818-25.

29. Brunner J, Parhofer KG, Schwandt P, Bronisch T. [Cholesterol, omega-3 fatty acids, and suicide risk: empirical evidence and pathophysiological hypotheses][Article in German] *Fortschr Neurol Psychiatr.* 2001 Oct;69(10):460-7.

30. Ellison LF, Morrison HI. Low serum cholesterol concentration and risk of suicide. *Epidemiology.* 2001 Mar;12(2):168-72.

31. Boston PF, Dursun SM, Reveley MA. Cholesterol and mental disorder. *Br J Psychiatry.* 1996 Dec;169(6):682-9.

32. Wei M, Macera CA, Davis DR, Hornung CA, Nankin HR, Blair SN. Total cholesterol and high density lipoprotein cholesterol as important predictors of erectile dysfunction. *Am J Epidemiol.* 1994 Nov 15;140(10):930-7.

33. Nikoobakht M, Pourkasmaee M, Nasseh H. The relationship between lipid profile and erectile dysfunction. *Urol J.* 2005 Winter;2(1):40-4.

34. Vrentzos GE, Paraskevas KI, Mikhailidis DP. Dyslipidemia as a risk factor for erectile dysfunction. *Curr Med Chem.* 2007;14(16):1765-70.

35. Padrón RS, Más J, Zamora R, Riverol F, Licea M, Mallea L, et al. Lipids and testicular function. *Int Urol Nephrol.* 1989;21(5):515-9.

36. Forette B, Tortrat D, Wolmark Y. Cholesterol as risk factor for mortality in elderly women. *Lancet.* 1989 Apr 22;1(8643):868-70.

37. Weverling-Rijnsburger AW, Blauw GJ, Lagaay AM, Knook DL, Meinders AE, Westendorp RG. Total cholesterol and risk of mortality in the oldest old. *Lancet.* 1997 Oct 18;350(9085):1119-23.

38. Olsen TS, Christensen RH, Kammersgaard LP, Andersen KK. Higher total serum cholesterol levels are associated with less severe strokes and lower all-cause mortality: ten-year follow-up of ischemic strokes in the Copenhagen Stroke Study. *Stroke.* 2007 Oct;38(10):2646-51. Epub 2007 Aug 30.

39. Corti MC, Guralnik JM, Salive ME, Harris T, Ferrucci L, Glynn RJ, et al. Clarifying the direct relation between total cholesterol levels and death from coronary heart disease in older persons. *Ann Intern Med.* 1997 May 15;126(10):753-60.

40. Krumholz HM, Seeman TE, Merrill SS, Mendes de Leon CF, Vaccarino V, Silverman DI, et al. Lack of association between cholesterol and coronary heart disease mortality and morbidity and all-cause mortality in persons older than 70 years. *JAMA.* 1994 Nov 2;272(17):1335-40.

41. Iribarren C, Reed DM, Burchfiel CM, Dwyer JH. Serum total cholesterol and mortality. Confounding factors and risk modification in Japanese-American men. *JAMA.* 1995 Jun 28;273(24):1926-32.

42. Stemmermann GN, Chyou PH, Kagan A, Nomura AM, Jano K. Serum cholesterol and mortality among Japanese-American men. The Honolulu (Hawaii) Heart Program. *Arch Intern Med.* 1991 May;151(5):969-72.

43. Iso H, Naito Y, Kitamura A, Sato S, Kiyama M, Takayama Y, et al. Serum total cholesterol and mortality in a Japanese population. *J Clin Epidemiol.* 1994 Sep;47(9):961-9.

44. Sherwin RW, Wentworth DN, Cutler JA, Hulley SB, Kuller LH, Stamler J. Serum cholesterol levels and cancer mortality in 361,662 men screened for the Multiple Risk Factor Intervention Trial. *JAMA.* 1987 Feb 20;257(7):943-8.

45. Windler E, Ewers-Grabow U, Thiery J, Walli A, Seidel D, Greten H. The prognostic value of hypocholesterolemia in hospitalized patients. *Clin Investig.* 1994 Dec;72(12):939-43.

46. Onder G, Landi F, Volpato S, Fellin R, Carbonin P, Gambassi G, et al. Serum cholesterol levels and in-hospital mortality in the elderly. *Am J Med.* 2003 Sep;115(4):265-71.

47. Glueck CJ, Kuller FE, Hamer T, Rodriguez R, Sosa F, Sieve-Smith L, et al. Hypocholesterolemia, hypertriglyceridemia, suicide, and suicide ideation in children hospitalized for psychiatric diseases. *Pediatr Res.* 1994 May;35(5):602-10.

48. Maccari S, Bassi C, Zanoni P, Plancher AC. Plasma cholesterol and triglycerides in heroin addicts. *Drug Alcohol Depend.* 1991 Dec 31;29(2):183-7.

49. Wilczek H, Ceska R, Zlatohlávek L. Serum lipids in drug addicts. *Vnitr Lek.* 2004 Aug;50(8):584-6.

50. Ho WK, Wen HL, Fung KP, Ng YH, Au KK, Ma L. Comparison of plasma hormonal levels between heroin-addicted and normal subjects. *Clin Chim Acta.* 1977 Mar 15;75(3):415-9.

51. Wannamethee G, Shaper AG, Whincup PH, Walker M. Low serum total cholesterol concentrations and mortality in middle aged British men. *BMJ.* 1995 Aug 12;311(7002):409-13.

52. Oganov RG, Shestov DB, Deev AD, Zhukovskiĭ GS, Klimov AN, Perova NV, et al. Increased risk of death from coronary heart disease in men with low blood concentration of total cholesterol and low density lipoprotein cholesterol according to data from a prospective epidemiologic study in Moscow and Leningrad within the framework of Soviet-American cooperation. *Ter Arkh.* 1991;63(1):6-11.

53. Corti MC, Guralnik JM, Salive ME, Harris T, Ferrucci L, Glynn RJ, et al. Clarifying the direct relation between total cholesterol levels and death from coronary heart disease in older persons. *Ann Intern Med.* 1997 May 15;126(10):753-60.

54. Lee M-LT, Rosner BA, Weiss ST, Vokonas PS, Gaziano JM. Predictors of Cardiovascular Death: The Normative Aging Study – 1963-1998. *Clinical Geriatrics.* 1999;7(9): (www.mmhc.com/cg/articles/CG9909/lee.html)

55. Schatz IJ, Masaki K, Yano K, Chen R, Rodriguez BL, Curb JD. Cholesterol and all-cause mortality in elderly people from the Honolulu Heart Program: a cohort study. *Lancet.* 2001 Aug 4;358(9279):351-5.

56. Iribarren C, Reed DM, Chen R, Yano K, Dwyer JH. Low serum cholesterol and mortality. Which is the cause and which is the effect? *Circulation.* 1995 Nov 1;92(9):2396-403.

57. Behar S, Graff E, Reicher-Reiss H, Boyko V, Benderly M, Shotan A, et al. Low total cholesterol is associated with high total mortality in patients with coronary heart disease. The Bezafibrate Infarction Prevention (BIP) Study Group. *Eur Heart J.* 1997 Jan;18(1):52-9.

58. Siemianowicz K, Gminski J, Stajszczyk M, Wojakowski W, Goss M, Machalski M, et al. Serum total cholesterol and triglycerides levels in patients with lung cancer. *Int J Mol Med.* 2000 Feb;5(2):201-5.

59. Williams RR, Sorlie PD, Feinleib M, McNamara PM, Kannel WB, Dawber TR. Cancer incidence by levels of cholesterol. *JAMA.* 1981 Jan 16;245(3):247-52.

60. Törnberg SA, Carstensen JM, Holm LE. Risk of stomach cancer in association with serum cholesterol and beta-lipoprotein. *Acta Oncol.* 1988;27(1):39-42.

61. Knekt P, Reunanen A, Aromaa A, Heliövaara M, Hakulinen T, Hakama M. Serum cholesterol and risk of cancer in a cohort of 39,000 men and women. *Clin Epidemiol.* 1988;41(6):519-30.

62. Goldstein MR, Mascitelli L. Do statins decrease cardiovascular disease at the expense of increasing cancer? *Int J Cardiol.* 2009 Apr 3;133(2):254-5. Epub 2007 Dec 31.

63. Neaton JD, Blackburn H, Jacobs D, Kuller L, Lee DJ, Sherwin R, et al. Serum cholesterol level and mortality findings for men screened in the Multiple Risk Factor Intervention Trial. Multiple Risk Factor Intervention Trial Research Group. *Arch Intern Med.* 1992 Jul;152(7):1490-500.

64. Iribarren C, Jacobs DR Jr, Sidney S, Claxton AJ, Gross MD, Sadler M, et al. Serum total cholesterol and risk of hospitalization, and death from respiratory disease. *Int J Epidemiol.* 1997 Dec;26(6):1191-202.

65. Fraunberger P, Schaefer S, Werdan K, Walli AK, Seidel D. Reduction of circulating cholesterol and apolipoprotein levels during sepsis. *Clin Chem Lab Med.* 1999 Mar;37(3):357-62.

66. Claxton AJ, Jacobs DR Jr, Iribarren C, Welles SL, Sidney S, Feingold KR. Association between serum total cholesterol and HIV infection in a high-risk cohort of young men. *J Acquir Immune Defic Syndr Hum Retrovirol.* 1998 Jan 1;17(1):51-7.

67. Shor-Posner G, Basit A, Lu Y, Cabrejos C, Chang J, Fletcher M, et al. Hypocholesterolemia is associated with immune dysfunction in early human immunodeficiency virus-1 infection. *Am J Med.* 1993 May;94(5):515-9.

68. Iribarren C, Jacobs DR Jr, Sidney S, Claxton AJ, Feingold KR. Cohort study of serum total cholesterol and in-hospital incidence of infectious diseases. *Epidemiol Infect.* 1998 Oct;121(2):335-47.

69. Leardi S, Altilia F, Delmonaco S, Cianca G, Pietroletti R, Simi M. Blood levels of cholesterol and postoperative septic complications. *Ann Ital Chir.* 2000 Mar-Apr;71(2):233-7.

Chapter 4

1. Jacobson TA. Clinical context: current concepts of coronary heart disease management. *Am J Med.* 2001 Apr 16;110 Suppl 6A:3S-11S.

2. Chung N, Cho SY, Choi DH, Zhu JR, Lee K, Lee PY, et al. STATT: a titrate-to-goal study of simvastatin in Asian patients with coronary heart disease. Simvastatin Treats Asians to Target. *Clin Ther.* 2001 Jun;23(6):858-70.

3. Hunninghake D, Insull W, Knopp R, Davidson M, Lohrbauer L, Jones P, et al. Comparison of the efficacy of atorvastatin versus cerivastatin in primary hypercholesterolemia. *Am J Cardiol.* 2001 Sep 15;88(6):635-9.

4. Bakker-Arkema RG, Nawrocki JW, Black DM. Safety profile of atorvastatin-treated patients with low LDL-cholesterol levels. *Atherosclerosis.* 2000 Mar;149(1):123-9.

5. Wierzbicki AS, Lumb PJ, Semra Y, Chik G, Christ ER, Crook MA. Atorvastatin compared with simvastatin-based therapies in the management of severe familial hyperlipidaemias. *QJM.* 1999 Jul;92(7):387-94.

6. McPherson R, Hanna K, Agro A, Braeken A; Canadian Cerivastatin Study Group. Cerivastatin versus branded pravastatin in the treatment of primary hypercholesterolemia in primary care practice in Canada: a one-year, open-label, randomized, comparative study of efficacy, safety, and cost-effectiveness. *Clin Ther.* 2001 Sep;23(9):1492-507.

7. McKenney JM. New guidelines for managing hypercholesterolemia. *J Am Pharm Assoc (Wash).* 2001 Jul-Aug;41(4):596-607.

8. Simons LA, Levis G, Simons J. Apparent discontinuation rates in patients prescribed lipid-lowering drugs. *Med J Aust.* 1996 Feb 19;164(4):208-11.

9. Tomlinson B, Chan P, Lan W. How well tolerated are lipid-lowering drugs? *Drugs Aging.* 2001;18(9):665-83.

10. Rizvi K, Hampson JP, Harvey JN. Do lipid-lowering drugs cause erectile dysfunction? A systematic review. *Fam Pract.* 2002 Feb;19(1):95-8.

11. Carvajal A, Macias D, Sáinz M, Ortega S, Martín Arias LH, Velasco A, et al. HMG CoA reductase inhibitors and impotence: two case series from the Spanish and French drug monitoring systems. *Drug Saf.* 2006;29(2):143-9.

12. Jacquet A, Colomes M, Ferrieres J, Denat M, Douste-Blazy P, Monstastruc JL. [A one-year prospective and intensive pharmacovigilance of antilipemic drugs in an hospital consultation for prevention of risk factors]. *Therapie.* 1993 Sep-Oct;48(5):509-12.

13. Chang JT, Staffa JA, Parks M, Green L. Rhabdomyolysis with HMG-CoA reductase inhibitors and gemfibrozil combination therapy. *Pharmacoepidemiol Drug Saf.* 2004 Jul;13(7):417-26.

14. Scheen AJ. Fatal rhabdomyolysis caused by cerivastatin. *Rev Med Liege.* 2001 Aug;56(8):592-4.

15. Borrego FJ, Liébana A, Borrego J, Pérez del Barrio P, Gil JM, García Cortés MJ, et al. Rhabdomyolysis and acute renal failure secondary to statins. *Nefrologia.* 2001 May-Jun;21(3):309-13.

16. Omar MA, Wilson JP, Cox TS. Rhabdomyolysis and HMG-CoA reductase inhibitors. *Ann Pharmacother.* 2001 Sep;35(9):1096-107.

17. Ahmad A, Fletcher MT, Roy TM. Simvastatin-induced lupus-like syndrome. *Tenn Med.* 2000 Jan;93(1):21-2.

18. Cromwell WC, Ziajka PE. Development of tachyphylaxis among patients taking HMG CoA reductase inhibitors. *Am J Cardiol.* 2000 Nov 15;86(10):1123-7.

19. Silver MA, Langsjoen PH, Szabo S, Patil H, Zelinger A. Statin cardiomyopathy? A potential role for Co-Enzyme Q10 therapy for statin-induced changes in diastolic LV performance: description of a clinical protocol. *Biofactors.* 2003;18(1-4):125-7.

20. Available at: http://www.anma.org/mon62.html Accessed February 19, 2008.

21. Horlitz M, Sigwart U, Niebauer J. Statins do not prevent restenosis after coronary angioplasty: where to go from here? *Herz.* 2001 Mar;26(2):119-28.

22. Sirvent P, Mercier J, Lacampagne A. New insights into mechanisms of statin-associated myotoxicity. *Curr Opin Pharmacol.* 2008 Jun;8(3):333-8. Epub 2008 Feb 1.

23. Tiwari A, Bansal V, Chugh A, Mookhtiar K. Statins and myotoxicity: a therapeutic limitation. *Expert Opin Drug Saf.* 2006 Sep;5(5):651-66.

24. Ormiston T, Wolkowitz OM, Reus VI, Johnson R, Manfredi F. Hormonal changes with cholesterol reduction: a double-blind pilot study. *J Clin Pharm Ther.* 2004 Feb;29(1):71-3.

25. Hall SA, Page ST, Travison TG, Montgomery RB, Link CL, McKinlay JB. Do statins affect androgen levels in men? Results from the Boston area community health survey. *Cancer Epidemiol Biomarkers Prev.* 2007 Aug;16(8):1587-94.

26. Izquierdo D, Foyouzi N, Kwintkiewicz J, Duleba AJ. Mevastatin inhibits ovarian theca-interstitial cell proliferation and steroidogenesis. *Fertil Steril.* 2004 Oct;82 Suppl 3:1193-7.

27. Mastroberardino G, Costa C, Gavelli MS, Vitaliano E, Rossi F, Catalano A, et al. Plasma cortisol and testosterone in hypercholesterolaemia treated with clofibrate and lovastatin. *J Int Med Res.* 1989 Jul-Aug;17(4):388-94.

28. Golomb BA, Kane T, Dimsdale JE. Severe irritability associated with statin cholesterol-lowering drugs. *QJM.* 2004 Apr;97(4):229-35.

29. Muldoon MF, Ryan CM, Flory JD, Manuck SB. Effects of simvastatin on cognitive functioning. Presented at the American Heart Association Scientific Sessions. Chicago, IL, USA; 2002, Nov. 17-20.

30. Wagstaff LR, Mitton MW, Arvik BM, Doraiswamy PM. Statin-associated memory loss: analysis of 60 case reports and review of the literature. *Pharmacotherapy*. 2003 Jul;23(7):871-80.

31. King DS, Wilburn AJ, Wofford MR, Harrell TK, Lindley BJ, Jones DW. Cognitive impairment associated with atorvastatin and simvastatin. *Pharmacotherapy*. 2003 Dec;23(12):1663-7.

32. Orsi A, Sherman O, Woldeselassie Z. Simvastatin-associated memory loss. *Pharmacotherapy*. 2001 Jun;21(6):767-9.

33. Gaist D, García Rodríguez LA, Huerta C, Hallas J, Sindrup SH. Are users of lipid-lowering drugs at increased risk of peripheral neuropathy? *Eur J Clin Pharmacol*. 2001 Mar;56(12):931-3.

34. Posvar EL, Radulovic LL, Cilla DD Jr, Whitfield LR, Sedman AJ. Tolerance and pharmacokinetics of single-dose atorvastatin, a potent inhibitor of HMG-CoA reductase, in healthy subjects. *J Clin Pharmacol*. 1996 Aug;36(8):728-31.

35. Walsh KM, Albassam MA, Clarke DE. Subchronic toxicity of atorvastatin, a hydroxymethylglutaryl-coenzyme A reductase inhibitor, in beagle dogs. *Toxicol Pathol*. 1996 Jul-Aug;24(4):468-76.

36. von Keutz E, Schlüter G. Preclinical safety evaluation of cerivastatin, a novel HMG-CoA reductase inhibitor. *Am J Cardiol*. 1998 Aug 27;82(4B):11J-17J.

37. Farnsworth WH, Hoeg JM, Maher M, Brittain EH, Sherins RJ, Brewer HB Jr. Testicular function in type II hyperlipoproteinemic patients treated with lovastatin (mevinolin) or neomycin. *J Clin Endocrinol Metab*. 1987 Sep;65(3):546-50.

38. Newman TB, Hulley SB. Carcinogenicity of lipid-lowering drugs. *JAMA*. 1996 Jan 3;275(1):55-60.

39. Available at:
    http://baycollitigation.com/news/news_page_3.htm Accessed
    February 19, 2008.

40. Goldstein MR, Mascitelli L. Do statins decrease cardiovascular
    disease at the expense of increasing cancer? *Int J Cardiol.* 2009 Apr
    3;133(2):254-5. Epub 2007 Dec 31.

41. Childs M, Girardot G. Evaluation of acquired data on long-term
    risk of hypolipidemic treatments. *Arch Mal Coeur Vaiss.* 1992
    Sep;85 Spec No 2:129-33.

42. Saito A, Saito N, Mol W, Furukawa H, Tsutsumida A, Oyama A, et
    al. Simvastatin inhibits growth via apoptosis and the induction of
    cell cycle arrest in human melanoma cells. *Melanoma Res.* 2008
    Apr;18(2):85-94.

43. Tomiyama N, Matzno S, Kitada C, Nishiguchi E, Okamura
    N, Matsuyama K. The possibility of simvastatin as a
    chemotherapeutic agent for all-trans retinoic acid-resistant
    promyelocytic leukemia. *Biol Pharm Bull.* 2008 Mar;31(3):369-74.

44. Gould AL, Rossouw JE, Santanello NC, Heyse JF, Furberg CD.
    Cholesterol reduction yields clinical benefit. A new look at old
    data. *Circulation.* 1995 Apr 15;91(8):2274-82.

45. Papassotiropoulos A, Hawellek B, Frahnert C, Rao GS, Rao ML.
    The risk of acute suicidality in psychiatric inpatients increases with
    low plasma cholesterol. *Pharmacopsychiatry.* 1999 Jan;32(1):1-4.

46. Pignone M, Phillips C, Mulrow C. Use of lipid lowering drugs for
    primary prevention of coronary heart disease: meta-analysis of
    randomised trials. *BMJ.* 2000 Oct 21;321(7267):983-6.

47. Deller M, Huth K. Prevention of coronary heart disease by therapy
    of hyperlipidemia. Between cholesterol hysteria and therapeutic
    realism. *Fortschr Med.* 1992 Sep 10;110(25):463-6.

48. Smith GD, Song F, Sheldon TA. Cholesterol lowering and
    mortality: the importance of considering initial level of risk. *BMJ.*
    1993 May 22;306(6889):1367-73.

49. Geurian KL. The cholesterol controversy. *Ann Pharmacother*. 1996 May;30(5):495-500.

50. Law MR, Thompson SG, Wakd NJ. Assessing possible hazards of reducing serum cholesterol. *BMJ*. 1994 Feb 5;308(6925):373-9.

51. Ravnskov U. Cholesterol lowering trials in coronary heart disease: frequency of citation and outcome. *BMJ*. 1992 Jul 4;305(6844):15-9.

52. Ravnskov U. Frequency of citation and outcome of cholesterol lowering trials. *BMJ*. 1992 Sep 19;305(6855):717.

Chapter 5

1. Dzugan SA, Smith RA. Hypercholesterolemia treatment: a new hypothesis or just an accident. *Med Hypotheses*. 2002;59:751-6.

2. Yokoyama C, Wang X, Briggs MR, Admon A, Wu J, Hua X, et al. SREBP-1, a basic-helix-loop-helix-leucine zipper protein that controls transcription of the low density lipoprotein receptor gene. *Cell*. 1993 Oct 8;75(1):187-97.

3. Tapiero H, Mathé G, Couvreur P, Tew KD. I. Arginine. *Biomed Pharmacother*. 2002 Nov;56(9):439-45.

4. Bhilwade HN, Tatewaki N, Nishida H, Konishi T. Squalene as novel food factor. *Curr Pharm Biotechnol*. 2010 Dec;11(8):875-80.

Chapter 6

1. Paul SM, Purdy RH. Neuroactive steroids. *FASEB J*. 1992 Mar;6(6):2311-22.

2. Do Rego JL, Seong JY, Burel D, Leprince J, Luu-The V, Tsutsui K, et al. Neurosteroid biosynthesis: enzymatic pathways and neuroendocrine regulation by neurotransmitters and neuropeptides. *Front Neuroendocrinol*. 2009 Aug;30(3):259-301. Epub 2009 Jun 6.

3. Ritsner MS, Gibel A, Shleifer T, Boguslavsky I, Zayed A, Maayan R, et al. Pregnenolone and dehydroepiandrosterone as an adjunctive treatment in schizophrenia and schizoaffective disorder: an 8-week, double-blind, randomized, controlled, 2-center, parallel-group trial. *J Clin Psychiatry*. 2010 Oct;71(10):1351-62. Epub 2010 Jun 15.

4. Roberts E, Fitten LJ. Serum steroid levels in two old men with Alzheimer's disease (AD) before and after oral administration of dehydroepiandrosterone (DHEA). Pregnenolone synthesis may be ratelimiting in aging. In: Kalimi M, Regelson W, editors. *The Biological Role of Dehydroepiandrosterone (DHEA)*. Berlin , de Gruyter, 1990, 43–63.

5. Semeniuk T, Jhangri GS, Le Mellédo JM. Neuroactive steroid levels in patients with generalized anxiety disorder. *J Neuropsychiatry Clin Neurosci*. 2001 Summer;13(3):396-8.

6. Heydari B, Le Mellédo JM. Low pregnenolone sulphate plasma concentrations in patients with generalized social phobia. *Psychol Med*. 2002 Jul;32(5):929-33.

7. Osuji IJ, Vera-Bolaños E, Carmody TJ, Brown ES. Pregnenolone for cognition and mood in dual diagnosis patients. *Psychiatry Res*. 2010 Jul 30;178(2):309-12. Epub 2010 May 21.

8. George MS, Guidotti A, Rubinow D, Pan B, Mikalauskas K, Post RM. CSF neuroactive steroids in affective disorders: pregnenolone, progesterone, and DBI. *Biol Psychiatry*. 1994 May 15;35(10):775-80.

9. Myers GN. Pregnenolone in the treatment of rheumatoid arthritis. *Ann Rheum Dis*. 1951 Mar;10(1):32-45.

10. McGavack TH, Chevalley J, Weissberg J. The use of delta 5-pregnenolone in various clinical disorders. *J Clin Endocrinol Metab*. 1951 Jun;11(6):559-77.

11. Roberts E. Pregnenolone—from Selye to Alzheimer and a model of the pregnenolone sulfate binding site on the GABAA receptor. *Biochem Pharmacol*. 1995 Jan 6;49(1):1-16.

12. Dharia S, Parker CR Jr. Adrenal androgens and aging. *Semin Reprod Med.* 2004 Nov;22(4):361-8.

13. Bélanger A, Candas B, Dupont A, Cusan L, Diamond P, Gomez JL, et al. Changes in serum concentrations of conjugated and unconjugated steroids in 40- to 80-year-old men. *J Clin Endocrinol Metab.* 1994Oct;79(4):1086-90.

14. Labrie F, Bélanger A, Cusan L, Gomez JL, Candas B. Marked decline in serum concentrations of adrenal C19 sex steroid precursors and conjugated androgen metabolites during aging. *J Clin Endocrinol Metab.* 1997 Aug;82(8):2396-402.

15. Barrett-Connor E, Khaw KT Yen SS. A prospective study of dehydroepiandrosterone sulfate, mortality, and cardiovascular disease. *N Eng J Med.* 1986 Dec;315:1519-24.

16. Barad D, Brill H, Gleicher N. Update on the use of dehydroepiandrosterone supplementation among women with diminished ovarian function. *J Assist Reprod Genet.* 2007 Dec;24(12):629-34.

17. Berr C, Lafont S, Debuire B, Dartigues JF, Baulieu EE. Relationships of dehydroepiandrosterone sulfate in the elderly with functional, psychological, and mental status, and short-term mortality: a French community-based study. *Proc Natl Acad Sci USA.* 1996 Nov 12;93(23):13410-5.

18. Leng SX, Cappola AR, Andersen RE, Blackman MR, Koenig K, Blair M, Walston JD. Serum levels of insulin-like growth factor-I (IGF-I) and dehydroepiandrosterone sulfate (DHEA-S), and their relationships with serum interleukin-6, in the geriatric syndrome of frailty. *Aging Clin Exp Res.* 2004 Apr;16(2):153-7.

19. Adachi M, Takayanagi R. Role of androgens and DHEA in bone metabolism. *Clin Calcium.* 2006 Jan;16(1):61-6.

20. Haden ST, Glowacki J, Hurwitz S, Rosen C, LeBoff MS. Effects of age on serum dehydroepiandrosterone sulfate, IGF-I, and IL-6 levels in women. *Calcif Tissue Int.* 2000 Jun;66(6):414-8.

21. Osmanagaoglu MA, Okumus B, Osmanagaoglu T, Bozkaya H. The relationship between serum dehydroepiandrosterone sulfate concentration and bone mineral density, lipids, and hormone replacement therapy in premenopausal and postmenopausal women. *J Womens Health (Larchmt)*. 2004 Nov;13(9):993-9.

22. Barad D, Brill H, Gleicher N. Update on the use of dehydroepiandrosterone supplementation among women with diminished ovarian function. *J Assist Reprod Genet*. 2007 Dec;24(12):629-34.

23. Chang DM, Chu SJ, Chen HC, Kuo SY, Lai JH. Dehydroepiandrosterone suppresses interleukin 10 synthesis in women with systemic lupus erythematosus. *Ann Rheum Dis*. 2004 Dec;63(12):1623-6.

24. Alhaj HA, Massey AE, McAllister-Williams RH. Effects of DHEA administration on episodic memory, cortisol and mood in healthy young men: a double-blind, placebo-controlled study. *Psychopharmacology (Berl)*. 2005 Oct 18;:1-11.

25. Bloch M, Schmidt PJ, Danaceau MA, Adams LF, Rubinow DR. Dehydroepiandrosterone treatment of midlife dysthymia. *Biol Psychiatry*. 1999 Jun 15;45(12):1533-41.

26. Wolkowitz OM, Reus VI, Roberts E, Manfredi F, Chan T, Raum WJ, et al. Dehydroepiandrosterone (DHEA) treatment of depression. *Biol Psychiatry*. 1997 Feb 1;41(3):311-8.

27. Rabkin JG, McElhiney MC, Rabkin R, McGrath PJ, Ferrando SJ. Placebo-controlled trial of dehydroepiandrosterone (DHEA) for treatment of nonmajor depression in patients with HIV/AIDS. *Am J Psychiatry*. 2006 Jan;163(1):59-66.

28. Oettel M, Mukhopadhyay AK. Progesterone: the forgotten hormone in men? *Aging Male*. 2004 Sep;7(3):236-57.

29. Singh M. Progestins and neuroprotection: are all progestins created equal? *Minerva Endocrinol*. 2007 Jun;32(2):95-102.

30. Fournier A, Berrino F, Clavel-Chapelon F. Unequal risks for breast cancer associated with different hormone replacement therapies: results from the E3N cohort study. *Breast Cancer Res Treat.* 2008 Jan;107(1):103-11. Epub 2007 Feb 27.

31. Sofuoglu M, Mouratidis M, Mooney M. Progesterone improves cognitive performance and attenuates smoking urges in abstinent smokers. *Psychoneuroendocrinology.* 2011 Jan;36(1):123-32. Epub 2010 Aug 2.

32. Sánchez MG, Bourque M, Morissette M, Di Paolo T. Steroids-dopamine interactions in the pathophysiology and treatment of CNS disorders. *CNS Neurosci Ther.* 2010 Jun;16(3):e43-71.

33. Stein DG, Wright DW. Progesterone in the clinical treatment of acute traumatic brain injury. *Expert Opin Investig Drugs.* 2010 Jul;19(7):847-57.

34. Hu Z, Li Y, Fang M, Wai MS, Yew DT. Exogenous progesterone: a potential therapeutic candidate in CNS injury and neurodegeneration. *Curr Med Chem.* 2009;16(11):1418-25.

35. Naghi JJ, Philip KJ, Dilibero D, Willix R, Schwarz ER. Testosterone Therapy: Treatment of Metabolic Disturbances in Heart Failure. *J Cardiovasc Pharmacol Ther.* 2011 Mar;16(1):14-23. Epub 2010 Nov 19.

36. Malkin CJ, Pugh PJ, Morris PD, Asif S, Jones TH, Channer KS. Low serum testosterone and increased mortality in men with coronary heart disease. *Heart.* 2010 Nov;96(22):1821-5. Epub 2010 Oct 19.

37. Iellamo F, Volterrani M, Caminiti G, Karam R, Massaro R, Fini M, et al. Testosterone therapy in women with chronic heart failure: a pilot double-blind, randomized, placebo-controlled study. *J Am Coll Cardiol.* 2010 Oct 12;56(16):1310-6.

38. Panay N, Al-Azzawi F, Bouchard C, Davis SR, Eden J, Lodhi I, et al. Testosterone treatment of HSDD in naturally menopausal women: the ADORE study. *Climacteric.* 2010 Apr;13(2):121-31.

39. Salom MG, Jabaloyas JM. [Testosterone deficit syndrome and erectile dysfunction]. *Arch Esp Urol.* 2010 Oct;63(8):663-70.

40. Morgentaler A, Bruning CO 3rd, DeWolf WC. Occult prostate cancer in men with low serum testosterone levels. *JAMA*. 1996 Dec 18;276(23):1904-6.

41. Schatzl G, Madersbacher S, Haitel A, Gsur A, Preyer M, Haidinger G, et al. Associations of serum testosterone with microvessel density, androgen receptor density and androgen receptor gene polymorphism in prostate cancer. *J Urol*. 2003 Apr;169(4):1312-5.

42. Vatten LJ, Ursin G, Ross RK, Stanczyk FZ, Lobo RA, Harvei S, et al. Androgens in serum and the risk of prostate cancer: a nested case-control study from the Janus serum bank in Norway. *Cancer Epidemiol Biomarkers Prev*. 1997 Nov;6(11):967-9.

43. Chodak GW, Vogelzang NJ, Caplan RJ, Soloway M, Smith JA. Independent prognostic factors in patients with metastatic (stage D2) prostate cancer. The Zoladex Study Group. *JAMA*. 1991 Feb 6;265(5):618-21.

44. Rosario ER, Chang L, Stanczyk FZ, Pike CJ. Age-related testosterone depletion and the development of Alzheimer disease. *JAMA*. 2004 Sep 22;292(12):1431-2.

45. Okun MS, DeLong MR, Hanfelt J, Gearing M, Levey A. Plasma testosterone levels in Alzheimer and Parkinson diseases. *Neurology*. 2004 Feb 10;62(3):411-3.

46. Białek M, Zaremba P, Borowicz KK, Czuczwar SJ. Neuroprotective role of testosterone in the nervous system. *Pol J Pharmacol*. 2004 Sep-Oct;56(5):509-18.

47. Lu PH, Masterman DA, Mulnard R, Cotman C, Miller B, Yaffe K, et al. Effects of testosterone on cognition and mood in male patients with mild Alzheimer disease and healthy elderly men. *Arch Neurol*. 2006 Feb;63(2):177-85. Epub 2005 Dec 12.

48. Comijs HC, Gerritsen L, Penninx BW, Bremmer MA, Deeg DJ, Geerlings MI. The association between serum cortisol and cognitive decline in older persons. *Am J Geriatr Psychiatry*. 2010 Jan;18(1):42-50.

49. Schwabe L, Wolf OT. Learning under stress impairs memory formation. *Neurobiol Learn Mem.* 2010 Feb;93(2):183-8. Epub 2009 Sep 29.

50. Phillips AC, Batty GD, Gale CR, Lord JM, Arlt W, Carroll D. Major depressive disorder, generalised anxiety disorder, and their comorbidity: Associations with cortisol in the Vietnam Experience Study. *Psychoneuroendocrinology.* 2011 Jun;36(5):682-90. Epub 2010 Oct 16.

51. Anderson GL, Limacher M, Assaf AR, Bassford T, Beresford SA, Black H, et al. Effects of conjugated equine estrogen in postmenopausal women with hysterectomy: the Women's Health Initiative randomized controlled trial. *JAMA.* 2004 Apr 14;291(14):1701-12.

52. Rossouw JE, Anderson GL, Prentice RL, LaCroix AZ, Kooperberg C, Stefanick ML, et al. Risks and benefits of estrogen plus progestin in healthy postmenopausal women: principal results From the Women's Health Initiative randomized controlled trial. *JAMA.* 2002 Jul 17;288(3):321-33.

53. Becker KL. Principles and practice of endocrinology and metabolism. 1990, p.786. Lippincott Company. Philadelphia, USA.

54. Helguero LA, Faulds MH, Gustafsson JA, Haldosén LA. Estrogen receptors alfa (ERalpha) and beta (ERbeta) differentially regulate proliferation and apoptosis of the normal murine mammary epithelial cell line HC11. *Oncogene.* 2005 Oct 6;24(44):6605-16.

55. Bardin A, Boulle N, Lazennec G, Vignon F, Pujol P. Loss of ERbeta expression as a common step in estrogen-dependent tumor progression. *Endocr Relat Cancer.* 2004 Sep;11(3):537-51.

56. Isaksson E, Wang H, Sahlin L, von Schoultz B, Masironi B, von Schoultz E, et al. Expression of estrogen receptors (alpha, beta) and insulin-like growth factor-I in breast tissue from surgically postmenopausal cynomolgus macaques after long-term treatment with HRT and tamoxifen. *Breast.* 2002 Aug;11(4):295-300.

57. Weatherman RV, Clegg NJ, Scanlan TS. Differential SERM activation of the estrogen receptors (ERalpha and ERbeta) at AP-1 sites. *Chem Biol.* 2001 May;8(5):427-36.

58. Pettersson K, Delaunay F, Gustafsson JA. Estrogen receptor beta acts as a dominant regulator of estrogen signaling. *Oncogene.* 2000 Oct 12;19(43):4970-8.

59. Saji S, Jensen EV, Nilsson S, Rylander T, Warner M, Gustafsson JA. Estrogen receptors alpha and beta in the rodent mammary gland. *Proc Natl Acad Sci USA.* 2000 Jan 4;97(1):337-42.

60. Zhu BT, Han GZ, Shim JY, Wen Y, Jiang XR. Quantitative structure-activity relationship of various endogenous estrogen metabolites for human estrogen receptor alpha and beta subtypes: Insights into the structural determinants favoring a differential subtype binding. *Endocrinology.* 2006 Sep;147(9):4132-50.

61. Rich RL, Hoth LR, Geoghegan KF, Brown TA, LeMotte PK, Simons SP, et al. Kinetic analysis of estrogen receptor/ligand interactions. *Proc Natl Acad Sci USA.* 2002 Jun 25;99(13):8562-7.

62. Sitieri PK, Sholtz PI, Cirillo PM, et al. Prospective study of estrogens during pregnancy and the risk of breast cancer. Unpublished study performed in at the Public Health Institute in Oakland, California, and funded by the US Army Medical Research and Material Command under DAMD 17- 99-1-9358.

63. Sniekers YH, Weinans H, van Osch GJ, van Leeuwen JP. Oestrogen is important for maintenance of cartilage and subchondral bone in a murine model of knee osteoarthritis. *Arthritis Res Ther.* 2010;12(5):R182. Epub 2010 Oct 5.

64. Craig MC, Murphy DG. Estrogen therapy and Alzheimer's dementia. *Ann N Y Acad Sci.* 2010 Sep;1205:245-53. doi: 10.1111/j.1749-6632.2010.05673.x.

65. Kojima T, Lindheim SR, Duffy DM, Vijod MA, Stanczyk FZ, Lobo RA. Insulin sensitivity is decreased in normal women by doses of ethinyl estradiol used in oral contraceptives. *Am J Obstet Gynecol.* 1993 Dec;169(6):1540-4.

66. Seely EW, Walsh BW, Gerhard MD, Williams GH. Estradiol with or without progesterone and ambulatory blood pressure in postmenopausal women. *Hypertension.* 1999 May;33(5):1190-4.

67. McManus J, McEneny J, Young IS, Thompson W. The effect of various oestrogens and progestogens on the susceptibility of low density lipoproteins to oxidation in vitro. *Maturitas.* 1996 Oct;25(2):125-31.

Chapter 7

1. Dzugan SA, Smith RA. Hypercholesterolemia treatment: a new hypothesis or just an accident. *Med Hypotheses.* 2002;59:751-6.

2. Dzugan SA, Rozakis GW, Dzugan KS, Emhof L, Dzugan SS, Xydas C, et al. Correction of Steroidopenia as a New Method of Hypercholesterolemia Treatment. *Neuroendocrinol Lett (NEL).* 2011;32(1):77-81.

Chapter 8

1. Dzugan SA, Rozakis GW, Dzugan SS, Smith RA. Hormonorestorative therapy is a promising method for hypercholesterolemia treatment. *Approaches to Aging Control.* 2009;13:12-9.

2. Dzugan SA, Rozakis GW, Dzugan KS, Emhof L, Dzugan SS, Xydas C, et al. Correction of Steroidopenia as a New Method of Hypercholesterolemia Treatment. *Neuroendocrinol Lett (NEL).* 2011;32(1):77-81.

3. Smith D. Cardiovascular disease: a historic perspective. *Jpn J Vet Res.* 2000 Nov;48(2-3):147-66

4. Jacobson TA. Clinical context: current concepts of coronary heart disease management. *Am J Med.* 2001 Apr 16;110 Suppl 6A:3S-11S

5. Weiner SD, Reis ED, Kerstein MD. Peripheral arterial disease. Medical management in primary care practice. *Geriartrics.* 2001 Apr;56(4):20-2, 25-6, 29-30.

6. Soska V. Pharmacotherapy of hyperlipoproteinemia. *Vnitr Lek.* 2000 Sep;46(9):565-8.

7. Hanefeld M, Hora C, Schulze J, Rothe G, Barthel U, Haller H. Reduced incidence of cardiovascular complications and mortality in hyperlipoproteinemia (HLP) with effective lipid correction. The Dresden HLP study. *Atherosclerosis.* 1984 Oct;53(1):47-58.

8. Vogel RA, Corretti MC, Gellman J. Cholesterol, cholesterol lowering, and endothelial function. *Prog Cardiovasc Dis.* 1998 Sep-Oct;41(2):117-36.

9. Lopez-Sendon JL, Rubio R, Lopez de Sa E, Delcan JL. Why the cardiologists should be interested in lipids? *Rev Esp Cardiol.* 1995;48 Suppl 2:23-32.

10. Hughes K. Screening for and treatment of hypercholesterolemia – a review. *Ann Acad Med Singapore.* 1997 Mar;26(2):215-20.

11. Yang YH, Kao SM, Chan KW. A retrospective drug utilization of antihyperlipidaemic agents in a medical center in Taiwan. *J Clin Pharm Ther.* 1997 Aug;22(4):291-9.

12. Turpin G, Bruckert E. Management of atherogenic hyperlipidemia. *Ann Cardiol Angeiol (Paris).* 1998 Nov;47(9):627-32.

13. Bancarz A, Jolda-Mydlovska B, Swidnicka-Szuszkowska. Pharmacological treatment of lipid disorders according to present clinical studies. *Pol Merkur Lekarski.* 1998 Sep;5(27):162-6.

14. Bachmann GA. Androgen cotherapy in menopause: evolving benefits and challenges. *Am J Obstet Gynecol.* 1999 Mar;180(3 Pt 2):S308-11.

15. Ciepluch R, Czestochowska E. Hormonal replacement therapy and body weight in postmenopausal women. *Pol Merkur Lekarski*. 1997 Jan;2(9):188-90.

16. Regelson W, Loria R, Kalimi M. Hormonal intervention: "buffer hormones" or "state dependency". The role of dehydroepiandrosterone (DHEA), thyroid hormone, estrogen and hypophysectomy in aging. *Ann NY Acad Sci*. 1988;521:260-73 .

17. Morales AJ, Nolan JJ, Nelson JC, Yen SS. Effects of replacement dose of dehydroepiandrosterone in men and women of advancing age. *J Clin Endocrinol Metab*. 1994. Jun;78(6):1360-7.

18. Takahashi K, Manabe A, Okada M, Kurioka H, Kanasaki H, Miyazaki K. Efficacy and safety of oral estriol for managing postmenopausal symptoms. *Maturitas*. 2000 Feb 15;34(2):169-77.

19. Haddock BL, Marshak HP, Mason JJ, Blix G. The effect of hormone replacement therapy and exercise on cardiovascular disease risk factors in postmenopausal women. *Sports Med*. 2000. Jan;29(1):39-49.

20. Calaf i Alsina J. Benefits of hormone replacement therapy – overview and update. *Int J Fertil Womens Med*. 1997;42 Suppl 2:329-46.

21. Havranek EP. Primary prevention of CHD: nine ways to reduce risk. *Am Fam Physician*. 1999;59:1455-63,1466.

22. Blakely JA. The heart and estrogen/progestin replacement study revisited: hormone replacement therapy produced net harm, consistent with the observational data. *Arch Intern Med*. 2000;160:2897-900.

23. Morales AJ, Nolan JJ, Nelson JC, Yen SS. Effects of replacement dose of dehydroepiandrosterone in men and women of advancing age. *J Clin Endocrinol Metab*. 1994;78:1360-7.

24. Smolarczyk R, Romejko E, Wójcicka-Jagodzińska J, Czajkowski K, Teliga-Czajkowska J, Piekarski P. The effect of total estrogens and lactogen hormone on lipid metabolism in women during normal pregnancy. *Ginekol Pol.* 1996;67:438-42.

25. Chiang AN, Yang ML, Hung JH, Chou P, Shyn SK, Ng HT. Alterations of serum lipid levels and their biological relevances during and after pregnancy. *Life Sci.* 1995;56:2367-75.

26. Smolarczyk R, Romejko E, Wójcicka-Jagodzińska J, Czajkowski K, Teliga-Czajkowska J, Piekarski P. Lipid metabolism in women with threatened abortion. *Ginekol Pol.* 1996;67:481-7.

27. Jacobs DR Jr, Iribarren C. Invited commentary: low cholesterol and nonatherosclerotic disease risk: a persistently perplexing question. *Am J Epidemiol.* 2000;151:748-51.

28. Mastroberardino G, Costa C, Gavelli MS, Vitaliano E, Rossi F, Catalano A, et al. Plasma cortisol and testosterone in hypercholesterolaemia treated with clofibrate and lovastatin. *J Int Med Res.* 1989;17:388-94.

29. Boizel R, de Peretti E, Cathiard AM, Halimi S, Bost M, Berthezene F, et al. Pattern of plasma levels of cortisol, dehydroepiandrosterone and pregnenolone sulphate in normal subjects and in patients with homozygous familial hypercholesterolaemia during ACTH infusion. *Clin Endocrinol.* 1986;25:363-71.

30. Broitman SA. Dietary cholesterol, serum cholesterol, and colon cancer: a review. *Adv Exp Med Biol.* 1986;206:137-52.

31. Epstein FH. Low serum cholesterol, cancer and other noncardiovascular disorders. *Atherosclerosis.* 1992;94:1-12.

32. Rabe-Jablonska J, Poplawska I. Levels of serum total cholesterol and LDL-cholesterol in patients with major depression in acute period and remission. *Med Sci Monit.* 2000;6:539-47.

33. McGovern ME, Mellies MJ. Long-term experience with pravastatin in clinical research trials. *Clin Ther.* 1993;15:57-64.

34. Kummerow FA, Olinescu RM, Fleischer L, Handler B, Shinkareva SV. The relationship of oxidized lipids to coronary artery stenosis. *Atherosclerosis*. 2000;149:181-90.

35. Bratus' VV, Talaieva TV, Lomakovs'kyĭ OM, Tretiak IV, Radalovs'ka NV. Modified lipoproteins – their types and role in atherogenesis. *Fiziol Zh*. 2000;46:73-81.

36. George MS, Guidotti A, Rubinow D, Pan B, Mikalauskas K, Post RM. CSF neuroactive steroids in affective disorders: pregnenolone, progesterone and DBI. *Biological Psychiatry*. 1994;35:775-80.

37. Legros JJ. Towards a consensus regarding androgen substitution therapy for andropause. *Rev Med Liege*. 2000;55:449-53.

38. Haug A, Hostmark AT, Spydevold O. Plasma lipoprotein responses to castration and androgen substitution in rats. *Metabolism*. 1984;33:465-70.

39. Hänggi W, Birkhäuser MH, Malek A, Peheim E, von Hospenthal JU. Cyclical gestagen (MPA) supplement for continuous transdermal or oral estrogen substitution in postmenopause: modification of serum lipids. *Geburtshilfe Frauenheilkd*. 1993;53:709-14.

40. Bhatnagar D, Soran H, Durrington PN. Hypercholesterolaemia and its management. *BMJ*. 2008;337: a993.

41. Schuff-Werner P, Kohlschein P. Current therapy of hypercholesterolemia. How much statin does your patient need? *MMW Fortschr Med*. 2002;144: 24-6.

42. Manzoli A, Patti G, D'Ambrosio A, Montesanti R, Calabrese V, Abbate A, et al. Statins: from hypocholesteremic drugs to antiatherogenic agents. *Clin Ter*. 2001;152: 307-13.

43. Dzugan SA, Smith RA. Broad spectrum restoration in natural steroid hormones as possible treatment for hypercholesterolemia. *Bull Urg Rec Med*. 2002;3: 278-84.

44. Dzugan SA, Smith RA. Hypercholesterolemia treatment: a new hypothesis or just an accident? *Med Hypotheses*. 2002;59: 751-6.

45. Dzugan SA (2004). Hypercholesterolemia treatment: a new hypothesis or just an accident. In: Anti-Aging Therapeutics. Vol. 6. Chicago, IL, USA; p. 89-98.

46. Dzugan SA, Smith RA, Kuznetsov AS. A new statin free method of hypercholesterolemia. *Health Donbass*. 2004;4: 19-25.

47. Dzugan SA (2007). Hypercholesterolemia Treatment: a New Statin Free Method. In: Anti-Aging Therapeutics. Vol. 9. Chicago, IL, USA; p. 117-25.

48. Dzugan SA, Rozakis GW, Dzugan SS, Smith RA. Hormonorestorative therapy is a promising method for hypercholesterolemia treatment. *Approaches to Aging Control*. 2009;13: 12-9.

49. Smith RG, Betancourt L, Sun Y. Molecular endocrinology and physiology of the aging central nervous system. *Endocr Rev*. 2005;26: 203-250.

50. Ravnskov U. Cholesterol lowering trials in coronary heart disease: frequency of citation and outcome. *BMJ*. 1992 Jul 4;305(6844):15-9.

51. Ravnskov U. Quotation bias in reviews of the diet-heart idea. *J Clin Epidemiol*. 1995 May;48(5):713-9.

Chapter 9

1. Castelli WP. The new pathophysiology of coronary artery disease. *Am J Cardiol*. 1998 Nov 26;82(10B):60T-65T.

2. Lehto S, Palomäki P, Miettinen H, Penttilä I, Salomaa V, Tuomilehto J, et al. Serum cholesterol and high density lipoprotein cholesterol distributions in patients with acute myocardial infarction and in the general population of Kuopio province, eastern Finland. *J Intern Med*. 1993 Feb;233(2):179-85.

3. van Aalst-Cohen Es, Jansen AC, de Jongh S, de Sauvage Nolting PR, Kastelein JJ. Clinical, diagnostic, and therapeutic aspects of familial hypercholesterolemia. *Semin Vasc Med*. 2004 Feb;4(1):31-41.

4. Marks D, Thorogood M, Neil HA, Humphries SE. A review on the diagnosis, natural history, and treatment of familial hypercholesterolemia. *Atherosclerosis*. 2003 May;168(1):1-14.

5. Rader DJ, Cohen J, Hobbs HH. Monogenic hypercholesterolemia: new insights in pathogenesis and treatment. *J Clin Invest*. 2003 Jun;111(12):1795-803.

6. Risch N, Tang H, Katzenstein H, Ekstein J. Geographic distribution of disease mutations in the Ashkenazi Jewish population supports genetic drift over selection. *Am J Hum Genet*. 2003 Apr;72(4):812-22.

7. Sijbrands EJ, Westendorp RG, Defesche JC, de Meier PH, Smelt AH, Kastelein JJ. Mortality over two centuries in large pedigree with familial hypercholesterolaemia: family tree mortality study. *BMJ*. 2001 April;322:1019-23.

8. Austin MA, Hutter CM, Zimmern RL, Humphries SE. Familial hypercholesterolemia and coronary heart disease: a HuGE association review. *Am J Epidemiol*. 2004 Sep;160(5):421-9.

9. Alonso R, Mata N, Mata P. Benefits and risks assessment of simvastatin in familial hypercholesterolaemia. *Expert Opin Drug Saf*. 2005 Mar;4(2):171-81.

10. Brown MS, Goldstein JL. A receptor-mediated pathway for cholesterol homeostasis. *Science*. 1986 Apr;232(4746):34-47.

11. de Jongh S, Ose L, Szamosi T, Gagné C, Lambert M, Scott R, et al. Efficacy and safety of statin therapy in children with familial hypercholesterolemia: a randomized, double-blind, placebo-controlled trial with simvastatin. Circulation. 2002 Oct;106(17):2231-7.

12. Burnett JR, Ravine D, van Bockxmeer FM, Watts GF. Familial hypercholesterolaemia: a look back, a look ahead. *MJA* 2005;182(11):552-3.

13. Chung N, Cho SY, Choi DH, Zhu JR, Lee K, Lee PY, et al. STATT: a titrate-to-goal study of simvastatin in Asian patients with coronary heart disease. Simvastatin Treats Asians to Target. *Clin Ther.* 2001 Jun;23(6):858-70.

14. Scheen AJ. Fatal rhabdomyolysis caused by caused by cerivastatin. *Rev Med Liege.* 2001 Aug;56(8):592-4.

15. Muldoon MF, Manuck SB, Matthews KA. Lowering cholesterol concentrations and mortality: a quantitative review of primary prevention trials. *BMJ.* 1990 Aug;301(6747):309-14.

16. Law MR, Thompson SG, Wald NJ. Assessing possible hazards of reducing serum cholesterol. *BMJ.* 1994 Feb;308(6925):373-9.

17. Erkkola R, Viikari J, Irjala K, Solakivi-Jaakkola T. One year follow-up of lipoprotein metabolism after pregnancy. *Biol Res Pregnancy Perinatol.* 1986;7(2):47-51.

18. Martin U, Davies C, Hayavi S, Hartland A, Dunne F. Is normal pregnancy atherogenic? *Clin Sci (Lond).* 1999 Apr;96(4):421-5.

19. Loke DF, Viegas OA, Kek LP, Rauff M, Thai AC, Ratnam SS. Lipid profiles during and after normal pregnancy. *Gynecol Obstet Invest.* 1991;32(3):144-7.

20. Tschudi MR, Noll G, Lüscher TP. Pharmacotherapy of arteriosclerosis and its complications. Effect of ACE inhibitors and HMG-CoA-reductase inhibitors. *Schweiz Med Wochenschr.* 1997 Apr 12;127(15):636-49.

21. Kaunitz H. The significance of dietary fat in arteriosclerosis. An outmoded theory? *MMW Munch Med Wochenschr.* 1977 Apr 22;119(16):539-42.

22. Rifkind BM, Levy RI. Testing the lipid hypothesis. Clinical trials. *Arch Surg.* 1978 Jan;113(1):80-3.

Image Credits

- Information Overload: © James Group Studios
- Pharmacy - Entering Information: © Digital Planet Design
- Defocused lights: © Nicholas Monu
- Mature couple smiling: © HannaMonika
- Cholesterol lowering pills: © Erickson Photography
- Dollars, Pills & Syringe: © Richcano
- Emergency Sign: © Photos by Jim
- Laboratory: © Alex Raths
- Healthy Living: © Perkmeup Imagery
- Female scientist working in a lab: © Yuri Arcurs
- Sun and life: © Plainview
- Drawing Blood: © Alex Raths
- At the laboratory: © Alex Raths
- Father and Daughter: © Michael DeLeon Photography
- Cholesterol in artery: © Eduard Härkönen
- Clipboard series: © Peepo
- Adult Couple Standing Affectionately: © Neustock

All images from iStockphoto LP

Index

About The Authors

Sergey A. Dzugan, MD, PhD

Dr. Dzugan graduated from the Donetsk State Medical Institute (Ukraine) with a Doctorate of Medicine in 1979. After medical school, he performed his residency in general and cardiovascular surgery and became the Head of Heart Services in 1985. Dr. Dzugan has had special training in vascular surgery, combustiology, microsurgery, arrhythmology, heart surgery, genetic testing, pedagogics, and psychology. Dr. Dzugan was a distinguished and highly trained educator, physician, and surgeon in Ukraine.

In 1990, he received his PhD in Medical Science concerning heart rhythm disorder and subsequently became Assistant Professor at the Donetsk State Medical Institute. In May of 1991, he became the first Chief of the Department of cardiovascular Surgery and senior Heart Surgeon, at the Donetsk District Regional Hospital, Ukraine.

In March of 1993, he became an Associate Professor at Donetsk State Medical University. Dr. Dzugan performed a wide spectrum of operations on children and adults, including congenital and acquired heart diseases, and rhythm disorders. As the Head of Heart Surgery he had the highest medical skills and qualifications which can be awarded in his former country. As a practicing physician, Dr. Dzugan always found himself more in favor of holistic and natural medicines rather than synthetic. He always believed that strengthening one's immune system would do more to improve health than treating problems after they occur. Because of this, while performing heart surgeries, Dr. Dzugan became more interested in the preventive aspects of heart disease and began studying hormone treatments.

Dr. Dzugan moved to the United States from Ukraine in 1995 and in 1996, became a scientific consultant to Dr. Arnold Smith at the North Central Mississippi Regional Center in Greenwood, Mississippi. His role there was to stay current on the latest advances in nutraceutical treatments with a particular focus on such to improve immunity and the ability of patients to fight cancer. Dr. Dzugan worked with the Cancer Center for more than 7 years and was a principle consultant of Anti-Aging strategy and biological therapy of cancer. The Cancer Center was active in clinical research and Dr. Dzugan's scholarly background as a clinical researcher helped this proceed in a more organized and scientific fashion. In 1998, he had become board certified by the American Academy of Anti-Aging Medicine. His employer at the North Central Mississippi Regional Cancer Center had expressly stated that "Dr. Dzugan is extremely valuable to patient care and his role differentiates the North Central Mississippi Regional Cancer Center from that of any other centers in the states, because no other center has a full time well qualified staff person to meet the same function." Dr. Smith believes that "Dr. Dzugan is a brilliant, gifted physician whose talents we believe would make a significant contribution to the nation."

In 2001, Dr. Dzugan suggested a new hypothesis of hypercholesterolemia and developed a new statin-free method of high cholesterol treatment. At the same time he also developed a unique multimodal program for migraine management.

In October 2003, he moved to Ft. Lauderdale, Florida, and became the Manager of the Advisory Department at the Life

Extension Foundation. Later, he became President of Life Extension Scientific Information Inc. In August 2006, Dr. Dzugan left the Life Extensions Foundation to create a scientific organization that consults physicians to develop the program for their patients to optimize physiology.

Dr. Dzugan was accepted (June, 30 2006) to the International Academy of Creative Endeavors (Moscow, Russia) as a Corresponding Member of the Academy for the outstanding contribution to the development of new methods of hypercholesterolemia and migraine treatment. One year later, the Academy awarded Dr. Dzugan with the honorary title of Academician. In December 2007, Dr. Dzugan was rewarded with Honoree Medal by this Academy for the personal input into the acquisition of science, culture, physical betterment of nation and strengthening of friendship between nations. He performed presentations multiple times at the prestigious International Congress on Anti-Aging Medicine. The topics of his presentations were related to cholesterol disorders, migraine, physiology optimization, stem cell therapy, cancer, immunorestorative and hormonorestorative therapy.

Dr. Dzugan is the author of 146 publications in medical journals and these publications include surgical, oncological, academic, and anti-aging topics. Also, several articles were published in health related magazines, such as Life Extension Magazine and The South African Journal of Natural Medicine. He is the author of "Migraine Cure", "Dzugan Method | Restorative Medicine" and "Your Blood Doesn't Lie!" books and is a holder of 3 patents (all related to heart surgery). Dr. Dzugan is a Member of the Editorial Board of the Neuroendocrinology Letters and a member of the Medical Advisory Board at Life Extension Magazine. He is co-founder and President of iPOMS

(International Physiology Optimization Medical Society).

Dr. Dzugan's current primary interests are physiologic therapy for elevated cholesterol, migraine, fatigue, fibromyalgia, behavioral and hormonal disorders.

Konstantine S. Dzugan

Konstantine graduated from Florida Atlantic University in 2010.

He is the author of 2 publications in medical journals and his primary interest is development of programs for physiology optimization.

P 128 - Estradiol
P 148 - Tinnitus

For more information

please visit us on the web:

themagicofcholesterolnumbers.com

or call

866-225-4877